Praise for
Breaking the Conspiracy of Silence

"*Breaking the Conspiracy of Silence* provides a forthright and challenging analysis of how the teachings of Jesus Christ can be used by Christians of all denominations to mobilize in new ways in the global struggle against the global AIDS pandemic. Messer offers visionary teachings and perspectives that are essential for all people of faith who believe that together we can create a better world."
—**Dr. Paul Zeitz, Global AIDS Alliance**

"*Breaking the Conspiracy of Silence* is the finest book I have read on the role of the church in this struggle with HIV/AIDS. Challenging our cherished beliefs, illuminating our darkest fears, confronting our secret complacency, and questioning our commitment, he directs us to the compassionate Lord Jesus. I feel every pastor needs to read this book."
—**Allan R. Handysides, Director, Health Ministries**
General Conference of Seventh-day Adventists World Church

"For too long the church has been asleep to the AIDS crisis taking place across our planet. Messer provides a much-needed wake-up call to Christians everywhere that not only must something be done, but also it can be done—beginning with you and me. This is a must read for every believing Christian."
—**Margaret Feinberg, author of *twentysomething* and *Simple Acts of Faith***

"Messer calls for a 'new holy boldness' and for a spirit of 'apostolic-like' risk-taking that the churches have scarcely tapped. He tackles our parochial and prejudicial boundaries around sexuality and risk-taking behaviors and calls for an empowering interfaith vision of hope. An important work at a time when 'compassion fatigue' in the West is deep and the global pandemic threatens obliteration of entire communities. Required reading for our communities of faith."
—**Dr. Jon A. Lacey, Interim Director, Council of Religious AIDS Networks**

"*Breaking the Conspiracy of Silence* is a call for action, covering all the topics on which Christians need to be informed. Messer addresses boldly and directly the sensitive topics of sexuality, homosexuality, and gender inequity, and the sometimes unhelpful attitudes of the church, which too often demonstrate more love of laws than the law of love. *Breaking the Conspiracy of Silence* is personal and readable as it calls for a paradigm shift in the church's traditional perception of AIDS."
—**Ray Martin, Executive Director**
Christian Connections for International Health

Other titles in

PRISMS

BREAKING THE CONSPIRACY OF
SILENCE

Christian Churches and the
Global **AIDS** Crisis

Donald E. Messer

Fortress Press /Minneapolis

BREAKING THE CONSPIRACY OF SILENCE
Christian Churches and the Global AIDS Crisis

Scripture quotations are from the New Revised Standard Version Bible, copyright © 1989 by the Division of Christian Education of the National Council of the Churches of Christ in the USA and used by permission.

Cover photograph: © Louise Gubb/CORBIS SABA. Photographer: Louise Gubb. Date Photographed: September 2000. Location Information: Ipusukilo, Zambia. *Students assemble before class at Ipusukilo Community School. The school was set up by a local non-governmental organization, Copperbelt Health and Education Project (CHEP), for the town's children, many of whom have been orphaned by AIDS. Seventy percent of the world's HIV-infected people live in sub-Saharan Africa, and more than a million children have been orphaned by parents who have succumbed to AIDS in Zambia alone.*

Cover and book design: Zan Ceeley

Lyrics of Bob Dylan, "Saving Grace," from the album *Saved*. Copyright © 1980 by Special Rider Music. All rights reserved. International copyright secured. Reprinted by permission.

ISBN 0-8006-3641-4

The paper used in this publication meets the minimum requirements of American National Standard for Information Sciences — Permanence of Paper for Printed Library Materials, ANSI Z329.48-1984.

Manufactured in the U.S.A.
08   07   06   05   04   1   2   3   4   5   6   7   8   9   10

To my esteemed friend
N. M. Samuel, MD
Chennai, India

my beloved grandchildren
Rachel C. Gallagher
Noah C. Gallagher
Madeline K. Messer
Gabriel E. Gallagher

Contents

Introduction

How do we hear the voice of God speaking to us? As Christians we believe we hear the words of God as we read the Word of God in the Old and New Testaments. Other times we discern the still small voice of God through prayer and meditation. At other moments we may hear God speaking to us as we worship or listen to a sermon or face a crisis moment in our lives. Sometimes, as the Irish playwright Sean O'Casey has written, God may be "a shout in the street."[1]

The Voice of God

Just before Christmas 2001, I heard the voice of God speaking to me like "a shout in the street." This time it was in the faces of more than 800 Indian men, women, and children who are struggling to live with HIV/AIDS (human immunodeficiency virus/acquired immune deficiency syndrome). I was in southern India visiting the largest public hospital for AIDS patients in Tambaram, a suburb of Chennai (formerly known as Madras). With fellow Christians, I walked through the wards of this overcrowded hospital and distributed Christmas gifts to every person with AIDS. As we greeted one another with traditional Indian words, and as I looked into their faces, I heard God calling me to a new mission and ministry.

As I knelt down beside a young man lying on a mat, I saw the pain of his suffering. As I reached out to touch a sick child upon a bed with another hurting child, I felt their loneliness. As I exchanged Christmas greetings with a woman clutching a large Bible in her arms, I heard her hopelessness; her church and family had abandoned her. As I held babies with AIDS in my arms, I heard their cries for care and love. A beautiful young woman, age nineteen, asked why the Western world could have heart transplants but no medical treatment for the millions of persons with HIV/AIDS in India, Africa, and elsewhere.

At one point a little girl swept past me in the hospital ward and ran to her mother's mat. In that moment my heart broke and tears overwhelmed me.

Yes, I knew the grim global statistics about HIV/AIDS: 46 million people are infected worldwide; 7,000 people die daily, 16,000 new persons each day are infected. More than 20 million persons have already died; 65 million more will die by the year 2020. Africa has 28.5 million persons living with HIV/AIDS, but fewer than 30,000 have received treatment. By 2010, some public health officials project, there will be 20–25 million persons with HIV/AIDS in India alone.

I knew the statistics but not the reality. In that particular moment, all those millions became personalized for me in the little girl, as her mother on the mat embraced her. I did not know their names, but I realized they were somebody's daughter and granddaughter. What if they were my daughter, Christine, and my granddaughter, Rachel?

Each of us is a part of God's family—in Christ we are one. The world may separate us by countries, cultures, races, borders, and even denominations, but in truth we are all the children of a loving God who cares for every one of us. The suffering persons I met in the Tambaram hospital and the next day at a rural clinic in Namakkal are our brothers and sisters.

They are good, hardworking people struggling to earn enough money to support themselves and their families. Often they do not have the benefit of an education, so they don't know how they got HIV/AIDS or how they could have prevented others from getting infected from them. They are trapped in a discriminatory social system and a culture of poverty that limit freedom and opportunities.

Because of widespread illiteracy and indifference, they and millions more in Africa, Asia, and Latin America suffer the fate of an incurable disease that is sweeping the world. But this does not have to be the case. It is not inevitable that this disease should triumph. The powers of disease and death are great but, to borrow words from Esther, "for such a time as this" God calls us for a new mission and ministry in our churches, theological seminaries, and religious institutions.

Jesus in the AIDS Hospital

This book seeks to motivate and challenge Christians, both laity and clergy, to take leadership and form partnerships with Christians around the world in the struggle against HIV/AIDS. In writing it, I am grateful for the opportunity to share what I believe God is calling us to be and to do at this unprecedented, *kairotic* moment in human history. The New Testament term *kairos,* according to Robert McAfee Brown, refers to a "time of opportunity demanding a response: God offers us a new set of possibilities and we have to accept or decline."[2]

As Christians we affirm an understanding that mission is not something we do if we have a little extra time in the week. It is not just another program of the church or some special outside agency. No, mission is integral to what it means to be the church of Jesus Christ. As Emil Brunner declared long ago, "the church exists by mission, just as fire exists by burning."[3] Every church is a mission station and every Christian a missionary.

Christians define mission in many different ways, but fundamental to our perspective is the idea that God is at work in the world. The Bible tells the story of the mission of God (*missio Dei*). It is neither our mission nor the church's mission, but God's mission that we affirm.

Our challenge is to discern and to join in God's liberating and healing and loving initiatives in the world. Sri Lankan theologian D. T. Niles once wrote:

> You cannot take Jesus to India. You cannot take Jesus to Africa. The call to take Jesus to the heathen is ridiculous. We cannot take Jesus anywhere. He is already in Africa. He is already beside the mother in the hut in India. He is already there loving and healing and ministering.[4]

I did not take God to the AIDS hospital in Tambaram. God was already there seeking to offer comfort, care, and compassion. In my mind and heart, I felt Jesus' presence there, wiping the brows of so many who sweated profusely. Jesus was already there, comforting those whose bodies were shivering from pain-induced cold. Jesus was there in the comforting presence of Indian nurses and doctors offering what limited medicines they had. And he was there crying with the children, praying with the hurting, feeling the pain of the crucifixion anew. Every new HIV infection is like another nail pounded into the body of our Lord.

But Christians are people of the resurrection, not Good Friday. We worship a God of life, not death; of hope, not despair; of love, not hate; of acceptance, not stigma and discrimination. God does not will that the people of Africa should be wiped off their continent by the dreaded disease of HIV/AIDS. God does not intend to decimate the people of Latin America or Eastern Europe by disease. God does not want to see the people of Asia wracked by pain and suffering, nor does God wish that India become the new AIDS capital of the world in the next few years. God does not want the church of Jesus Christ to stand idly by when the world faces the worst health crisis in 700 years.

I believe that God is at work in the world, calling us to join the divine in a liberating, healing, and loving mission. God is challenging us to think and to act decisively as Christians. Just as Jesus reached out to the lepers of his own time, and to all who were marginalized and suffering in his society, so in the twenty-first century our global challenge is to hear and respond to the voice of God calling Christians to lead a new healing mission and ministry to eradicate HIV/AIDS and its devastating effects.

Word Becomes Flesh

It is one thing to give lectures at international conferences, write resolutions, preach sermons, or even write a book about HIV/AIDS. It is another thing to look people in the eye as you kneel beside them—to look up and down the hall and see mother after mother aged seventeen, twenty-one, twenty-seven. Meeting young widows and orphans brings one face-to-face with the global AIDS pandemic. "And the Word became flesh and lived among us" (John 1:14).

I was among a group of Christians visiting the AIDS hospital that day. Our trip had been made possible by N. M. Samuel, MD, of India, Park Hill United Methodist Church in Denver, the United Methodist Board of Global Ministries, and the Center for Global Pastoral Ministry at Iliff School of Theology in Denver. The gifts that we distributed had been purchased using individual donations from people in Colorado, Kansas, Pennsylvania, and elsewhere.

My colleague Susan Brown, lay leader from Park Hill, said later that she saw the face of God in the eyes of the people. I found myself asking repeatedly: Where is God amid this suffering? Where is the church of Jesus Christ?

We walked from ward to ward individually presenting the gifts. Outside the men's wards, women (mothers and wives of the sick) looked through the bar-like windows at what we were doing. Once we stepped outside, they greeted us with smiles and gestures of appreciation for the gifts. But outside the women's wards, no one looked through the windows. Those inside were terribly alone. I was told some husbands and families visit, but we certainly didn't see any. At the Third International AIDS India Conference, I learned that men spread the disease to their spouses and girlfriends, but the women are blamed and often tossed out of the home. They not only die, they die alone.

While in India, I gave two speeches at the International Conference and chaired a session with a Buddhist doctor and a Muslim cleric on interfaith-based care of people with HIV/AIDS. I also preached at two Indian churches on the theme of Advent and AIDS. These were important and powerful experiences, but the time in the hospital made flesh of the words spoken earlier at the churches and conference.

An Essay in Practical Theology

Recognizing that the world faces the worst health crisis in centuries, the United Nations General Assembly declared unanimously in 2001 that "the global HIV/AIDS epidemic . . . constitutes a global emergency." They called on every segment of society to come to the rescue, specifically mentioning faith-based groups as essential to the global effort. UN Secretary-General Kofi Annan says "the first battle" must be to "break the conspiracy of silence at every level."[5] He laments, "In too many countries an official conspiracy of silence about AIDS has denied people information that could have saved their lives."[6]

To date, the efforts of Christian congregations and denominations have been less than minimal. More than twenty years into the global pandemic, most denominations have passed compassionate-sounding resolutions, but few have become involved significantly in God's mission and ministry of healing.

A bottom-line test is to examine the expenditures of a congregation, conference, or denomination. Budgets reveal values, be they managerial, maintenance, or missional. Only a few congregations and denominations have allocated a miniscule portion of funds to a mission and ministry of healing directed at the global HIV/AIDS crisis. May the compassionate character of Christianity awaken in the coming years. It is late since the global crisis began, but as an African proverb says, "The best time to plant a tree is twenty years ago. The next best time is today."

This book is not a medical textbook, a counseling manual, or a public policy strategy. It is an essay in practical theology that seeks to motivate all Christians to take leadership and form partnerships with Christians around the world in the struggle against HIV/AIDS. Twenty years into the epidemic, Christians have remained curiously silent and tragically apathetic about the implications of a plague that has already killed 26 million people and is likely to eradicate 100 million more. As the General Secretary of the Lutheran World Federation, Rev. Dr. Ishmael Noko, declared: "Silence and all forms of myths about the reality of HIV/AIDS amount to an affront of what God has achieved for us in Christ."[7]

Several years ago Christians in South Africa issued a famous document based on the *kairos* of apartheid, calling God's people everywhere to join them in the battle against racism, segregation, and violence. The thunder and lightning of that proclamation forced Christians worldwide to rethink their attitudes and to renew their political, social, economic, and missional activities. Apartheid was labeled a sin and abolished; democracy dawned and a new day was launched. Now the South African theologian Ronald Nicolson argues that global AIDS is "a time of *kairos*" that "will, or should, change the way we think about God, about Jesus, about the church, about life and death and sexuality."[8] Another South African theologian, Bonginjalo Goba, says the AIDS epidemic leaves us with more questions than answers, challenging "all of our philosophical or theological presuppositions. To encounter those who have openly come to terms with the challenge of AIDS is to participate in a deep spiritual pilgrimage which attempts to redefine the ultimate meaning of human existence."[9] Mother Teresa was even more forthright, saying that AIDS was a word from God and that "God is speaking to us through this disease."[10]

This book emphasizes three major themes: *First, just as people must change their behavior in order to prevent and eliminate AIDS, church leaders also must change their own behavior.* Compassion, not condemnation; involvement, not indifference, must prevail. The days of denial and discrimination must end. Global AIDS education, prevention, treatment, and care must become a priority agenda in the church's mission.

Second, churches must increase financial resource allocations for AIDS education and prevention programs. Meaningful participation in God's healing mission in the world requires substantial new resources. After the September 11, 2001, terrorist attacks on the United States, vast amounts of money were raised in all churches and denominations in response to the emergency situation. An appeal from the bishops of my denomination yielded some $15 million. I keep wondering what would happen if the United Methodist Council of Bishops would make a special appeal for global AIDS as it does for other world emergencies. Some efforts are under way, as reflected by the special efforts of the Lutheran World Federation, Samaritan's Purse, Church World Service, World Council of Churches, and others. But most mainline denominations and congregations remain apathetic and uninvolved.

Third, ecumenical organizations, denominations, and local churches need to respond imaginatively to this global emergency. Educational pro-

grams at all levels of the church supporting orphan outreach programs, speaking out for global social justice in health care programs,
and participating in volunteer mission programs are but a few examples of what can be done. This is not a partisan issue, but a call by
God to respond to an urgent human crisis with the healing spirit of
Jesus Christ.

In Christian scholarship an *apologia* is a straightforward appeal, or
even polemic, designed to argue as persuasively as possible certain
Christian teachings, beliefs, or doctrines. This book is offered as an
apologia for Christian involvement in addressing global HIV/AIDS,
motivated by the belief that God is calling us to join in this divine
mission. The very soul of the church is at stake if we fail to reflect the
deepest values and vision of Jesus, the Great Physician. In a world
filled with suffering, abandoned orphans and widows, it is incompre-
hensible that Bible-believing people would fail to act.When 46 million people are HIV-infected and most are destined to die premature
deaths, surely Christians will respond if they hear anew Jesus' words:
"I was sick and you took care of me," and "Just as you did it to one of
the least of these who are members of my family, you did it to me"
(Matthew 25:36, 40).

In the following pages, chapter 1 introduces the nature of the
global emergency the church faces. Chapter 2 invites Christians to
break out of thinking in "we-they" categories and to imagine oneself
as HIV-positive. Chapter 3 notes that certain human realities, particularly related to sex, are difficult for Christians to acknowledge,
much less accept or tolerate; yet, understanding is required to
address the AIDS pandemic. Chapter 4 struggles with stigmatization
and discrimination as sins contrary to the will of God. Chapters 5, 6,
7, and 8 cite specific challenges facing Christians who seek to promote awareness, education, prevention, care, and treatment of persons living with HIV/AIDS. The final chapter outlines a vision of
how Christians can respond to this global emergency and become
partners in God's mission and ministry of hope and healing in the
twenty-first century. An appendix and bibliography of helpful documents conclude the volume.

Defining Terms: HIV/AIDS

HIV/AIDS is the widely used acronym for *human immunodeficiency virus* and *acquired immune deficiency syndrome*.[11] The virus destroys the human immune system and causes AIDS. Technically AIDS is not a single disease since AIDS patients usually have many diseases, each with their own signs and symptoms. When the body cannot produce a sufficient number of immune-specific cells, it becomes very vulnerable to infection, which leads to terminal illness.

Persons infected with HIV are said to be HIV-positive and those who are not are HIV-negative. It appears that not everyone who is HIV-positive will develop AIDS. Some estimate that 5 percent of the HIV-infected population will not develop AIDS. From a scientific or medical perspective, people do not die from AIDS, but of opportunistic infections, cancers, and organ failures prompted by an inadequate immune system. In ordinary language, however, we say that HIV causes AIDS and that people die from HIV/AIDS or AIDS.

Words of Gratitude

This book does not simply emerge from my seminary teaching and research, but out of the countless experiences I have shared with persons living with HIV/AIDS and persons who are committed to ending this pandemic. In Africa, Latin America, Europe, Australia, and the United States, I have met with many persons and spoken at various conferences focused on the church and global AIDS. To each of them I am deeply indebted.

No book is ever written without the support and assistance of countless persons. Just mentioning their names is an insufficient expression of gratitude for their assistance, but failing to acknowledge in print their contribution would be especially egregious.

Thanks especially are due to N. M. Samuel, MD, Ashok Pillai, Youngsook Kang, Randolph Nugent, Sally B. Geis, Suzanne Calvin, Maggi Mahan, Paul and Paula Murphy, John and Elaine Blinn, Jong Chun Park, Gilbert Caldwell, Bishop "Fritz" and Etta Mae Mutti,

Bruce and Carol Robbins, Edward Antonio, Susan Brown, Janet Everhart, Sue Burnett, Nora Boots, Mortimer and Beatrice Arias, Ryan Bee-
man, B. J. Stiles, Daniel Marutle, and Bonnie J. Messer.

Publication would not have been possible without the expertise
and support of Fortress Press, with particular thanks to Harold Rast,
Bob Todd, and Zan Ceeley.

I also extend gratitude to the Iliff School of Theology, Park Hill
United Methodist Church, and the United Methodist General Board
of Global Ministries for their support of the Center for the Church
and Global AIDS.

I encourage persons seeking more information and/or involvement opportunities to contact me at the Center for the Church and
Global AIDS (dmesser@iliff.edu).

1

The Church and Global AIDS

If only the bite of a mosquito caused HIV/AIDS, then the Christian community would be in the global forefront of the struggle for prevention and care.

—N. M. Samuel, MD

Many years ago, at age twenty, I headed from the rural prairies of South Dakota to experience the crowded, teeming cities of India. While a student at Madras Christian College, I volunteered with my friend, N. M. Samuel, at a volunteer clinic ministering to lepers and their families. Each week men, women, and children with leprosy would come there to receive a little medicine and to have their bandages changed. Their social status and medical health were not remarkably different than those whom Jesus had encountered nearly twenty centuries earlier.

I returned to America and lost track of my friend. Then, after thirty years, we were reunited, and I learned that he had become a medical doctor and had devoted his life to caring for people with leprosy in India, Nepal, and Kenya. In recent years, however, his specialty had changed and he was now leading the fight in India against HIV/AIDS.

As a Christian—the son of a pastor—he was deeply disturbed by the contemporary church's inaction. Dr. Samuel kept asking me why the church had been in the forefront of the battle against leprosy— showing compassion and care when others were shunning and excluding—while in the campaign against AIDS, the church has been in the background, often showing condemnation and neglect. "Why, Don, won't the church face human reality and reach out in love?"

As a Christian layman, he knew the answer: "If only the bite of a mosquito caused HIV/AIDS, then the Christian community would be in the global forefront of the struggle for prevention and care."[1] But because the disease is spread primarily through sexual contact, the global church has failed to respond positively to efforts of prevention and care and has often been a stumbling block, contributing to the denial, discrimination, and suffering of infected people and their families.

Can the church continue to remain essentially aloof and detached? What does the gospel of Jesus Christ require? Has the global context changed so swiftly and dramatically that mission and ministry in the twenty-first century are drastically redefined? Is it enough simply to evangelize or to build schools when people are suffering and dying at alarmingly increasing rates? Do old attitudes that add to stigmatization, prejudice, and discrimination conform to God's will? What is God calling the church to be and to do?

Global Emergency

Facing the worst world health crisis in 700 years, the United Nation's General Assembly has endorsed a "Declaration of Commitment on HIV/AIDS."[2] Its key conclusion was that "the global HIV/AIDS epidemic, through its devastating scale and impact, constitutes a global emergency. . . ."[3] Speaking to the 180 signatory nations, United States Secretary of State Colin L. Powell declared: "No war on the face of the world is more destructive than the AIDS pandemic. I was a soldier, but I know of no enemy in war more insidious or vicious than AIDS, an enemy that poses a clear and present danger to the world."[4]

Addressing this health issue represents a major political breakthrough. It is a beginning step in attempting to mobilize governmental and non-governmental organizations, including faith-based groups like the church, to deal with this new global emergency. In the face of natural disasters like earthquakes, hurricanes, and typhoons, nations know how to rally together to meet human need. In times of war, and even in some peacekeeping operations, cooperative governmental and non-governmental efforts are combined for common objectives. Through the World Health Organization, efforts have been undertaken to conquer various diseases and to provide care. However, by elevating the imperative of fighting HIV/AIDS to the status of a global emergency, the United Nations has provided a new level of leadership and outlined a new challenge to every segment of human society.

Why did the United Nations declare HIV/AIDS a global emergency rather than a major world disaster? Disasters have a foreseeable end, but the global HIV/AIDS pandemic is just beginning with no end in sight. Some 67 million people worldwide have been infected since the disease was first detected twenty years ago. It is now the leading killer among all known infectious diseases. Biologist Gerald J. Stine notes that if the world is "lucky" and breakthroughs in prevention, treatment, and vaccines occur, "by 2021 AIDS will be killing 5 million people a year. If not 'lucky,' the toll could be 12 million."[5] Who can understand or comprehend the suffering and misery these abstract numbers signify for the lives of individual women, men, and children?

The United Nations mentioned numerous reasons and concerns for calling this crisis a global emergency. Succinctly, eight can be cited. First, they noted the number of people estimated to be living with the disease—40 million when they met, and the 22 million they estimated had already died. Some 95 percent of those living with HIV/AIDS were in the Two-Thirds World (nonindustrialized nations, which constitute a majority of the world's population); 75 percent were in sub-Saharan Africa.

Second, the UN expressed "grave concern that all people, rich and poor, without distinction of age, gender or race are affected by the HIV/AIDS epidemic." They noted that women, young adults, and children—girls in particular—are the most vulnerable. HIV/AIDS also impacts everyone, whether infected or not, because it "threatens development, social cohesion, political stability, food security, and life expectancy and imposes a devastating economic burden" especially in Africa and other parts of the Two-Thirds World.

Citing alarming statistics from around the world (from the Caribbean to sub-Saharan Africa, to Latin America, Asia-Pacific, and Central and Eastern Europe), the UN General Assembly forecasted, third, that a rapid escalation of the epidemic was forthcoming and the impact would be devastating if specific measures of prevention, treatment, and care were not taken immediately. Within the short time period of 1999 through 2001, about 17 million new infections were reported. Some 16,000 new infections occur every day. This disease had caused Africa alone to have 12.1 million orphans by 2002, with estimates that in eight years that number will escalate to 40 million (the same number as children enrolled in public schools in the United States).

A fourth reason emphasized that "stigmatization, silence, discrimination, and denial, as well as lack of confidentiality, undermine prevention, care, and treatment efforts," increasing the impact of the epidemic on individuals, families, communities, and nations. Often people with HIV/AIDS have been marginalized as societal pariahs, religious sinners, sexual deviants, or worse. These prejudicial practices and attitudes not only harm the well-being of individuals but undermine the well-being of society.

Fifth, the UN stressed that gender inequality facilitates the global HIV/AIDS pandemic. In a world where women are the most impoverished and have the least control over their own destinies, the vulnerability of women and girls across the world to HIV/AIDS must be addressed. The report stresses that the "full realization of human rights and fundamental freedoms for all is essential" to fighting the HIV/AIDS pandemic.

Sixth, a fundamental element in the struggle is lack of access to medication for the treatment and care of people with HIV/AIDS. Currently, of the 30 million people in the Two-Thirds World with the disease, only 50,000 are receiving treatment. The cost of pharmaceutical drugs is prohibitive in most of the world. Clearly a global emergency exists when only the rich get treatment and the rest of the world is condemned to suffering and death.

Seventh, the external debt and debt servicing problems of the poorer nations of the world stymies health care and services. Nations straddled with overwhelming debt have no resources to expend for the health and education of their citizens. Programs of prevention, treatment, and care are impossible in countries lacking medical infrastructure and funds to create or sustain such facilities and services.

Government alone cannot control or conquer HIV/AIDS, and, therefore, eighth, "the important role of cultural, family, ethical, and religious factors in the prevention of the epidemic, and in treatment, care, and support . . ." was emphasized. Priority should be given to the creation of partnerships among governments, non-governmental organizations, people living with HIV/AIDS, groups vulnerable to the disease, foundations, medical, scientific, and educational institutions, businesses and labor unions, and faith-based organizations. Perhaps for the first time ever, the United Nations called on the leadership of churches, synagogues, mosques, temples, and other religious groups to help others tackle this global emergency. As United Methodist Bishop Felton E. May has said, "Churches cannot conquer AIDS alone, but it will not happen without us."[6]

UN Secretary-General Kofi Annan is credited with moving the United Nations to acknowledge and act regarding this global crisis. Specifically, he called for the creation of a new global fund of $10 billion yearly to combat HIV/AIDS, tuberculosis, and malaria. However, from the beginning, political rhetoric regarding the global emergency has not been matched by new dollars being donated for the cause. For example, only $2.2 billion was available in 2002, though initial requests from around the world exceeded $7.9 billion. One question was whether this was new money for HIV/AIDS or money simply diverted from other important social welfare funds. For example, Great Britain's $200 million might sound generous, but actually, cash was diverted from other parts of the government's development budget and was scheduled to be disbursed over five years. Whether other nations are also "robbing Peter to pay Paul" is yet undetermined. While the United States pledged more than any other nation, this fact has to be compared to the more than $1 billion a week expenditure the United States is making to sustain its occupation of Iraq.

From Denial to Constructive Engagement

Jonathan Mann, the first director of the World Health Organization Global Program on AIDS, once suggested that every person and society undergoes three stages of reaction to HIV/AIDS: (1) denial that there is a problem, (2) minimization of the problem's significance, and (3) emergence of constructive engagement to resolve the challenges. Religious leaders and communities of all faiths appear to be no exception to this process, except that it seems to take them even longer than public authorities to become constructively engaged. Worse yet, they often not only contribute to the denial and minimization stages but also promote and reinforce levels of discrimination and stigmatization. In a global emergency, the question, "How can we stimulate, educate, and motivate religious faith communities, especially Christian congregations, to become constructively engaged?" is critical.

The resistance and reticence of Christians to become involved in the AIDS crisis is reflected in an informal survey conducted within two diverse Christian populations in recent years by N. M. Samuel, MD, Chennai, India. He questioned a sampling of people from around the world who had gathered in late 1998 in Harare, Zimbabwe, for the World Council of Churches (WCC) Assembly. He also questioned Christians in his home country of India. Though the leadership of the WCC has long been a progressive voice in the struggle against HIV/AIDS, individual members or delegates do not always reflect positive, accepting attitudes. These are his findings:

As a church leader will you support your members infected
    with HIV/AIDS?
48 percent WCC in Harare versus 52 percent in India

How will your church respond to those whose sexual orientation
    is different in nature?
30 percent WCC in Harare will interact versus 22 percent in India

Will you support human rights issues raised by HIV?
45 percent WCC in Harare versus 65 percent in India

Do you consider HIV/AIDS as punishment from God?
68 percent WCC in Harare versus 40 percent in India

Will you use the church to educate youth about sex and
    drug abuse?
25 percent WCC in Harare versus 20 percent in India

We hope, of course, that these attitudes are now reversing. Nevertheless, these attitudes serve as a glaring benchmark of the necessary work not only at the grassroots level of the Christian church, but also among those who are put forward as leaders of the faith.

Committed Christians around the world are struggling to move Christian communities into the forefront of this global emergency. For example, the Institute for Contextual Theology in Johannesburg, South Africa, the ecumenical agency that developed the famous *kairos* document in the struggle against apartheid, has switched its focus to combating HIV/AIDS and mobilizing the church for action. The former director of the Institute, Nontando Hadebe, wrote about the frustrations they experience and their need for assistance from theologians and church leaders outside their own country. She described a meeting of academic theologians and church workers who relate daily to people affected by HIV. "The cry was for a theological understanding of the pandemic. We looked at each other and felt bankrupt—we are doing care work and counseling but not theological reflection to examine those elements in our beliefs that make it difficult for us to accept people affected with HIV/AIDS and where to go from there." The vision is not only to develop a theological framework for responding to the pandemic, but helping to create a just society that affirms the equality of women, stresses healthy sexuality and family life, affirms the dignity of persons regardless of disease, and holds the government accountable in caring for all of its people, especially the most vulnerable.[7]

A Global Portrait of HIV/AIDS

The statistics that have been quoted are actually conservative estimates, often based on figures supplied by countries that either do not have accurate means of forecasting or that, in a state of denial or minimization, fear to tell the truth to their citizens. When I share such statistics in sermons or public speeches, the audience seems skeptical, quietly suggesting that I am exaggerating in order to make a point. However, when I return years later to my manuscripts, I discover that the figures I used were actually (and tragically) underestimates. For example, in a 1988 sermon I noted with alarm that "in eight African capitals more than 5 percent of the population has already contracted the virus." Today, if only 5 percent of the population had HIV/AIDS, it would be considered a sign of good news. Instead, in seven African nations, one adult in five now suffers from the HIV virus, with Botswana's infected adult population at almost 40 percent of the entire population!

The Web site sponsored by the organization Stop Global AIDS flashes a sobering reminder of the global AIDS crisis: "Every minute of every hour—five more people die of AIDS—and another nine are newly infected." Without attempting to highlight every place and problem, what follows are some estimated global statistics and some commentary.

Canada and the United States
More than twenty years have now passed since the first public signs of the disease were identified in Canada and the United States. Since then about 450,000 people have died in the United States from AIDS. In 2002 there were an estimated 931,000 people living with HIV/AIDS in the United States and about 49,000 in Canada.

With the advent of new medicines, HIV/AIDS is now viewed as a "chronic manageable disease" in North America, but with many side effects and unforeseen long-term consequences. Reports circulate that younger generations of gay white men, lacking the sobering experiences of loss and death of the 1980s and early 1990s, are engaging in riskier sexual practices.

Public attention has diminished and efforts to raise awareness and funds for HIV/AIDS agencies have become more difficult. Few churches, for example, were ever on the forefront of efforts for prevention and care, and now even greater complacency and apathy exist.

Yet some 45,000 new infections occur yearly in the United States. What has happened is that many of the people suffering in the United States are publicly invisible and intensely isolated. The disease, for example, is spreading disproportionately among the poor and persons of color, particularly African Americans. Black women make up 7 percent of the nation's population, but 64 percent of women in the United States diagnosed in 2001 with HIV were African American. In 1999 African American men made up 35 percent, white men 27 percent, Latino men 14 percent, and white and Latino women were each 4 percent.[8] The Centers for Disease Control believes that one in every 50 African American men is infected with HIV, and one in every 160 African American women. By comparison, one in every 250 white men is infected, and one in every 3,000 white women.[9] African American children represent almost two-thirds of all reported pediatric AIDS cases. In Canada aboriginal persons make up only 3 percent of the population, but 9 percent of the new infections in 1999. Education and prevention programs often fail to target specific racial and ethnic groups.

The death rate from AIDS in the United States has been declining, but not proportionally among racial groups and between genders. For example, though death declined 21 percent among whites in 1996, it declined only 2 percent among African Americans and increased by 3 percent among women. This raises serious issues of racism and sexism and reflects differences in access to modern medical treatment. AIDS-related illnesses in 2002 were the leading cause of death for African American men aged twenty-five to forty-four and the third leading cause of death for Hispanic men in the same age category.

Persons with hearing impairments are often overlooked in programs of HIV/AIDS education and prevention. Little is known about the transmission of HIV within the deaf population, yet between 8,000 to 40,000 hearing impaired people are estimated to be infected. These dramatically different statistics result from two very limited studies in the United States. What is clearly known is that deaf high school students have much less knowledge about HIV transmission than do their hearing peers.

Africa

Currently African nations, particularly those south of the Sahara, are most impacted. Seventy percent of the adults and 80 percent of children infected with HIV/AIDS in the world are from Africa. Three-fourths of those who have died have been in Africa. In 2003 there were sixteen African countries where more than one-tenth of the population aged fifteen to forty-nine were infected. This has prompted President Olusegun Obasanjo of Nigeria to say: "With this trend in statistics, the future of our continent is bleak, to say the least, and the prospect of extinction of the entire continent looms larger and larger."[10] Senegalese president Abdoulaye Wade contends his nation has kept HIV infection rates to 1 percent among adults by "breaking the conspiracy of silence about it."[11]

In particular, South Africa suffers immensely with one out of every five adults infected. In 2003 South Africa had the largest number of people living with HIV/AIDS in the world. Five million currently are infected; 26 percent are men and 12 percent are women aged 20 to 24; 36 percent are women and 23 percent are men aged 25 to 29. Estimates are that 6–7.5 million will be infected by 2010 in South Africa. Recently it was reported that outsiders discovered a whole village of children with no living adults. One newspaper account stated that "sixty percent of students at the largest university are HIV-positive."[12]

Many factors compound the crisis in South Africa. President Thabo Mbeki refused to attend the United Nations General Assembly on HIV/AIDS, since he was skeptical whether the virus leads to the disease. Roman Catholic bishops in southern Africa denounced condoms as "the heart of evil." Some doctors have had to flee for their lives in certain areas because people believe they were injected with the virus while being tested. South African racists see AIDS as an answer to their prayers; it could lead to a white majority government in power. "AIDS will succeed where apartheid failed," says one white South African.[13] When I reported this observation made by the South African satirist Pieter-Dirk Uys in one of my lectures, I was approached by a woman who told of meeting a white couple from South Africa while vacationing in Amsterdam. To her shock, she said they confidently announced: "You know, in South Africa, we won't have a black problem much longer; it is being taken care of by AIDS."

In neighboring Zimbabwe, caught in other political quandaries, one in three adults is believed infected. Some 800,000 orphans already struggle for care and survival. Some companies and organizations reportedly train three people for a single job because they are uncertain of life expectancy of employees. In Kenya the incidence rate in 2003 had reached double-digit percentages and continues to rise. At least 3.5 million are infected, seven of ten HIV-positive being Kenyans between the ages of eighteen and twenty-five. Six hundred Kenyans die daily, according to estimates from The Balm in Gilead, an AIDS advocacy organization.[14] One Kenyan commented that "there is no one in the church that has not suffered an HIV infection or AIDS death in their family."

Life expectancy rates are decreasing in many African countries. For example, in Tanzania it has already decreased from sixty-one to forty-six years due to AIDS. In Zambia it is down to forty years. In the past twenty years the average life expectancy for all Africans has decreased by fifteen years.

The prime minister of Mozambique, Pascoal Mocumbi, wrote in the *New York Times*: "The United Nations estimates that 37 percent of the sixteen-year-olds in my country will die of AIDS before they are thirty."[15] He further notes:

> In Mozambique, the overall rate of HIV infection among girls and young women—15 percent—is twice that of boys their age, not because the girls are promiscuous, but because nearly three out of five are married by age eighteen, 40 percent of them to much older, sexually experienced men who may expose their wives to HIV and sexually transmitted diseases.[16]

With an aggressive prevention campaign led by President Museveni, Uganda has reduced its estimated infection rate from 21 percent in 1992 to 6 percent in 2000, but the suffering continues at a high level. The Reverend Fred Taabu, a Ugandan pastor, offers this eyewitness account:

> Last Friday I attended four funerals. One of the women who died was only twenty-eight and left five orphans. This family is one that has suffered hard. On December 31, 1997, the father to this girl died of AIDS; after four days his wife died. In February this year their eldest daughter died and now the last born of their children, and these due to AIDS. The worst thing is that they have left thirteen orphans under the care of a young twenty-two-year-old unmarried man. Pray for this family and for the Church on whose neck the burden of care for the orphans is left.

The next great wave of HIV/AIDS in the world is expected to include Nigeria and Ethiopia. Predictions are that Nigeria will have 10 to 15 million cases and Ethiopia 7 to 10 million by 2010.[17] In Nigeria, the most populous country in Africa, the reported rate varies significantly by region, with the lowest rates in the northern, more Muslim parts of the country. By 2010 some 18 to 26 percent of all adults are likely to be infected. Ethiopia already has between 10 to 18 percent of adults infected.

War, poverty, drought, malnutrition, limited health care, lack of education, and diseases have facilitated the spread of HIV in Ethiopia. As the border conflict with Eritrea diminishes, soldiers, who already have a high infection rate, will return to their homes across the country, thereby spreading HIV to the broader population. In 2000, Nigeria had an estimated 2.6 million children orphaned by AIDS. In both Ethiopia and Nigeria the number of orphans is expected to escalate dramatically, overwhelming available caretakers.[18] It should be noted that the more "Christian-dominated" countries of Africa have a much higher prevalence of HIV than "Muslim-dominated countries."

Asia

In the early years of the twenty-first century, the epicenter of the epidemic in sheer numbers is expected to shift to Asia, home of more than half of the world's population. A small increase in infection rates can impact millions and millions of people. By 2003 South and Southeast Asia had an estimated 6 million people living with HIV/AIDS (36 percent women), and eastern Asia and the Pacific had 1.2 million (24 percent women).

Thailand, with about a million people infected, has long struggled to combat the disease with aggressive prevention efforts. By doing so, in contrast to South Africa, it has kept the infection rate relatively low over the past decade. Yet HIV/AIDS remains the leading cause of death in the country. The government makes anti-retroviral drugs available at less than a dollar per day—but that is beyond the reach of the poor.

Other countries in Southeast Asia are facing serious problems. For example, 3 percent of the adult population of Cambodia is now infected. But some health experts fear that the death rate may exceed the genocide committed by the Khmer Rouge from 1975–79, when more than 1 million were massacred.[19]

The governments of the two most populous nations of the world, China and India, have long been in a state of denial about the seriousness of the health situation within their borders. Knowledge about China remains limited, but information is increasingly emerging to suggest that HIV/AIDS is more widespread than previously reported. A top Chinese government official, Deputy Health Minister Yin Dakui, openly admitted that China is "facing a very serious epidemic of HIV/AIDS" and the government has "not effectively stemmed the epidemic."[20] Statistics vary widely, with the Chinese government claiming 600,000 people were infected at the end of 2000 while the United Nations estimates there were more than 1 million. The government's goal is to contain the number of HIV/AIDS cases to less than 1.5 million in 2010, while some project 10 to 15 million cases and the United Nations expects the number could be 20 million in 2010, if current trends continue there.[21] Several factors influence China's growth of infections: 100 million uprooted rural migrants seeking employment in crowded cities, rising intravenous drug usage, the practice of selling and mixing blood plasma, widespread ignorance about HIV/AIDS, and cultural taboos regarding sexual matters.[22]

Likewise, in India denial reigns supreme not only among government officials but also much of the general population. Officially, the number of people infected is reported at nearly 5 million. Other health experts suggest the number is closer to 10 million. Knowledgeable experts predict between 20 to 25 million by 2010.[23] A *Washington Post* article even suggested that by 2005 the number will be about 35 million in India! Whatever the number, India surpasses South Africa as the nation with the greatest incidence of HIV/AIDS.

In this ancient land of more than a billion people, accurate statistics may never be forthcoming due to the multiplicity of health problems, lack of medical infrastructure, and acute poverty. But regardless of mass statistics, individual persons suffering from AIDS in India experience not only the pain and agony of their illness but also a high level of discrimination and isolation. Many Christian hospitals until recently did not even accept HIV/AIDS patients!

The Bill and Melinda Gates Foundation has committed over $200 million to prevention programs in India, emphasizing voluntary counseling and testing, condom distribution, treatment of sexually transmitted diseases, and reduction of fear and stigma. Heterosexual transmission in India is the primary cause of HIV infections, though intravenous drug use is an important factor in certain areas. HIV incidence rates for truckers, soldiers, migrant workers, and sex workers are ten times higher than the national average. Bill Gates believes we know how to prevent the spread of HIV/AIDS. He says, "The choice now is clear and stark: India can either be the home of the world's largest and most devastating AIDS epidemic—or, with the support of the rest of the world, it can become the best example of how this virus can be defeated."[24]

Latin America and the Caribbean
By the end of 2002, Latin America had 1.5 million people infected with HIV and the Caribbean some 420,000. Deaths in Latin America numbered 60,000 in 2002, and new HIV cases numbered 150,000. At an AIDS conference in Uruguay, I met and spoke with overwhelmed church health workers from almost every Latin American country. I spent time in Costa Rica visiting men dying in an AIDS hospice—most of whom had been abandoned by their families. A Christian nurse from Panama told me how HIV/AIDS patients were sometimes dropped off anonymously and no one ever came to see them.

Several Caribbean island states suffer worse epidemics than anywhere except sub-Saharan Africa. In Haiti over 8 percent of adults in urban areas and 4 percent in rural areas live with HIV; in the Bahamas the rate is over 4 percent. By the end of 2001, it was estimated that 200,000 Haitian children had lost one or both parents to AIDS. The heterosexual epidemic is fueled by a deadly combination of early sexual activity and frequent partner exchange among young people. HIV rates are five times higher for girls than boys aged fifteen to nineteen in Trinidad and Tobago because of intergenerational sex. Young men have sex with women their own age or younger, but 28 percent of young girls report sex with older men.

Rates of heterosexual and homosexual transmission of HIV vary from country to country in Latin America. Infection in Mexico, Argentina, and Colombia has been primarily among men who have sex with men and among intravenous drug users. In Costa Rica the epidemic primarily impacts men who have sex with other men. To date, low rates of infection have been reported in the Andean countries, but Honduras, Guatemala, and Belize are experiencing a fast-growing epidemic with incidence rates among adults between 1 and 2 percent.

Three Latin American countries—Argentina, Brazil, and Mexico—are attempting to provide anti-retroviral therapy for all people suffering from HIV/AIDS. By the end of 2001, Brazil, for example, was providing about 105,000 Brazilians with free anti-retroviral treatment. Brazil, with an estimated 600,000 people living with HIV/AIDS, has also reduced infections among intravenous drug users by promoting programs for safer injection habits. Sustained education and prevention efforts have significantly increased condom usage in Brazil.

Russia and Eastern Europe

According to every indication, the rate of HIV infection in Russia is quickening. The top Russian government AIDS expert, Vadim V. Pokrovsky, estimates that between 500,000 to 1.5 million, or more than 1 percent of the population, are carrying the virus. Within five years the number could escalate to over 7 million, one in every twenty-five Russians. UNAIDS (the Joint United Nations Program on HIV/AIDS) reports that there were 25,000 deaths from AIDS in 2002 and 250,000 new cases reported. The crisis is mainly fueled by intravenous drug use of young men, most of whom are sexually active. Initially, an estimated 80 to 90 percent of all Russian infection was related to intravenous drug use. Men comprise 77 percent of those infected, with 60 percent between the ages of seventeen and twenty-five.

Russian prisons serve as incubators of HIV since illegal drugs are easily accessible there. Reports from Ekaterinburg, Russia, show that in one year alone the number of inmates with HIV increased by over 300 percent! Once prisoners are released into the general society, the virus spreads rapidly through sexual relationships. Combine this with an inadequate health care infrastructure and it is anticipated that the crisis will escalate rapidly.[25] Government and public AIDS prevention messages in Russia have been minimal. Seeking to break the conspiracy of silence in Russia, Pokrovsky warned: "The problems related to H.I.V. infection are like a snowball, and the longer we look at how it rolls down the slope, the larger it will be when it stops if we do not come out altogether to stop this avalanche."[26]

Escalating drug use and unsafe heterosexual practices are also blamed for the rapid rise of HIV/AIDS in countries that were formerly part of the Soviet Union. Countries like Estonia, the Ukraine, and Kazakhstan are cited as having one of the fastest growing HIV epidemics in the world.

Western Europe, Australia, and New Zealand

Because of contemporary medical therapies and prevention strategies, HIV/AIDS is a more manageable disease in Western Europe, Australia, and New Zealand. At the end of 2002 Western Europe had

570,000 people (25 percent women) living with HIV/AIDS and Australia/New Zealand had 15,000. These countries have low HIV infection rates among heterosexuals in the general population.

Some signs exist, however, that complacency and risky sexual practices may have returned. Sweden, with one of the lowest rates of HIV infection in the world, suddenly experienced a 48 percent increase of new HIV cases early in 2001. In Australia and some other high-income countries, the availability of anti-retroviral drugs apparently has misled some young gay men to engage in unprotected anal sex.

European countries with the highest numbers of people estimated to be living with HIV/AIDS are Spain with 131,000, France with 101,000, Italy with 100,000, Portugal with 36,000, and the United Kingdom with 49,500.[27]

North Africa and the Middle East
Medical surveillance systems in North Africa and the Middle East are inadequate, so estimates of infection rates are very uncertain. UNAIDS projects there were an estimated 550,000 people living with HIV/AIDS in this region at the end of 2002. Women constitute about 55 percent of the infected adult population. In 2002, 37,000 people died of HIV/AIDS and another 83,000 were newly infected.

Denial prevails in many of the countries and cultures in this region, so tracking the disease is difficult. Among the worst affected countries are Sudan with 140,000 people infected; Algeria, where a local study of HIV among pregnant women revealed 1 percent as HIV-positive; and Iran where intravenous drug use is high (200,000–300,000 people), injecting equipment is shared, and many allegedly engage in extramarital sex. Much remains unknown in this region of the world regarding human sexual behavior and the challenges to public health from HIV/AIDS.

Updating Global Statistics

Keeping abreast of the latest statistics and developments on global HIV/AIDS is a challenge. I hope the foregoing thumbnail sketch of statistics from around the world will prove exaggerated and that—thanks to creative programs in prevention, behavioral change, and treatment—the numbers predicted will not come to pass. Realistically, however, I worry they will be underestimates in most cases and that the health crisis will escalate beyond our greatest fears. The executive director of the United Nation's related Global Fund for AIDS says we are only at the beginning of the pandemic and that it will not peak until 2050 or 2060.[28]

To keep updated, I urge readers to seek out information from the many AIDS-related sites readily available on the Internet. Here are some helpful resources from among the many out there.

AIDS Map is a charity based in Great Britain, providing a broad range of articles and information from around the world. **www.aidsmap.com**

AIDS Org provides updated information, especially treatment news. **www.aids.org**

Artists Against AIDS Worldwide is an entertainment nonprofit organization that provides music, videos, and an instant accounting of AIDS deaths since the first of January of a given year. **www.aaaw.org**

Bill and Melinda Gates Foundation offers innovations in health and learning to the global community. **www.gatesfoundation.org**

Center for the Church and Global AIDS coordinates efforts of individuals and organizations committed to engaging churches in practical projects aimed at creating a world without AIDS. E-mail: **churchandglobalaids@yahoo.com** or **dmesser@iliff.edu**

Christian Connections for International Health promotes health and wholeness from a Christian perspective with an emphasis on HIV/AIDS, tuberculosis, and malaria. **www.ccih.org**

The Ecumenical Advocacy Alliance, based in Geneva in the World Council of Churches building, coordinates Christian advocacy efforts internationally. **www.e-alliance.ch**

Lutheran World Federation has launched a global campaign against HIV/AIDS.
www.lutheranworld.org

Stop Global AIDS offers an extensive network of agencies advocating progressive policies to combat AIDS.
www.stopglobalaids.org

UNAIDS, a joint United Nations program on HIV/AIDS, provides invaluable information and statistics.
www.UNAIDS.org

United Methodist HIV/AIDS Ministries Network provides updated information on the global AIDS pandemic.
www.gbgm-umc.org/health/aids

Toward a New AIDS Theology

Currently the church in the United States has little understanding of the global AIDS crisis and sees little, if any, relationship between what it means to be a disciple of Jesus Christ and an active advocate for the well-being and health of the billions of God's people on earth. The global emergency outlined by the United Nations is simply not on our religious radar, and otherwise good and compassionate Christians function as if they had no responsibility for making a difference. This attitudinal perspective and apathetic posture lead to almost no creative missional outreach to Christians and others in the Two-Thirds World. Tragically, this type of narrow theological thinking prevails not only among Christians in the so-called First World (the top industrialized nations) but often among Christians and many other religious traditions throughout the world.

Kabanda and Brigitte Syamalevwe of Zambia were caught in this theological mind-set. Both are committed Christians and both were infected with HIV. For years the church in Africa was silent about and sometimes condemning of HIV/AIDS. Kabanda and Brigitte had been married for thirty years, but they discovered their illness too late to take preventive steps. Nevertheless, they were determined to use their

HIV-positive status "for the glory of God." As a senior clinical officer for the public health service, Kabanda, the son of a tribal chief, became an advocate for men's participation in AIDS work, changed his thinking about women's issues, and sought to empower his wife. Brigitte, a schoolteacher, counselor, and artist became a consultant to the Ministry of Education.

At a conference of Christians in the United States, they were articulate spokespersons for the millions in the Two-Third's World who suffer without modern medical therapies. In one session, tension developed between the American and African participants, with the Syamalevwes saying that "the Americans did not really feel and share in the burden of AIDS weighing down the church and communities in Africa." Once effectively challenged and convicted, the Americans joined with their African friends in a period of crying, confession, forgiveness, and supplication. They gathered around the Syamalevwes, praying for them and each other, "allowing the Spirit of God to show that we are all in this struggle together." But without medical treatment, Kabanda died a year later, and soon after, his wife was buried beside him on their farm in Luanshya Ibenga, Zambia. They left behind ten children—orphans they had adopted over the course of a decade.[29]

During the first twenty-five years since the advent of HIV/AIDS on the global scene, Christian theology has been dominated by an exclusive, judgmental perspective, contradictory to the very character or essence of the church of Jesus Christ. In response to this global emergency, Christians should instead move toward a new AIDS theology that emphasizes inclusion, not exclusion—compassion, not condemnation. More Christian leaders must make the effort to link biblical teachings with the imperative of caring for people with HIV/AIDS and to embrace a theological perspective that harmonizes with the radical love and action epitomized in Jesus, the Christ.

The central logo at an ecumenical conference on global HIV/AIDS that I attended in Mumbai (Bombay), India, was the cross of Jesus Christ wrapped in the red ribbon symbolizing AIDS. It was a very dramatic way of saying that the church of Jesus Christ is called to be in the very heart of this global pandemic of pain and suffering. We have no choice; there is no escape; *the body of Christ has AIDS.*

Perhaps many of us, deep down in our hearts and minds, recoil at mixing the sacred symbol of the cross with the red ribbon of

HIV/AIDS. The cross may have become for us something beautiful, even decorative. Many people like to wear it as a fashion statement— the cross on a necklace or as earrings or a lapel pin. We decorate our churches with crosses and emblazon them on our denominational logos. The cross reminds us of the centrality of Christ's sacrifice for us all. We love to sing "In the cross of Christ I glory," and we cherish the music of "The Old Rugged Cross."

On the other hand, the red ribbon of HIV/AIDS reminds us of other issues that we often do not want to talk about in the church: human sexuality, intravenous drug use, condom distribution, disease, and death. During the 1980s and early 1990s, AIDS activists in America often wore the red ribbon that symbolizes AIDS. With advanced medical treatment in this country, however, the ribbon gradually disappeared from the clothes of even the most committed. But in India, I was confronted with the two symbols woven together. Placed on the background of a globe, this highlights both the need for a new theology and the new world challenge we face. It is a new way of restating Scottish theologian George MacLeod's claims:

> I simply argue that the Cross be raised again at the center of the market place as well as on the steeple of the church. I am recovering the claim that Jesus was not crucified in a Cathedral between two candles, but on a Cross between two thieves; on the town garbage heap; on a crossroads so cosmopolitan that they had to write his title in Hebrew and Latin and in Greek; at the kind of place where cynics talk smut and thieves curse, and soldiers gamble. Because that is where he died and that is what he died about. And that is where churchmen should be and what churchmen should be about.[30]

While the cross has become the central symbol of Christian faith, which itself is an intriguing irony and puzzling paradox, we need to remember that it was intended to humiliate the early Christian followers of Jesus. Used to execute Jesus, the cross was equivalent to a contemporary electric chair, a firing squad, or a guillotine. It was designed to show the weakness of Jesus and the helplessness of his followers. Christians cherish other symbols like the fish, the empty tomb, the cup of wine, and the loaf of bread. But somehow Christians have been drawn to a crucified Christ and have transformed the cross into their hope for life and redemption.

Paul recognized this intriguing irony and puzzling paradox when he wrote to the church in Corinth. It was already evident that people outside the Christian community had difficulty understanding the mysterious significance of Jesus the Christ being crucified. It seemed preposterous to them that God would so love the world that God would allow an only son to die a horrible death upon a cross. Thus Paul declared: "We proclaim Christ crucified, a stumbling block to Jews and foolishness to Gentiles." Yet, Paul said, Jesus' followers see this crucified Christ on a cross as "the power of God and the wisdom of God." Furthermore, "For God's foolishness is wiser than human wisdom, and God's weakness is stronger than human strength" (1 Corinthians 1:23-25).

A new holy boldness is required of the church in the age of AIDS. The cross wrapped in the red ribbon of AIDS reminds the church of God's saving mission in Christ and our ecclesial calling to join in God's liberating and loving ministry in the world. Doing so will require us to take apostolic risks of entering into previously controversial topics and ministries that demonstrate anew that the crucified Christ is "the power of God and the wisdom of God."

Reclaiming the Essence of the Church

The global AIDS emergency compels us to reclaim the essence of the church. The very being (*esse*) of the church of Jesus Christ requires the inclusion of all God's people. The church as *koinonia*—as true fellowship—is violated when some Christian believers are excluded and stigmatized and suffer discrimination because of the church's teachings and actions. The very essence of the church is at stake when people are excluded from God's mission and ministry.[31]

Inclusiveness is not an optional "extra" or "political correctness" for Christians. It is not simply discretional, useful, or theologically beneficial (*bene esse*). Inclusiveness is a way of being, living, working, and worshiping together in mission: a basic element of our faith in Jesus Christ and our Christian identity. To paraphrase Emil Brunner, whom we quoted in the introduction, inclusiveness is to the church as fire is to burning. Inclusiveness is a precondition for the church's distinguishing marks set forth in the Nicene Creed: "one, holy, catholic, and apostolic church." The unity, holiness, universality, and apostolicity of the church flow from Christ's inclusive gospel.

Historically the basis of the unity of the church has sometimes been lodged in the papacy, episcopacy, or some other juridical body. Augustine, however, identified a spiritual basis in the love poured out by Christ and the Holy Spirit. Church unity comes not from scripture, doctrine, or denominational polity but from God's redemptive action in Christ, "which is intrinsically nonprovincial in character, with no divisions or exclusions legitimated on the basis of race, nationality, location, sex, creed, language, or the like."[32] Inclusive love that tolerates and embraces diversity and difference is the precondition of unity.

Likewise, if the church is truly to be catholic, universal, or ecumenical, it cannot discriminate against other Christian persons of faith and goodwill. The early church was radically egalitarian and inclusive, a subversive threat to prevailing Jewish and Hellenistic religious and cultural patterns. The new *basileia* vision of Jesus (kingdom or realm of God) provided a new way of relating to people in the world: the inclusion of people without conditions, namely, women, the poor, the sick, and "sinners" of all sorts.[33] Galatians 3:28 epitomizes this vision: "Neither Jew nor Greek, neither slave nor free, neither male nor female, all are one in Christ Jesus." The holiness of the church, wrote Thomas Aquinas in his *Exposition on the Apostles' Creed,* is due to "the indwelling of the blessed Trinity." Holiness does not depend on the moral worthiness of any of its members, clergy or laity, whether heterosexual or homosexual, HIV-positive or HIV-negative. We are, in Martin Luther's words, *simul justus et peccator* (at once justified and sinful), both a communion of saints (*communio sanctorum*) and a community of sinners (*communio peccatorum*).[34]

Ultimately the apostolic nature of the church does not depend upon the theory of apostolic succession, but on the liberating inclusive paradigm of Jesus' ministry that reached out to all people, especially those most marginalized and stigmatized by their cultures and religions. This paradigm is at the heart of our mission as Christians combating AIDS in the twenty-first century.

The reason that the church has been "missing in action" regarding global AIDS is primarily because of its theology of exclusion toward homosexual persons. Instead of focusing on God's grief over AIDS,

Christians in many places have sought to sideline God's healing ministry by offering a judgmental rather than a compassionate gospel. While some of the writings of Richard B. Hays at Duke Divinity School are often cited to justify the exclusion of gays and lesbians from all levels of the life of the church, he nevertheless insists that "We all stand without excuse under God's judgment. Self-righteous judgment of homosexuality is just as sinful as the homosexual behavior itself."[35]

Luke Timothy Johnson of Emory University suggests that gay and lesbian people may reflect the ongoing revelation of God, calling the church to respond with Christ-like grace and justice. He notes that God does act in "surprising and unanticipated ways" to "upset human perceptions of God's scriptural precedents." He cites three examples: (1) a crucified and resurrected Messiah contrary to expectations and teachings in the Hebrew Bible, (2) the spread of the gospel to Gentiles without requiring circumcision or following the Torah, and (3) more recently the church allowing divorce even though Jesus forbade it.[36] God's ongoing revelation at first may be perceived as "dissonant with the symbols of Scripture," but by God's grace homosexuality may eventually be understood by the church as "consonant with those symbols and God's own fidelity."[37] Johnson asks, What if the church were to consider homosexual people as a social class akin to Gentiles, accepting them as full members of the body of Christ in all respects, similar to what happened in Acts 15?

Now HIV/AIDS is primarily transmitted heterosexually and the church remains paralyzed on the sideline, trapped by its initial exclusionary attitude, moralistic teachings, stone-throwing tendencies, and failure to remember the forgiving, compassionate spirit of Jesus. The global Christ we worship embraced especially those who were excluded at the religious table of others: women, tax collectors, Samaritans, lepers, and "sinners."

Discrimination and stigmatization of persons are immoral actions and attitudes contrary to the teachings of Jesus. Whenever and wherever they occur, they cause personal and social harm. A primary example has been the church's failure to address the global HIV/AIDS emergency. Though clearly the global crisis is now primarily a heterosexual phenomenon, discriminatory and stigmatizing attitudes and actions toward gay persons by heterosexual Christians has shaped our general lack of response and compassion. African bishops and other church leaders declared at a World Council of Churches consultation in Nairobi, Kenya, in December 2001, that the global pandemic of HIV/AIDS has "exposed fault lines that reach to the heart of our theology, our ethics, our liturgy and our practice of ministry. Today, churches are being obliged to acknowledge that we have—however unwittingly—contributed both actively and passively to the spread of the virus. Our difficulty in addressing issues of sex and sexuality has often made it painful for us to engage, in any honest and realistic way, with issues of sex education and HIV prevention." Further, it was noted:

> Our tendency to exclude others, our interpretation of the scriptures and our theology of sin have all combined to promote the stigmatization, exclusion, and suffering of people with HIV or AIDS. This has undermined the effectiveness of care, education, and prevention efforts and inflicted additional suffering on those already affected by HIV. Given the extreme urgency of the situation and the conviction that the churches do have a distinctive role to play in the response to the pandemic, what is needed is a rethinking of our mission, and the transformation of our structures and ways of working.[38]

An Ecumenical and Interfaith Response

Such theological rethinking and structural transformation must not only be individual and denominational but also ecumenical and interfaith. Instead of being positive and progressive forces in the global battle against HIV/AIDS, religious leaders and communities too often prove negative and reactionary. Instead of accenting central core values like love, forgiveness, and healing (found in most of the major world religions), too often people with HIV/AIDS experience the opposite when religious leaders and communities contribute to denial and discrimination. This only compounds public health and personal well-being issues. Long before AIDS emerged on the world stage, Martin Luther King Jr. declared that we have inherited a "world house in which we have to live together—black and white, Easterner and Westerner, Gentile and Jew, Catholic and Protestant, Moslem and Hindu—

a family unduly separated in ideas, culture and interest, who, because we can never again live apart, must learn somehow to live with each other in peace." He warned that unless we learn to live together as sisters and brothers, "we will be forced to perish as fools."[39]

How can we avoid perishing "as fools"? One possibility has already been modeled. In recent years world religious leaders have gathered together at the invitation of Pope John Paul II and others to pray and to seek creative responses to urgent issues related to justice, peace, and the integrity of creation. As a new century dawns, there is an ever urgent need for a similar gathering focused exclusively on addressing the international crisis of HIV/AIDS.

One by One by One

While a global pandemic calls upon national and international bodies of both church and state to become responsibly involved, it is yet imperative to accent the role every individual can and must play in the process. It is not enough simply to support policy resolutions or write one's public officials—important as these steps are. What remains fundamental is that committed Christians and other people of faith and goodwill become personally involved.

During a trip to India, I spent some time at Kalighat, a home for the destitute and dying in Calcutta established by Mother Teresa. Fifty years ago she came across an abandoned woman dying in the streets with rats and ants consuming her. She took her to a hospital, but the woman was refused entrance. Thus began Mother Teresa's ministry to the poorest of the poor. She identified the suffering poor with the crucifixion of Christ. She began the Missionaries of Charity, which now has more than 3,000 members working in 52 countries, many addressing HIV/AIDS.

Every day volunteers from around the world go out on the streets of India and pick up people who are desperately ill and hopelessly alone. They bring them to Kalighat and care for them. After she won the Nobel Peace Prize, Mother Teresa returned to toil with the volunteers, caring for patients, scrubbing the floors, hand washing the blankets, and ministering to the dead and dying. When I was there, I saw about fifty men and fifty women lying on mats on the floor.

Beside them were people bathing them, holding their hands, comforting them in their last moments of life. I was reminded of these words of Mother Teresa:

> I never look at the masses as my responsibility.
> I look at the individual. I can love only one person at a time. I can feed only one person at a time.
> Just one, one, one.
> You get closer to Christ by coming closer to each other. As Jesus said, "Whatever you do to the least of my brethren, you do to me."
> So you begin . . . I began.
> I picked up one person—
> Maybe if I didn't pick up that one person I wouldn't have picked up 42,000.
> . . .
> Just begin . . . one, one, one.[40]

When I ponder the overwhelming statistics of global AIDS—such as 46 million people infected worldwide—I sometimes grow numb and feel paralyzed. There is remoteness to such staggering statistics as numbers replace faces and percentages take the place of people. I know Mother Teresa has been criticized as lacking a sufficient political or social Christian ethic, yet I also know the beneficial and enduring missional strategy of Mother Teresa—one by one by one.

The day I visited her home for the destitute and dying, they had just brought in patient number 77,441. One by one since she began, they have logged in each person needing care and love. In this one house, in this one place, all these people have felt the merciful ministry of people who care.

If the church is to effectively address global HIV/AIDS, then a theological revolution must occur. Christian behavioral change will result as people are converted—one by one by one—from an old theology of exclusion and condemnation to a new theology of inclusion and compassion. And the one, holy, catholic, and apostolic church will once again become the "church militant," but this time in the war to liberate the world from AIDS.

2

We Are All HIV-positive

Sexuality is a topic the church has found difficult to address. Its silent and joyless condemnation of sexuality in general has been a contributing factor in the spread of AIDS.

—Canon Susan Cole-King

About forty years ago at the beginning of the struggle for justice and civil rights in the United States, John Howard Griffin wrote a controversial, yet popular, book entitled *Black Like Me* (the thirty-fifth anniversary edition was published in 1996).[1] What made the book controversial was that Griffin was a white man who temporarily darkened his skin and treated his hair to attempt to live as an African American in a racially segregated society. Critics rightfully pointed out that no white person in such a temporary situation could even begin to appreciate the outrages of racism and the personal pain of discrimination. What made it popular, however, was that for the first time many white readers began the process of understanding the experience of racism and its demeaning and terrible structures of segregation.

Perhaps for many of us, if we are to get "up close and personal" with the dilemmas and discrimination of persons with HIV/AIDS, we need to at least imagine, if not acknowledge, that we too are HIV-positive. Instead of an "us" and "them" perspective, we need to attempt to enter into the daily experiences of those living with HIV/AIDS. Recognizing the limits of such an approach, let me share what it might be like for me, and I would invite you to think about your own situation.

Facing Stigmatization and Discrimination

If I were to publicly acknowledge that I am HIV-positive, I think my world would begin to crumble. Besides the fear and pain and anxiety I would feel inside, I realize that my many relationships would be tested to the utmost. I don't know what would happen and how far I might tumble. I don't really know what family and friends would say or do.

If I am diagnosed with cancer tomorrow, I have no doubt that people wouldn't care how I got it, but people would care for me unconditionally. But if I'm diagnosed as HIV-positive, I know many people would care how I got it, and people would care for me conditionally.

Inevitably, the questions that would be raised in my presence, and especially behind my back, would focus on what I did to get the disease. I hope that, eventually, care would come from family and friends, but probably only after a painful process of questioning, anger, blaming, apologizing, and who knows what else. The acceptance and care I anticipate would be conditional.

Ramifications in the work world would probably be worse. Being a United Methodist clergyman means that if the source of my illness were sex-related, I know that my denomination would be condemning and unaccepting. Despite giving lip service to support, the vast majority of my friends in the ministry would simply disappear at the moment of my greatest crisis. Possibly the church would push me to either quietly retire from the ministry or be threatened with a public trial to remove me from the United Methodist clergy.

Life would be changed permanently. How would people respond to my hugs? How would my dentist or doctors react? Would my insurance be enough? How would I handle my feelings—emotionally and sexually? What would I tell people? What do I need to tell them? What treatments are available? What do I want to take? What can I afford? Do I need to find a new church or give up on God completely? How do I struggle to survive? How much pain and illness can I tolerate? How much hatred and rejection can I endure? Or do I just decide there is no viable future?

This stream of questions would be only the beginning of a flood of anxious questions and decisions that I would be forced to face. Even as grim as I imagine my own situation, I realize that for most of the 46 million people worldwide who are HIV-positive, my circumstances would be light-years better than their situation today. I have advantages that they simply do not have.

We know that far too many persons who have lived and died with AIDS in the United States have faced discrimination and outright hatred. Parents have rejected their children. Life partners have been excluded and treatments denied. The government has moved slowly and the church reluctantly at best. When the famous tennis player, Arthur Ashe, learned he was infected due to a blood transfusion, he so feared discrimination against himself and his family that he lived with the knowledge for three and one-half years before revealing he had the disease.[2]

If a person is HIV-positive or has AIDS in many parts of Africa, Asia, or South America, his or her plight is even more precarious. I have heard testimonies about people dropped off at hospitals in Panama and Thailand forever abandoned by their families. I know that in many rural African hospitals there are no medicines or clean needles available. In India there is often no medical care now for the poor, so little hope exists for the 5 to 20 million now HIV-positive.

Even as we see some signs of hope in the United States, we need to remember that 90 percent of all HIV infections are outside the industrialized First World, but only about 10 percent of all the resources are used to benefit those 95 percent. The HIV virus daily infects 16,000 people worldwide, but only 5 percent will have a chance to use the latest medicines. Some 2.9 million people around the globe died of AIDS in 1999. In some countries, like Zimbabwe, one out of three adults is infected and 800,000 orphans cry out for care. A fifteen-year-old in South Africa has only a fifty-fifty chance of living to age thirty.

We Are All Dying

The singer Diamánda Galás created a trilogy of albums called *The Masque of Red Death* against the AIDS epidemic that claimed her playwright brother.[3] Reportedly she tattooed on her knuckles the words "We are all HIV+." Her point was political, but mine is theological. HIV/AIDS symbolizes death in our generation—a fatal disease for which no cure has yet been discovered. But, in fact, we are all destined to die—most of us just don't yet know what fatal disease or accident will prompt our demise.

Thus by making the beginning point for our Christian understanding of the AIDS crisis the acknowledgment that, theologically, we are all HIV-positive, we first of all acknowledge the sovereignty of God. God is the giver of life; we are not the absolute owners of our lives and destinies. God is the creator and ruler of the universe, and we have been blessed with life. Because God is the giver of life, all human life is sacred and inviolable. Ultimately, life and death are within the sovereignty of God. So, with the apostle Paul we can declare: "We do not live to ourselves, and we do not die to ourselves. If we live, we live to the Lord, and if we die, we die to the Lord; so then, whether we live or whether we die, we are the Lord's. For to this end Christ died and lived again, so that he might be Lord of both the dead and the living" (Romans 14:7-9).

This emphasis on the sovereignty of God serves as a poignant reminder of the preciousness of life. What makes life so cherished and valued is the absence of life. What makes life so precious is the knowledge that all life has an ending. Therefore, we are called to appreciate, protect, nurture, and celebrate the life we all have been given.

The Least of These My Brethren is a medical doctor's story of hope and miracles on an inner-city AIDS ward in New York City. This doctor, Daniel J. Baxter, provides a gripping account of what it means to live and die with HIV/AIDS for the most marginalized of our society—prisoners, drug addicts, transsexuals, and the homeless. When asked how he deals daily with the incredible pain and pressures of dealing with difficult patients and facing the ugly spectacle of death, Baxter affirms how profoundly special are his patient's lives and his own as a caregiver—how special "*all* human life is."[4] He explains:

> This sense of life's preciousness . . . is how I can survive
> the daily spectre of disease and death. It is how I can

maintain my emotional perspective day in and day out. Not only do I never fear the daily reminders of my own frail mortality, but I am grateful for this exposure, this realization that *we are all ultimately HIV-positive,* in that we are all going to die sooner or later. I acutely realize that someday, regardless of my own final disease or injury, I, too, will join my many patients on the sickbeds. The poignant stories transpiring every day on my AIDS ward, my crucible of despair and hope, have taught me that living a life that denies the relevancy and imminency of death actually robs that life of the wonder it should really have. Indeed, I have come to believe that a content life is one that gracefully carries death on its shoulder as a friend and not a feared adversary.[5]

Further, when we acknowledge we are all HIV-positive, we discover a new solidarity with all our brothers and sisters in Christ. In the words of Paul, we all are brothers and sisters in Christ and stand under the parenthood and authority of God. From a Christian perspective we are all "members one of another," and what inflicts my brother or sister also afflicts me. Or, as Albert Schweitzer used to say, Christians are united in a solidarity of suffering.

Let us remember that the ground at the foot of the cross is level and that we all stand under the judgment of God. Paul makes it abundantly clear that we all are accountable to God. Thus Paul asks us: "Why do you pass judgment on your brother or sister? Or you, why do you despise your brother or sister? For we will all stand before the judgment seat of God" (Romans 14:10).

The judgmentalism of so many people toward persons with HIV/AIDS stands in stark contrast to this biblical injunction. One would think we would realize that the differences between people are so slight when we stand before the righteousness of God that we will be unable to measure any distinctions.

A Buddhist friend, José Cabezón, also points out that we are all dying. He notes that "whether our demise is brought about by AIDS or through some other cause, we will all end up in the same place." That, says Cabezón, is but one "of the many good Buddhist reasons for not discriminating against women and men who are HIV-positive."[6]

However, too often Christians forget that judgment rests with God. I never will forget what happened in an Atlanta hospital. A young gay man with AIDS was very much alone as he faced the final moments of his life. Hospital personnel sent out a call for a pastor. But much to their horror, a preacher came but only stood in the doorway. He shouted out a prayer asking God's forgiveness for this prodigal son, expressing judgment and disapproval.

When hearing of this incident, a young seminarian named Sally rushed to the room. She embraced the dying man and spent the remaining hours with him. Later, when friends asked her what she did, she replied, "Oh, I just held him, sang hymns, prayed, and kept telling him over and over again, how much God loved him."

By accepting that we are all HIV-positive, we affirm both the sovereignty of God and our solidarity with our brothers and sisters in Christ.

Courage and Hope of HIV/AIDS Victims

After John Howard Griffin published his successful book *Black Like Me*, he was invited throughout America to share his insights about race relations. What exasperated him and African Americans was that time and time again white people turned to him for explanations instead of to knowledgeable black persons who truly understood the experience of racism and segregation. African American perspectives as shared by themselves or presented in their newspapers and other media were ignored.

If we are to truly empathize with persons having HIV/AIDS, then we need to listen actively to their stories and the stories of their beloved partners and families. We need to read their newspapers and their books. We need to hear their personal spiritual testimonies and their political cries for social justice.

In doing so, I have been surprised by the incredible strength and courage and hope of those who are living with HIV/AIDS. Too much of what I have written about HIV/AIDS has been negative. This needs to be counterbalanced by the winsome witness and triumphant testimony of those who have discovered God's grace even amid this horrendous epidemic.

Thus in the autobiographical pages of Janice A. Burns's *Sarah's Song: A True Story of Love and Courage*, I was touched by how she and her husband both battled against AIDS and cared for one another with transformative and transcendent love.[7] And I remember how I was humbled by the confident faith of a man with AIDS named Ralph when I visited him in a Denver AIDS hospital. Though racked with pain as he rode the "misery-go-round" of cancer, pneumonia, and blindness, he constantly affirmed that God was with him. He repeatedly told me: "Never give up hope! Someday a breakthrough—a miracle—will come."

A Jewish rabbi asked his students at what point night turned into day. One student said, "It's when you can look out into the distance and tell the difference between a sheep and a dog." "No," said the rabbi, "that's not it." Another student claimed, "It's when you can look into the distance and tell the difference between a peach tree and a fig tree." Again the rabbi said no. Instead, the rabbi claimed, "It's dawn when you can look into the face of another human being and recognize him or her as your brother or sister. Then you know the night is over."[8]

The dark night of disease and death will be over and a new day of health and life will have arrived when Christians can look into the face of strangers, even those most marginalized and oppressed and ill—the "least of these my brethren"—and recognize them as brothers and sisters in the family of God. Recognize that we are all HIV-positive.

It's Not Our Problem

Tragically, Christians in many places throughout the world have failed to hear the summons of God to Christian compassion and action. AIDS is a global emergency, yet instead of being Good Samaritans reaching out to persons who have been struck down on the roadside of life, too often the church has epitomized the priests and Levites who busily hurried by, doing their spiritual business as usual.

The reasons for resistance and reticence on the part of Christians are many. Let me cite but three common excuses. First, "it's not our problem." Too often Christians have tried to stick their heads in the sand and pretend that HIV/AIDS strikes only persons in the families of other people. Instead of empathetically imagining ourselves as HIV-positive, with sickness and death impending, we have walked by. We have forgotten that the church of Jesus Christ is composed of human beings and that Christians in the church are not immune

from HIV/AIDS. But the truth is that many Christian people throughout the world already have the disease or will soon contract it.

Because the disease first manifested particularly in the United States
and Europe, many political and cultural leaders deluded themselves
into thinking it was only a "gay cancer" or a "Western disease" and
that their countries would escape the sweep of the pandemic. But in
an age of globalization, there is no place to hide. In the old "tropical
disease" model of medical thinking, we could delude ourselves into
thinking that a disease could be quarantined or isolated to a particular
region. A colonial mind-set permitted people to think of themselves as
"healthy" and others in some distant country or continent as "diseased."[9] But in the new world of international travel, commerce, and
association, national borders are no protection against disease.

Long ago African Americans coined the saying, "When the white
man sneezes, the black man gets pneumonia." The impact is always
greater for the poor and the marginalized, regardless of the illness.
The suffering of the impoverished is always immensely greater, since
people in the Two-Thirds World lack financial and medical resources.
Some 30 million people in Africa have AIDS, but only 30,000 Africans
have access to medications. Theoretically, almost everyone (except
the poorest and the most marginalized) in the so-called First World
has access to current anti-retroviral therapies. Cindy Patton, author
of *Globalizing AIDS,* reports that global health economics operates on
the logic that "the rich get health, and the poor are expendable. . . .
No matter how one looks at it, life—or rather, losing it—is cheap for
all but the most privileged."[10]

It's Not Christian to Talk about Sex

A second reason for church resistance and reticence is the belief that
it's not Christian to talk about sex. Sex-talk has long been a forbidden
topic among Christians almost everywhere in the world. Christian
missionaries were not always very effective in spreading the good
news of the gospel, but the bad news of sexuality somehow reinforced previously existing taboos or was successfully implanted in
churches and cultures. Theologically, we affirm God's good gift of sex,
but simultaneously we have been embarrassed and fearful of the practices and pleasures accompanying sexual relationships. Christians

have no problem talking about blood transfusions, organ transplants, cancer, or even war, but typically are tongue-tied and hesitant to talk about condoms, "safer sex," or oral and anal sex. It is almost as if we have been programmed into a conspiracy of silence about sexuality, lest we be misunderstood or misinterpreted as less than spiritual persons and leaders.

But this conspiracy of silence and secrecy has been deadly. Public health advocates have made clear that silence equals death. The 13th International AIDS Conference in South Africa emphasized a critical theme: "Break the Silence" to save human life. The United Nations says the conspiracy of silence is one of the main reasons for this global catastrophe.

People have become infected and suffered immensely with HIV/AIDS because of this silence and the lack of proper sex education. Persons throughout the world are infected daily because of lack of information and ignorance about how the disease can be prevented. Are we really being good pastors and leaders if we do not help people to understand their own bodies and sexual feelings—if we deny them education that will save them from suffering and death? If we have information about how to have a healthy life, how can we ethically deny others the same data? What better and more wholesome place than the church, schools, and theological seminaries to provide education for human loving that will respect the dignity of persons, emphasize Christian values, and teach prevention of diseases like HIV/AIDS? Is God calling us to collaborate in a conspiracy of silence or to speak out as pastors, teachers, and leaders?

It's Somebody Else's Responsibility

Third, Christian resistance and reticence is grounded in the belief that it's somebody else's responsibility. Already the burdens of responsibility on congregations, church leaders, and theological schools are great, and the resources are limited. Getting involved in HIV/AIDS education is to invite conflict and controversy, to risk misunderstandings and misinterpretations, and to stretch the church's mission and ministry beyond previous expectations.

I remember seeing a cartoon showing a person obviously wounded and hurt, dragging himself away from an automobile accident. The caption recorded him mumbling, "I don't want to get involved." Like the musical "Stop the World! I Want to Get Off!" many of us would like to think that our neighbor will respond to this global emergency, and we can continue our business-as-usual churchy activities. Too often churches duck the tough issues of life, hoping that governmental agencies or charities will respond. Then they stand back and criticize such organizations for their methods. For example, churches generally avoid sex education or condom distributions but are quick to criticize others for failing to emphasize abstinence or for promoting "safer sex" strategies. Thinking global AIDS is somebody else's responsibility is a serious evasion of the Christian ethic to love one's neighbor.

But again God's call is like "a shout in the street." The governmental leadership of every nation in the world joined together at the United Nations to urge "faith-based organizations" to get involved and take responsibility for combating this disease. Do we hear the call of God in the voice of the United Nations when they emphasize "the important role of cultural, family, ethical and religious factors in the prevention of the epidemic, and in treatment, care and support"?

Likewise is God like "a shout in the street" coming from the more than 46 million people throughout the world living with AIDS? Do we hear the divine speaking to us in the resolution emerging from the Christian Conference of Asia in 2001 at a consultation in Chiang Mai, Thailand? The participants, reflecting on the 15 million people living with AIDS in Asia, declared that "Jesus the great and beloved physician, the good shepherd, the rock and the refuge, calls us to be the good and compassionate neighbor, the loyal and faithful friends who lowered their sick friend from the roof of the house." Further they envisioned the church as a healing community, modeling compassion and love for all. Specifically, they contended that the church at all levels has an important role to play in the fight against AIDS:

> Challenging the negative, judgmental attitudes that still exist toward people with HIV/AIDS

> Decreasing fear and misconceptions about HIV/AIDS

> Providing accurate information about HIV/AIDS, including prevention information and information about HIV services that may assist persons living with HIV/AIDS (PLWHA)

Providing practical and pastoral support for people living with HIV/AIDS and their families, especially to women and children

Engaging in prayerful dialogue and networking with other churches, faith communities, and secular organizations to help them encourage each other in the ongoing struggle to meet the challenge of HIV/AIDS.[11]

Compassion, Self-Interest, and Challenges Ahead

Moving others and ourselves from thinking of global AIDS as an "I-and-us" rather than a "you-and-them" predicament probably requires a conversion experience for most of us. "Walking in another person's moccasins," as Native Americans have long advocated, rarely is easy or comfortable. It requires a spiritual leap or transformation to empathetically stand in solidarity with the life and suffering of others. Thinking of oneself as HIV-positive is a theological exercise that brings us closer to our infected sisters and brothers.

Of course, all those who have become involved in the great global struggle against AIDS have not been moved by care and compassion. Frankly, self-interest has prompted many non-governmental organizations (NGOs), pharmaceutical companies, businesses and corporations, and governments to engage. The military Joint Chiefs of Staff of the United States presumably were not motivated to get involved by theological teachings about the sisterhood and brotherhood of humanity, but rather by serious strategic concerns about world order and security.

At some point, Christians legitimately might ask similar self-interest questions about the future well-being of the Christian community. What good will it do to support Christian schools in Africa or Asia if there are no teachers due to death and illness from HIV/AIDS? What value is there in producing young leaders in Christian universities if they die shortly afterwards? How helpful is it to spend money evangelizing if persons are too ill to hear the message? How can we upgrade the role and status of girls and women worldwide if they are the most vulnerable to this epidemic? Clearly, HIV/AIDS education, prevention, treatment, and care serve the church's self-interest and should be an integral dimension of the church's outreach and mission everywhere.

The next several chapters explore the challenges facing Christians and their communities of faith if, or as, they become constructively engaged in the global AIDS pandemic. More is involved than simply advocating sexual abstinence or providing condoms. Education for behavioral change is a complicated process, and combating HIV/AIDS requires a multi-level, simultaneous approach that calls for the church to be in missional partnership with persons of other cultures and countries, non-governmental organizations, medical and educational organizations, government bodies, and so forth.

Everyone need not be in lock step with each other. Differing perspectives and approaches can be expected, and not every Christian or church body will have the same priorities. Unity in spirit and intent, not in every action or program, is the goal. For example, not every Christian is likely to feel that the promotion of condoms is appropriate. Possibly, talking about abstinence would also be uncomfortable. But that doesn't mean that the person cannot be a warrior in the fight against AIDS. Caring for the 12.1 million orphans in Africa, for example, would be a great contribution worthy of the name of Jesus Christ.

Around the world, committed Christians are struggling to move Christian communities into the vanguard of helping and healing during this global emergency. Their struggle is great; they must assist the church through six main challenges: (1) recognize human realities, (2) declare stigmatization and discrimination as sins, (3) advance the status of women and children, (4) promote the ABCs of prevention, (5) advocate social justice, and (6) ensure supportive care, testing, treatment, and counseling for persons living with HIV/AIDS. What is needed is a Christian breakthrough from indifference to involvement, from apathy to action, from silence to speaking out.

But the starting point of this mission and ministry is admitting that ultimately we are all HIV-positive. As long as we deny our own vulnerability and risk, rebuff our own oneness with the suffering of the world, and pretend we are separate from our infected and affected sisters and brothers, then perhaps we best step aside. Otherwise, we are likely to be of more harm than help in God's healing ministry in the world. Turn the page only if you can honestly say "we are all HIV-positive."

3

Facing and Responding to Sexual Realities

Silence kills. Breaking the silence is a powerful way that people at all levels of society can combat the disease. I do not minimize the courage it can take to come forward, to challenge taboos and change traditions. But that kind of courage is needed or more people will die.

—Colin L. Powell

After a number of airplane delays and diversions to unexpected airports, I arrived in India after thirty-six hours of flying from Colorado. I grabbed two hours of sleep before I preached at the crowded 7:30 a.m. service of St. George's Cathedral. Following that lengthy liturgy, I was whisked away from this traditional Church of South India with its Anglican style of worship to a contemporary Pentecostal service complete with young people in blue jeans playing guitars. They had been singing, praying, and praising God for several hours, so they were ready for a sermon.

Just before introducing me, the pastor in charge leaned over and said, "Our people expect a forty-five-minute sermon followed by an altar call." Surprised, I said okay and soon found myself abandoning my sport coat and preaching in my shirtsleeves. If my energy and voice held up, I figured I could easily expand a twenty-minute Christmas sermon on people living with HIV/AIDS finding "no room" in people's hearts. The challenge was the altar call. Though I had been preaching for some forty years, I am a seminary professor—and liberal academics don't give altar calls! But I had not flown halfway around the world to disappoint anyone.

So I ended with a passionate call for people to give their lives to Christ and demonstrate compassionate caring for people living with HIV/AIDS. I was stunned at the response as people came forward and lined up to speak and pray with me. Their honest and heartfelt testimonies melted my heart. Some spoke of how they had tried to care for people with AIDS but experienced burnout. Another expressed feelings of judgment, finding it hard to care for people who "got what they deserved." One man asked, "Why would a good God allow such a terrible disease?" A woman questioned whether AIDS is God's punishment. Several businesspeople asked how they could get involved in helping people with HIV/AIDS. One nurse tearfully said that she cared for AIDS patients but that she found it hard to be accepting and loving with *hijras* (the Indian term describing transsexuals or transvestites). She asked me to pray with her that God would help her be more compassionate. These Christians struggled to reconcile their faith and ethics with the human realities they face in the context of HIV/AIDS.

AIDS and Sexual Behavior

This experience was a vivid reminder to me of how difficult it is for Christians to be involved in an AIDS mission and ministry. While our faith teaches us that we are all brothers and sisters—one in Christ Jesus—yet we are often unable to understand or accept persons whose lifestyles or backgrounds are radically different from our own.

When I went to seminary years ago, we were required to read William James's *Varieties of Religious Experience*, but we were provided no information or insight into the varied worlds of human sexual behavior. It was assumed that people were diverse in their religious perspectives and behaviors—stereotypically that Catholics cherished liturgy, Protestants preaching, Buddhists meditation, Muslims prayer, Hindus sacrifices, and so forth. But when it came to sexual expression, it was presumed that heterosexual relations within marriage were normative and everything else was "abnormal." Diversity was not acknowledged. The so-called abnormal was neither discussed nor introduced into theological discussions. As daring as we got was to discuss reproduction, acknowledging that Catholics and Mormons had large families and that Protestants practiced birth control using artificial contraception. Though the sexual revolution swept through the West and some other parts of the globe, the church and its leadership resisted facing its reality and even pretended Christians were immune or isolated from the varieties of human sexual behavior evident in humanity.

The AIDS phenomenon has forced everyone to look at the varieties of human sexual behavior around the globe that previously were hidden, disguised, or unknown. People's practices do not always conform to what they profess or what their society or religion proclaim as the ideal or norm. Most religions champion celibacy in singleness and fidelity in marriage, but there is overwhelming evidence in every culture that persons have multiple partners, experience same-sex relationships, frequent sex workers (prostitutes), and engage in sexual contacts outside of marriage.[1] Theologian Gillian Paterson bluntly contends that most cultures and religions officially expect abstinence and faithfulness, but "in practice, this is often a fiction and most people know it." This complicates the work of public health officials working on AIDS since they must address what people really do, "not what people wish were true."[2]

Researchers have had to dig into cultural closets to find out how often heterosexual men engage in sex outside of marriage—with other women or sex workers. Do men who have sex with men (MWM) come only from the gay or homosexual communities or do primarily heterosexual men sometimes engage in sex with other men? What is bisexuality? In all cultures and societies men apparently do indeed have sex with other men, whether this is labeled homosexuality or not. How has a disease like AIDS that at first seemed to be primarily in North American gay communities become so widespread in a world dominated by heterosexuals? Without attempting to transform this book into a sex or an HIV/AIDS manual, this chapter will focus briefly on how the disease is (and is not) transmitted, as well as the sexual practices of homosexual and heterosexual persons.

How Do You Get HIV/AIDS?

Christians often get tongue-tied when speaking publicly about human sexuality. Christian leaders, so steeped in shame and often lacking in scientific or medical understanding and terminology, typically sidestep the important and life-saving realm of sex education. Too embarrassed to be forthright and honest, they leave the educational work to others who may or may not share their same relational values or ethics of responsibility.

Gay and lesbian leaders and public health professionals, with varying degrees of government and non-governmental support, have launched vigorous educational programs to alert various populations about HIV/AIDS transmission. Because of genuine fears and sometimes mass hysteria, it also has been extremely important that education be spread about how people do *not* get HIV/AIDS.

The human immunodeficiency virus (HIV), like the common cold, readily mutates, making treatment and the development of an effective vaccine very difficult. It can lie dormant for years within a healthy-feeling person. This virus weakens the human immune system, prompting the body to be more susceptible to various infections, leading to acquired immune deficiency syndrome (AIDS). The virus is primarily transmitted from person to person by the body fluids of semen, blood, vaginal secretions, and breast milk. Persons may get infected while (1) having vaginal or anal sex, (2) using dirty needles during intravenous drug injections, (3) getting contaminated blood transfusions, (4) being born, and (5) experiencing careless or accidental medical procedures. Engaging in oral sex also can be a cause, but studies repeatedly show it is a very low-risk behavior for HIV/AIDS. Hugging, kissing, sneezing, coughing, using common toilets, being bitten by mosquitoes or other insects, sharing food and drinks, and giving blood do *not* transmit the disease.

Straightforward communication of this information—in language and terminology that readers and listeners understand—is essential, but very often church people grow totally inarticulate when topics like oral or anal sex are mentioned or someone asks how to use a condom. The appendix of this book includes a more explicit list of how one can and cannot get HIV, which can be circulated to encourage "safer" sex. (There is no such thing as "safe" sex—all of life has an element of risk, but it is possible to substantially reduce the likelihood of HIV infection by following the guidelines provided.) These guidelines apply equally to homosexual and heterosexual persons.

Besides helping to stem the tide of HIV infections, open and honest communication assists in combating AFRAIDS—the acute fear people often have about AIDS. AFRAIDS is nourished by fear of (a) the unknown, (b) infection or contamination, (c) sexual activity, (d) one's own mortality, and (e) being ostracized. These fears are rampant not only among infected persons but also their family and friends.[3]

Ralph, a young man living with HIV, told me that his parents in Ripon, Wisconsin, were so closeted that they were even afraid to get a book from the library to learn about the disease. A pioneer in Christian AIDS ministry, Cathie Lyons, repeatedly speaks of the conspiracy of silence and how fearful people are to admit to their families and pastors that they have the disease. "Fear that they would not find acceptance or understanding," says Lyons, leads "too many loved ones of persons with AIDS to live in painful prolonged silence."[4]

Pastorally, the church can help resolve this situation by better educating its members and clergy about AIDS and the global pandemic. Unfortunately, too many priests and pastors are afraid to preach or teach on the subject, fearing what people might think or say. They have never participated in the yearly World AIDS Day on December 1. Ask the average clergyperson for a copy of a sermon dealing entirely or in part with HIV/AIDS, and discover that more than twenty years into the pandemic he or she has said nothing publicly. Underneath much of this fear is a conscious or unconscious homophobia.

Homosexuality

Christians find it particularly difficult to accept gay and lesbian persons and their sexual practices. Since HIV/AIDS first emerged with intensity in the gay male community, the disease highlighted homosexuality or male-to-male transmission. For a while it was even known as the "gay disease," and this prompted many a church and government to ignore the illness because of contempt for gay persons and their sexual preferences.

Some years ago Andres Tapai wrote in *Christianity Today*, "To avoid much pain and confusion, those who want to minister to people with AIDS should resolve their theology and philosophy about homosexuality before starting."[5] Like the Pentecostal nurse that answered my altar call in India, if one is perplexed, or finds gay sexual practices repugnant, or deems one's own sexual preferences highly superior, then engagement in a meaningful and helpful AIDS ministry is problematic.

The traditional conservative Christian response is to claim one "loves the sinner but hates the sin." Gay people reject such claims as contrary to Christian love. Trusting your health and well-being to someone who approaches you with a spirit of moral superiority and exclusiveness is risky. "Loving the sinner while hating the sin," says Michael J. Christensen, a professor at Drew University, "is a well-meaning attempt to separate a valued person from despised behavior, but is unlikely to succeed. Scripture reminds us that sin is not purely behavior but proceeds from the heart. Hatred of sin implies judgment of the sinner."[6] Such a judgmental spirit separates us from the very person with whom we want to stand in solidarity.

No one knows what percentage of the human population has a homosexual orientation. Some have said, "If one day all gay people turned purple, you'd be shocked to see how many people around you are gay."[7] What happened with the HIV/AIDS epidemic is that people did not turn purple, but many gays did become sick and die.

The global HIV/AIDS pandemic has forced Christians to articulate and rethink their views regarding sexuality, sin, and disease. Asserting that sexuality is a good and gracious gift of a creator God, Christians, however, differ as to whether they believe that homosexuality is a gift of God's grace. This difference stems from whether they deem homosexuality a sin or not. Those who consider it a sin interpret various negative verses of Scripture as proof that the practice is contrary to God's will.

The basic stance of Roman Catholicism and most Protestant churches is that if individuals have a same-sex orientation, they should pledge themselves to a life of heterosexual relations, chastity, or celibacy. Those who do not deem homosexual practice sinful interpret the Bible differently and insist that homosexuality is the result of God's loving creation, not simply a matter of personal choice. John J. McNeill contends that "only a sadistic God would create millions of humans as gay with no choice in the matter and no hope of changing and then deny them the right to express their gayness in a loving relationship for the rest of their lives under the threat of eternal damnation."[8]

My own theological understanding remains a minority view within Christianity but corresponds with the perspective expressed by United Methodist Bishop Melvin E. Wheatley:

> Homosexuality, quite like heterosexuality, is neither a
> virtue nor an accomplishment. It is a mysterious gift of
> God's grace communicated through an exceedingly com-
> plex set of chemical, biological, chromosomal, hormonal,
> environmental, developmental factors totally outside my
> homosexual friend's control. His or her homosexuality is a
> gift—neither a virtue nor a sin. What she/he does with
> their homosexuality, however, is their personal, moral,
> and spiritual responsibility. Their behavior as a homosex-
> ual may therefore be very sinful—brutal, exploitative, self-
> ish, promiscuous, superficial. Their behavior on the other
> hand, may be beautiful—tender, considerate, loyal, other-
> centered, profound.[9]

While the church seems to think it has the right and luxury of
debating the propriety of homosexual relationships from decade to
decade, offering either the option of life-long chastity or "miraculous" transformation from homosexuality to heterosexuality (called
"reparative therapy"), generation after generation of gay persons
around the world have to find ways of expressing themselves sexually
without becoming infected with HIV.[10] When it comes to this form of
life saving, the church universal has proved a miserable failure, leaving the work of educating about "safer" and "life-saving" sex up to
others.

I once believed that my own denomination would become more
open and honest about human sexuality and HIV/AIDS if people realized that the disease was more prevalent within the church community than previously realized. However, after a leading conservative
United Methodist leader, Bishop Finis A. Crutchfield of Houston,
Texas, died of AIDS in 1987, the barriers of silence and denial seemed
to rise even higher.[11] Lutheran theologian Martin E. Marty contends
that though the church changes slowly it eventually will change its
attitude. He writes:

> When every tenth fundamentalist preacher's son, every
> tenth evangelist's offspring, every tenth Pentecostal's
> child, every thirtieth priest falls to nonintravenously occa-
> sioned AIDS, the church will turn. It turns slowly and
> tardily, but when it turns, I have hopes for it. . . . Do not

underestimate the potential of the church when it brings together code and care, Leviticus and love, inherited attitudes and fresh understandings of need, awareness of both God's judgments and steadfast love.[12]

The late Roman Catholic priest and scholar Henri Nouwen, writing in *The Road to Daybreak: A Spiritual Journey* in the late 1980s, expressed his pastoral concern for the gay community facing the AIDS threat and all the deep fear, suffering, and anguish involved:

> More than ever the Church has to live out Christ's love for the poor, the sinners, the publicans, the rejected, the possessed, and all who desperately need to be loved. . . . He revealed the total and unlimited love of God for humanity. This is the love that the Church is called to make visible, not by judging, condemning, or segregating, but by serving everyone in need. I often wonder if the many heated debates about the morality of homosexuality do not prevent the Christian community from reaching out fearlessly to its suffering fellow human beings.[13]

Clearly these debates have paralyzed the church and prohibited it from meaningful involvement in the struggle against global HIV/AIDS.

Heterosexuality
In its first stages HIV/AIDS may have been centered primarily in the gay male community, but now it is overwhelmingly transmitted between heterosexual partners. Of the 46 million people infected internationally, more than an estimated 75 percent are heterosexual.[14] Of this number a certain small percentage inevitably were infected through bisexual relationships, but the primary route of transmission continues to be by male and female intercourse.

Persons within the heterosexual community are highly unlikely to get infected if they (a) abstain from sex before marriage, (b) faithfully have sex only with their married partner who also never had sex with anyone else, and (c) practice abstinence again after divorce or their partner's death. This has been the ideal set forth by the Christian church over the years, and, when followed by both partners, can prevent transmission of HIV. But the church over the centuries has also recognized that celibacy is actually a "special gift" of God, and not many men and women are able to live completely chaste lives. Thus celibacy has been reserved primarily for priests and others in religious vocations. Like condoms, vows of abstinence get broken, so there is no absolutely "fail-safe" prevention of HIV.

Of course, sex outside of marriage may be premarital, within marriage, and after marriage. Many young people in all cultures are known to experiment sexually. For example, in the United States 45.6 percent of high school students and 79.5 percent of college students reportedly have had sexual intercourse.[15] If they are not educated about how the HIV virus is transmitted, they are indeed vulnerable to infection. Contrary to past perceptions, older people do not quit having sex. In fact, in the United States the face of AIDS is aging, with 11 percent of all people with AIDS over the age of fifty. Five thousand people over the age of seventy are infected. With the popular advent of medicines to treat impotency, there is no reason to believe this trend will diminish. AIDS education must be addressed to every generation.

Prostitution

For most persons in the middle- and upper-class worlds of the West, opportunities for sexual expression exist without paying for services. Mutual agreement among adults enables persons to freely choose a variety of sexual partners. Clearly a subculture of male and female "escort" services exists, but for most people, knowledge about prostitutes is secondhand and distant. Wrapped in secrecy and past history, it is certainly not discussed in "polite" society or church Sunday schools!

Prostitution, however, is often called the world's oldest profession, since no matter what cultural or religious taboos have been proclaimed, human propensities and needs seem to have prevailed. The practice of selling sexual services is so endemic to the world scene today that government and non-governmental agencies speak of the vocation of sex workers rather than using the more pejorative term "prostitute."

Intertwined with gnawing poverty and hunger, vast numbers of young girls and women are entrapped in this sexual work as the only opportunity they have to eek out even a small income for personal and familial survival. Sexual slavery exists, as young people are recruited from poor rural areas and find themselves literally imprisoned in filthy, crowded urban slums with seemingly no way out. Exploitation is rampant. They have basically no protection from authorities and no health care or education, and they live highly dependent upon those who exploit them. As rumors have spread about the likelihood of HIV infection among sex workers, the demand for even younger girls has escalated. In parts of Africa, one rampant persistent myth suggests that a man can "cure" himself of HIV by having unprotected sex with a young "virgin."

In a land like India, with 1 billion people, the complexities of prostitution are beyond the scope of this book. Until recently there was little acknowledgment of the widespread practice of male heterosexuals engaging sex workers. But as HIV/AIDS threatens the culture and society, social scientists have discovered, for example, that because of "arranged" marriages, many people may not be happy or satisfied within their marital sexual arrangement. Married men are estimated to represent at least 50 percent of sex workers' customers.

In Africa, Asia, and Latin America, poor villagers often are away three or four months at a time doing extremely hard and lonely work as laborers in the city or driving old trucks down rough roads throughout the country, and thus situations that make prostitution tempting increase exponentially. A high percentage of these prostitutes—themselves very poor people struggling for just enough money to eat and to feed their families—are infected with HIV/AIDS. Then when the laborers and truck drivers return home after many months away, they inadvertently bring the disease into their villages and communities.

The varieties of sexual behavior among heterosexual and homosexual people worldwide, both in and outside the Christian faith community, obviously are greater than frequently acknowledged. These realities significantly impact the church's understanding of how HIV/AIDS needs to be addressed in the contemporary world. These realities challenge the very fundamental understanding of what it means for a Christian to love his or her neighbor and for the church to participate in the *missio Dei*—the liberating and loving activity of God in the world.[16]

Responding with Christian Love

While Christians express differing judgments regarding sexuality and sin, they do, however, share a fundamental understanding of a God of "agape" or "self-giving love," who cares for all of creation. Christians are called to be people who exemplify this same spirit of love in the way they reach out to people, especially the poor, the marginalized, and the ill. Throughout the centuries, Christians have sought to be in the forefront of the fight against disease, believing they have been called to be healers like Jesus among the lepers.

Christian love cannot be just some spiritual placebo or individualized panacea, but must be manifest in our missional concern for justice and community health care. In the remainder of this chapter, four meanings of Christian love are explored in terms of their consequences for the global HIV/AIDS pandemic.

Christian Love Means Facing Facts

Christian love in a time of global AIDS challenges us to face the facts of human existence. If we are to combat disease and promote health, we must gain all the medical and social science information possible. This knowledge is God's great gift to us. We cannot show love to anybody if, like ostriches, we stick our heads in the sand and pretend certain realities do not exist. Christian love requires us to seek to understand what is actually happening to people in our communities and cultures. It does not necessarily mean we need to approve or endorse particular behavior.

Certain human realities are difficult for religious persons to recognize, much less accept or tolerate. Recognition of the varieties of sexual expression and practice do not require approval or endorsement. Though Christians speak of humanity's sinful or fallen nature, a strong streak of naïve idealism tends to overwhelm a realistic understanding of human nature and behavior. The church's ideals have led to two responses: denunciation and denial. Denouncing certain sexual behavior has the value of setting norms and appropriate boundaries. It provides a kind of ethical sexual marker for persons to determine what is right and wrong. Saying no to certain behaviors can avoid sinful sexual behavior, what Bishop Wheatley identified as "brutal, exploitative, selfish, promiscuous, superficial." It provides helpful guidelines to educate people toward sexuality that Bishop

Wheatley describes as mutually "beautiful—tender, considerate, loyal, other-centered, profound" as well as "safer" in terms of disease prevention.[17]

However, denunciation often slides into talk of damnation and self-righteous religious presumptions and propositions that suggest God loves the person without HIV/AIDS more than the infected person. Judgmental preaching often rings louder than theological proclamations that all Christians are sinners kneeling at the foot of the cross, where we are all equal in seeking God's forgiveness, mercy, and grace.

Damnation preachers claim that HIV/AIDS is God's disease of retribution, suggesting God hates the sexual practices of homosexuals and also punishes some heterosexuals by giving them special diseases. A small but strident segment of the Christian community has declared that HIV/AIDS is God's retribution on sinful people. Since the disease spread first and foremost among gay men, some people were quick to suggest that God was inflicting the disease upon them because of their sexual preferences and practices. Further, it was argued that gay and bisexual men—along with other special at-risk populations (like drug addicts and prostitutes)—deserved such disease and death.

In response, reflective, caring Christians assert they worship a God of love that cares for all people and does not will disease and suffering on any population. Further, they might note that of all the people on earth, lesbian women are the least likely to become infected with HIV/AIDS. A logic that claimed that God disliked gay men would be forced to assert that God must like lesbian women the best of all persons!

Denial is another way Christians avoid the facts and thus underestimate the danger of HIV/AIDS in their communities and societies and contribute to a conspiracy of silence, apathy, and indifference. When I went to India in the early 1990s, my friend, N. M. Samuel, MD, said, "Society continues to pretend that gay and bisexual people don't exist in Indian society, but that is untrue." "Christians," Samuel reports, "particularly don't know how to deal with sexuality. We haven't learned to deal with how people actually feel and behave sexually."

Likewise, when I participated in an all-Latin American church conference in Uruguay, strong currents of denial were evident. At the time, some 2 million people were infected in Latin America and the

Caribbean, and the World Health Organization said infections transmitted sexually were skyrocketing. AIDS had already become the leading cause of death of men aged twenty-five to thirty-four in some countries in the Caribbean.[18] Yet people were struggling to accept that research had revealed more gay and bisexual behavior in Latin America and the Caribbean than previously known or acknowledged.[19]

Denial and discrimination offer no solutions to the dilemmas we face. Our challenge is to relate our religious traditions to educational issues of sexuality and health, realistically comprehend varieties of human sexual practices, understand the mysteries of God's creation, and chart new ways for preserving God's people by combating illness and preventing illness. If religious leaders and communities are going to be constructively engaged in fighting HIV/AIDS, then denunciation and denial must be overcome, without necessarily accepting or endorsing certain forms of human behavior.

Instead of being positive and progressive forces in the global battle against HIV/AIDS, too often religious leaders and communities prove to be negative and reactionary. Instead of accenting core values like love, forgiveness, and healing that are found in most of the major world religions at their best, too often we experience their worst when religious leaders and communities contribute to the denial and discrimination that only compounds public health issues and personal well-being.

Confessing Sins, Seeking New Life

Christian love means confessing sins and seeking a new life in Christ. In the ritual of the Lord's Supper with which I am most familiar, there is liturgical language that acknowledges personal and collective wrongdoing and sin and pledges sinners to seek a new life in Christ: "We do earnestly repent, and are heartily sorry for these our misdoings; the remembrance of them is grievous unto us. Have mercy upon us, have mercy upon us, most merciful Father. For thy Son our Lord Jesus Christ's sake, forgive us all that is past; and grant that we may ever hereafter serve and please thee in newness of life. . . ."[20]

In light of the threat HIV/AIDS poses for humanity, Christian communities around the world have slowly begun to respond to the pandemic, expressing their confession for failing to act more positively and quickly. In the early years of the crisis, Christians clearly responded in forms of denial, denunciation, fear, and apathy. Worse yet, even violence was tolerated. This was true when the HIV/AIDS epidemic first began to escalate in the early 1980s in the Western world. Three young hemophiliacs, Ricky, Robert, and Randy Ray, infected by blood transfusions, were firebombed out of their Florida home in the 1980s when neighbors discovered they had the disease.[21] Similar tragic incidences often have occurred in Africa, Asia, and Latin America.

One Christian theologian spoke out forcefully early in the HIV/AIDS pandemic about the need for the church to confess its failure to deal appropriately with faith, human sexuality, and the new disease. Like a voice crying in the wilderness, Ethicist James B. Nelson dared to say that Christians bore "major responsibility for the problems created by the AIDS crisis." In 1986, he called on the church to creatively and constructively repent of its sins: "Over the centuries we have given considerable religious sanction to homophobia. We have been the major institutional legitimizer of compulsory heterosexuality—and the punisher of those who did not conform to that heterosexual norm. Our *metanoia*, our creative repentance, calls us to constructive responses to the current tragedy."[22]

Years now have past and, belatedly, Christians and their leadership have begun to acknowledge that in almost all settings where they have been slow to act or failed to respond effectively, they have contributed to the AIDS pandemic.

There are two excellent illustrations of a new Christian response to HIV/AIDS. First is the remarkable declaration of confession by African church leaders in 2001 at an ecumenical gathering in Nairobi, Kenya:

> As the pandemic has unfolded, it has exposed fault lines that reach to the heart of our theology, our ethics, our liturgy, and our practice of ministry. Today, churches are being obliged to acknowledge that we have—however unwittingly—contributed both actively and passively to the spread of the virus. Our difficulty in addressing issues of sex and sexuality has often made it painful for us to engage, in any honest and realistic way, with issues of sex education and HIV prevention. Our tendency to exclude others, our interpretation of the scriptures, and our theology of sin have all combined to promote the stigmatization, exclusion, and suffering of people with HIV or AIDS.

> This has undermined the effectiveness of care, education, and prevention efforts and inflicted additional suffering on those already affected by the HIV.[23]

Instead of blaming others, church leaders formally acknowledged that they have contributed to the pandemic. The disease is not simply transferred by semen or other bodily fluid—it also is spread when people fail to provide information, prophylactics, or clean needles to protect a person in need. Infections happen when medicine is not provided to stop transmission from mother to child. Disease is spread when women are not empowered to say no and when men are not encouraged to practice "safer" sex. Church leaders silent in the face of prejudice and stigmatization might as well be actively distributing the virus—for discrimination kills both the body and the spirit.

The African church leaders, faced with enormous issues of illness, suffering, and death in their local communities, have belatedly realized that now is the time to act. They declared: "Given the extreme urgency of the situation, and the conviction that the churches do have a distinctive role to play in the response to the pandemic, what is needed is a rethinking of our mission, and the transformation of our structures and ways of working."[24]

To achieve such a remarkable transformation of their own missional thinking, structures, and ministry, the African church will need assistance from conscientious Christians around the world. The financial resources available to new and struggling churches in Africa are limited—especially in light of this overwhelming pandemic. Their good intentions to change their own behavior will have to be reinforced and financed by assistance from the global church.

A second illustration of a new Christian response comes from the son of Billy Graham, the influential evangelist Franklin Graham. Heading the charity Samaritan's Purse, he has made global HIV/AIDS a high priority in its understanding of Christian mission and ministry. In a remarkable statement, Graham is quoted as saying that how a person got HIV makes no difference. If embraced by others, this attitude could dramatically reverse the way Christians have responded to HIV/AIDS since its emergence on the global stage. Specifically, Graham said, "I don't care how you got AIDS—whether you got it from a needle, whether you got it through a blood transfusion, whether through homosexual contact, or whether just being careless." The fact is that people have it, and Christ's church "needs to be on the forefront of this issue with love, with compassion, with understanding and giving hope to those that don't have hope."[25]

Taken to heart by all Christians, this approach would signal a great reversal in the Christian response to HIV/AIDS.

Accenting Forgiveness and Healing

Christian love in the age of AIDS means accenting forgiveness and healing. Scholars of comparative religions could demonstrate how each major world religion in its own way emphasizes the values of love, forgiveness, and healing. Understandings are not the same, but a similar spirit undergirds all the great faiths of humankind; illustrations could be drawn from the Upanishads, Vedas, Koran, Torah, New Testament, teachings of Buddha, and other sacred texts. Lest I stray too far from the boundaries of my own knowledge and identity, however, I will draw illustrations only from Christianity.

Certainly Christians hold forgiveness and healing as core religious values. The teachings of Jesus epitomize the importance of self-giving love, reaching out in care and compassion to others. This love is to manifest itself even in loving one's enemies and forgiving other people, just as God forgives each of us for our mistakes and wrongdoing. Known as the Great Physician, Jesus often reached out to heal others. This healing ministry has long been at the heart of the Christian church's mission to provide hospitals, hospices, clinics, and medical colleges.

Unfortunately, however, sometimes in Christianity (as I suspect in many other religious traditions) these primary commitments to love, forgiveness, and healing are overshadowed by secondary teachings or traditions that suddenly become paramount in discussions about HIV/AIDS. Law overwhelms grace, and abstract principles rather than actual people become paramount. Rarely, for example, do Christians quote from Leviticus in the Old Testament for any purpose. Instead, most Christian leaders and churches prefer to speak about the loving parables of Jesus. Yet when conversations focus on issues related to sexuality, suddenly Christians start focusing almost exclusively on the limited biblical passages that speak negatively of same-sex relationships (such as in Leviticus) rather than the powerful, life-giving teachings of Jesus (who himself apparently never spoke about homosexuality).[26]

Christianity is divided among the Roman Catholics, Protestants, and Orthodox. While all three branches emphasize love, forgiveness, and healing, they differ in many respects on special issues of sexuality. Traditional Christian ethics have emphasized procreation, not pleasure, as the basic—if not sole—purpose of sexual relations. More contemporary Christian ethics recognizes sexual desire and pleasure as positive God-given "goods." Sexuality reflects more than genital activity and serves both the procreation and recreation interests of human beings and can be an avenue of ever deepening love and commitment. However, a unity exists among Christians that God calls the human family to be united in the struggle to conquer HIV/AIDS, since God wills that life flourish, disease be fought, and the ill be treated with care and compassion.

The critical moral issue for the Christian in the HIV/AIDS pandemic is whether we can change our behavior from condemnation to compassion. Roman Catholic Bishop Francis Quinn once observed that Jesus' harshest words were reserved for self-righteous people who condemned and rejected others. Quinn contends that Jesus thought those worthy of His kingdom would be judged on how they treated one another (Matt. 25), especially the "least among us": the hungry, the sick, prisoners, outcasts, rejects, and sinners.[27]

Early in the AIDS crisis Bishop Quinn administered the sacrament of anointing to a man with AIDS. Following ancient rituals, the person kneeled in the cathedral and the bishop placed oil on his forehead. Then Bishop Quinn helped the man to his feet. To the shock of the congregation, the bishop himself then kneeled and asked to be anointed by the person living with HIV/AIDS. His action provides all Christians with one of the best examples of the kind of healing and forgiveness we should provide and also receive.

Manifesting Hospitable Care for the Stranger

Christian love in a time of global AIDS manifests itself in hospitality and care for the stranger. In Exodus 23:9 we hear, "You shall not oppress a stranger; you know the heart of a stranger, for you were strangers in the land of Egypt." In Hebrews 13:2 comes this advice: "Do not neglect to show hospitality to strangers, for thereby some have entertained angels unaware."

The Bible emphasizes not only compassion for the person in need, but also expresses the idea of the stranger as a bearer of truth. God often appears in the face and the voice of the stranger. The stranger the dejected apostles met turned out to be the risen Christ. In Matthew 25:30-46, Jesus speaks of the poor, hungry, naked, diseased, and imprisoned as God incognito: "Just as you did it to one of the least of these . . . you did it to me" (25:40).

Loving hospitality to the stranger is a metaphor for the moral life. On the one hand, caring for another can mean providing sustenance and shelter, protecting against vulnerabilities, and promoting the well-being of a known neighbor. On the other hand, it offers a rich opportunity for meeting someone new, being challenged by differing perspectives, and possibly being personally transformed. Just as the stranger may need us, so we may need the stranger, for often strangers bear spiritual gifts.

Some years ago my son Kent and I visited Argentina. He was just beginning to learn Spanish. While I was participating in a church conference on the outskirts of Buenos Aires, he decided to take a train into the heart of the city. Along the way a stranger approached Kent and asked for alms. Kent gave the beggar some coins. After riding more than an hour, the train stopped and Kent got out with the other passengers. Much to his dismay he had gone in the wrong direction and was very far from the center of Buenos Aires.

Kent managed to cross the tracks and board another train going in the opposite direction. A bit later the same beggar came through the compartment. He was shocked and alarmed to see the lost "gringo." This time, instead of asking for money, he organized the other passengers to help Kent. When the train stopped at one place, a woman escorted Kent to a connecting train. Yes, at first the beggar stranger needed Kent, but later he needed the beggar stranger. Indeed, often strangers bring us unexpected and special gifts.

Christians who have become involved in HIV/AIDS ministries will testify unanimously that those "strangers" they have sought to help have gifted them. In a Buddhist monastery transformed into an AIDS hospice in Thailand, I heard Christian volunteers from the Netherlands tell how their spirits were touched and their lives transformed by dying patients. In Mother Teresa's home in Calcutta, India, Andrew, a young German, told me that if the Missionaries of Charity required it, he would pay five hundred (U.S.) dollars a month for the privilege of caring for "the lost, the least, and the last." Perhaps some "strangers" may eventually lead to the ultimate gift—a cure.

The Nairobi Prostitutes

My four-year-old grandson, Noah, loves to ask the question "what if?" From his vantage point, more possibilities exist in the world than his grandfather can imagine. "What if a cow jumped over the moon?" "What if I kissed Grandma all day?" "What if nobody ever got sick and died?"

I was reminded of Noah's "what if" scenarios when I read an article by Michael Specter in *The New Yorker* about "the Nairobi prostitutes" of Kenya.[28] In a land where one in six adults is infected with HIV (2.5 million people in total), scientific attention has been drawn to a small, but famous, cohort of research subjects—about 200 prostitutes who remain uninfected despite more than five years of high-risk sexual behavior. In some Kenyan cities, about 90 percent of the sex workers test positive for HIV. Why these women in Nairobi have not been diagnosed with HIV, fallen ill, and died of AIDS remains a mystery. Each of them has probably engaged with hundreds of HIV-positive men. One woman, Hala, at age forty-one, has five children and eight grandchildren and lives in an impoverished hut in the violent slums of Pumwani. She lost her husband to AIDS twenty years ago. One of her best customers over a seventeen-year period recently died of AIDS—and she reports he never used a condom! Hala and the others are generally undernourished and receive no special medications, yet they appear resistant to HIV/AIDS.

Scientists from around the world are asking "what if" questions about the Nairobi prostitutes. The Canadian infectious disease expert Francis Plummer asked if these women "harbored a rare defensive weapon within their immune systems," and concluded that they must.[29] It turns out these women possess high levels of a particular type of white blood cell that specifically kills HIV-infected cells. "What if" these women hold within themselves the key to a global vaccine? "What if" these unlikely sex workers were to help save the world? Would they be awarded the Templeton Prize in Religion or a Nobel honor?

These women must be acknowledged and respected for what unique gifts they may have to offer the world. As Kevin DeCock of the Centers for Disease Control notes, "You are not going to solve the AIDS crisis in a convent in Montana."[30] Fortunately, despite the stigma and discrimination and poverty and violence they have suffered in this world, these women still care about the rest of humanity and are cooperating in scientific tests. As Hala says, "I have no idea why I of all people have been spared. But if my luck can be useful to the doctors then I will be grateful." So in an academic laboratory at Oxford University, England, scientists Andrew McMichael and Sarah Rowland-Jones attempt to create a vaccine that would trigger the same kind of protection evident in the prostitutes. Whether they will be successful or not remains to be seen, as partially effective or universal vaccines still remain a distant dream.

What If?

Whether Hala and the other 200 Nairobi women will ever benefit is uncertain. Currently they cannot even stop having sex with HIV-positive men because, when they do, their immune systems lose the power to protect them from infection. If a vaccine for HIV/AIDS were to be developed, there is no assurance they or their fellow citizens will ever be able to afford the medication. Africans were essential in finding a vaccine for hepatitis B, but the international pharmaceutical companies priced it beyond their reach. Like the poor black men of the syphilis experiment, these women and their families may never receive assistance.

But "what if" the church became vigilant for the care and treatment of all God's children, including the marginalized sex workers of Nairobi and the rest of the world? What if the church moved beyond being tongue-tied about sexuality and became an effective voice advocating prevention? What if the church confessed its contribution to promoting the HIV/AIDS pandemic and moved from a stance of condemnation to compassion, from inaction to involvement?

Jesus taught his disciples to expect the unexpected and to imagine a "what if" world. The despised Samaritan was described as good, the prostitute was welcomed at his table, the prodigal son was welcomed home, and crucifixion was conquered by the resurrection. So let's pray for the unexpected: that the church of Christ will join in God's healing mission in the world. "What if" we had a world without AIDS?

4

Stigmatization and Discrimination

The ugliest word in the English language is the word exclusive.

—Carl Sandburg

Tens of thousands of neatly tied white bundles lay in front of a golden statue of Buddha in the Temple Wat Prabat Nampoo, located in the isolated hills of Lopburi Province seventy miles north of Bangkok, Thailand. Each package contains the cremated bones and ashes of a person who has died from AIDS. They have been abandoned because their families could not accept them.

On the other side of the world, deep in the heart of the United States, a woman in Kansas attended the funeral of a stranger. When asked why she was crying, she replied that her son had died of AIDS the previous week, but her husband would not permit them to have a Christian funeral. So she came to mourn near the casket of another family's son who had passed away because of AIDS.

In Samalkota, Andhra Pradesh, India, a landlord threw a poor man out of his house when it was discovered he was suffering from AIDS.

He was left for three days to die in a dumping ground, surrounded by garbage, where the pigs and dogs roamed freely. His wife, Laxmi, and their three little children brought him food and tried to care for him, but there was little they could do to comfort him in this dehumanizing situation. No one came to help him or his family.[1]

Stigmatization and Discrimination as Sins

These three stories dramatize the vicious sins of stigmatization and discrimination that are too often associated with HIV/AIDS. Even in death there is no dignity. People are denied even the right to grieve the loss of loved ones. Basic human rights are ignored. Fear and shame reign supreme, and the trauma of suffering is intensified.

Tragically, these three reports are not isolated incidents but reflect widespread antipathy toward people infected with HIV. Stigmatization and discrimination toward them and their families is not the particular response of people within one culture, country, or religion but unfortunately raise their ugly faces in almost every place.

People infected by HIV not only face the dilemma of illness but also the likelihood of discrimination. Throughout the world people lose jobs, friends, family, and even medical care when it is discovered they are suffering from HIV/AIDS. Their confidentiality is breached and their human rights ignored.

Religious communities, especially those in the minority in every culture, know what it means to suffer discrimination and loss of human rights. A sense of empathy, therefore, with the marginalized should serve as a useful reminder of the need to champion the cause of people with HIV/AIDS.

As the pandemic has swept across southern Africa, the church has had to confront AIDS on a human scale never before experienced. In the early stages of the disease many Christians sought to justify their judgmental noninvolvement with prevention efforts and care by blaming the infected for immoral behavior. Such negative treatment has also been common in the United States, and the Christian community has never expressed massive outrage to such prejudice.

A decade after HIV/AIDS emerged in the United States, a prominent Southern Baptist minister, Rev. Scott Allen, and his family faced unbelievable discrimination because his wife became infected with HIV during a blood transfusion and his two children were infected in the womb. Five times he and his family were discouraged from participating in local churches, and his children were denied entrance to church day cares and even Sunday school sessions. Though he was not HIV-positive, he was asked to leave the ministry when he was serving a church in Colorado Springs, Colorado. When he sees their bumper stickers declaring "You're Welcome in Our Church," he feels like suing them for false advertising. The church preaches a message of God's unconditional love, but Allen discovered "in practice, the love and acceptance are not unconditional. There are strings attached."[2]

Having HIV/AIDS is no longer likely to trigger quite the emotional fear in the United States that it did in the early years of the epidemic. In certain circles of society, acceptance and understanding prevail. Yet there remains enough antipathy and discriminatory practice that revealing one's HIV-positive status is still a traumatic experience, and fear keeps people from knowing the full love and care of the people of God. Fear also prohibits us from recognizing that global AIDS is not just an issue for somebody else in some distant place, but at our own very doorstep and perhaps in our very own households.

What was proclaimed at an ecumenical and global conference in Africa needs to be shouted from the pulpits of every congregation and taught in every church forum: "the most powerful contribution we can make to combating HIV transmission is the eradication of stigma and discrimination; a key that will, we believe, open the door for all those who dream of a viable and achievable way of living with HIV/AIDS and preventing the spread of the virus." Clearly it would signal a new day for the Christian community if we asserted: "We will condemn discrimination and stigmatization of people living with HIV/AIDS as a sin and as contrary to the will of God."[3]

Resisting Sin

In the words spoken by the youth of twenty-six countries at the United Nations General Assembly Special Session on HIV/AIDS. "We must be bold and assume leadership in breaking the conspiracy of silence and shame that drives AIDS underground and stigmatizes people living with HIV/AIDS"[4] Following are six ways for Christians to resist the sins of stigmatization and discrimination and thus break the conspiracy of silence and shame.

Follow Jesus' Example

By pointing to the life and ministry of Jesus, rank-and-file Christians can understand how sinful it is to discriminate and stigmatize people living with HIV/AIDS. Looking anew at the ways of Jesus reveals a vision of what God wills for our response. Paramount to this examination is to look at how Jesus responded to leprosy and lepers. In biblical times, those with leprosy experienced severe discrimination and stigmatization, yet Jesus boldly reached out and ministered to them.

Often the contemporary AIDS crisis has been compared to leprosy, especially in the way people have been treated. I am convinced that many Christians only read Leviticus when they want to find a proof text to condemn homosexuality—they endorse a couple of verses but ignore absolutely everything else in its twenty-seven chapters! One can also turn to Leviticus to understand the social-cultural-religious landscape and prejudices of the ancient world. For example, Leviticus offers a vivid portrait of the plight of the leper: "The person who has the leprous disease shall wear torn clothes and let the hair of his head be disheveled; and he shall cover his upper lip and cry out, 'Unclean, unclean.' He shall remain unclean as long as he has the disease; he is unclean. He shall live alone; his dwelling shall be outside the camp." (Leviticus 13:45-46).

Too often this is the experience of contemporary persons who have HIV/AIDS—they are ostracized and made to feel "unclean, unclean"— and they are not welcomed into the hearts, homes, and churches of Christians, but instead their "dwelling" is "outside the camp."

I am amazed by the radical difference between Jesus' approach to lepers and the dominant cultural and religious perspective of his time. To be a leper was to be an outcast—the lowest of the low. Lepers were excluded from many places, and leprosy was considered a punishment for sin (see Numbers 12:10-15; 2 Kings 5:27; 15:5; 2 Chronicles 26:20-21). Entering a leper's house was a cause for bathing, purification, and laundering. To associate with lepers was highly problematic behavior, certain to make you unpopular with powerful social and religious leaders. Thus how shocking to scan the ministry of Jesus and discover how repeatedly he reached out to heal people with leprosy (for example, see Matthew 8:1-4; Luke 17:11-19) and commissioned his disciples to do the same (Matthew 10:8). How amazing that two days before Passover, in the very moment when the plot to kill Jesus was brewing, Jesus deliberately chose to dine at the table of the home of Simon the leper (Mark 14:3-9).

Jesus crashed the barriers and smashed the bias of his time as he reached out both in compassion and companionship to the lepers of his time. Would he do otherwise today—as 46 million people suffer from HIV/AIDS worldwide? Clearly Jesus would be a compassionate companion and call us, his disciples, to join him whenever and wherever we can.

Respect Every Person's Worth and Dignity

Christian theology and ethics clearly condemns discrimination and stigmatization, affirming the essential worth and dignity of every person. Christians understand God as standing in loving solidarity, especially with those who suffer or who are abandoned (e.g., orphans, widows) or mistreated. Long identified with caring for the sick and caring for the suffering, Christians affirm the words of Hippocrates in *The Epidemics*: "As to diseases, make a habit of two things—to help, or at least do no harm."

The sacred value of every human being is based on the Christian belief in the *imago Dei*, the image of God, present in each and every person. Every person reflects the mystery and glory of God. To treat any person as less than valuable or as somehow disposable is to offend God. It is to deny the sacredness of every human life. Dehumanization is a blasphemous action against God as well as individual persons.

No one is treated more like a nonperson in today's world than an impoverished person living with HIV/AIDS. Treating anyone as a nonperson is contrary to the will and way of God, which, historically, church dogmatics tended to overlook. Duke theologian Frederick Herzog explains:

> Nicea and Chalcedon did not let Jesus the refugee, the homeless one, the "nonperson," through their lofty christological grid. In the dogmatic tradition, Jesus hardly appears as a particular human being, but rather as an

impersonal being (as in the old doctrinal notion of *enhy-postasia*). Nicea and Chalcedon dealt with the divinity of Jesus, but not with the "humanity of God" in the streets— God in solidarity with the poor, wretched human being.[5]

We need to affirm Herzog's assertion that "we are not allowed to reject even the most ragged shred of the human, for we do not so much hear the Word of God through 'nonpersons' as we meet the 'very God' in the 'nonperson' who struggles for justice."[6]

In this sense, the beginning of Christian mission is to identify with those treated as nonpersons and to reach out in caring ministry.[7] Christians always need to keep Jesus' parable of the Good Samaritan foremost in their minds. A contemporary paraphrase goes like this:

An HIV/AIDS afflicted person fell into a pit and couldn't get himself out.

A pharisaic fundamentalist came along and said, "You deserve your pit."

An apostate liberal came along and said, "Your pit is God's beautiful gift to you."

An activist came along and said, "Fight for your right to stay in your pit."

A researcher came along and said, "Discrimination against pits is illegal."

A charismatic came along and said, "Just confess that you're not in that pit."

"Respectable people" came along and said, "We don't associate with pit-dwellers."

His mother came along and said, "It's your father's fault you're in that pit."

His father came along and said, "It's your mother's fault you're in that pit."

Moralists came and said, "It's the fault of the company of friends you kept all these days."

But Jesus, seeing the man, loved him, and reaching into the pit, put his arms around the man, pulled him out and said, "Come my friend, share with me your painful story. . . ."[8]

As Christians we need to listen to the painful stories of those people who have experienced stigmatization and discrimination. If we think of the global pandemic only in terms of remote statistics and nameless numbers, we are unlikely to hear the voice of God speaking to us. But as we encounter individual persons living with HIV/AIDS and enter into their experience as empathetically as is humanly possible, our hearts will be broken and God's grace will permeate it with care and compassion.

When I visited the large AIDS hospital in Tambaram outside of Chennai, India, the administrator in charge warned me that the patients would be hoping that I was coming with some kind of miraculous cure. Expectations would be high and yet I would have so little to offer. The best I could do was to treat with dignity each person with AIDS. I could reach out and touch them and tell them God loved them. I could listen to their cries for help and their stories of anger and anguish. I could pray with a woman clutching her large Bible.

As they shared their painful stories and their great hope that I, as a representative of the church, could somehow help, I literally buried my head into my hands. Suddenly, I heard the voice of Jesus saying: "Come to me, all you that are weary and are carrying heavy burdens, and I will give you rest" (Matthew 11:28). They had come to me, but I wasn't Jesus. They had told their painful stories and they looked to me for hope and help. And what could I do?

I could respond, as so many traditional churches and church leaders have, as Gillian Paterson has described, with "thundering moral denunciations, and by victimizing and excluding those who are known to be living with HIV and their families." In effect, Paterson notes, they are saying, "Go away, you who labour and are heavy-laden. There is no rest for you here."[9] But I believe and worship a God of unconditional love and free grace, as do most other Christians.

Their faces and their voices and their stories haunt me. Remembering them, therefore, I seek to mobilize an apathetic church and an unresponsive political system to become constructively engaged in the global struggle against HIV/AIDS and *for* dignity. Being involved in an AIDS mission and ministry is to discover anew the image of God in all people.

I am persuaded that every person we meet is having a hard time and should be treated kindly. Scratch the surface of the most successful among us, and behind the greatest achievers often lies a painful story. True, our hard times are different than those who are most impoverished or marginalized or who suffer from HIV/AIDS, but nevertheless our sadness and suffering, agony and anguish, depression and despair, are real and genuine. The world is not divided between HIV-positive and HIV-negative people—certain universal human troubles bond us together as people:

- Pain and uncertainty of disease and declining health
- Burdens of caregiving that seem endless and often unappreciated
- Anxiety about problems facing our children, or parents, or loved ones
- Grief over losing a spouse, or friend, or child
- Fear of job insecurity or future employment
- Hurt from unkind remarks, unfair treatment, and insensitivity
- Heartbreak from broken relationships, separation, and divorce
- Personal struggles related to alcohol, drugs, or sexual addiction
- Loneliness
- Fear of death and dying

Thus I am drawn inexorably to the words of Jesus in Matthew 11:28-30. These words of comfort and hope were meant not only for the people of Jesus' day or for the "untouchables" of India or for those scarred by the "scarlet letters" of stigmatization and discrimination, but for every person. Hear anew Jesus saying: "Come to me, all you that are weary and are carrying heavy burdens, and I will give you rest. Take my yoke upon you, and learn from me; for I am gentle and humble in heart, and you will find rest for your souls. For my yoke is easy, and my burden is light" (Matthew 11:28-30).

Jesus sees each one of us, loves us, reaches into whatever "pit" we dwell, puts his arms around us, pulls us out, and says, "Come my friend, tell me your painful story." Christians can do the same by first respecting the worth and dignity of every person.

Take Loving Action

Christians can respond to God's call to combat stigmatization and discrimination in the church and world by offering love, acceptance, forgiveness, and healing, not judgment and prejudice. Every segment of society can contribute in its own way to overcoming this preventable disease. Religious communities will never have enough financial resources to provide all the funds necessary for promoting education, prevention, treatment, and care, but they can commit their share. As Calle Almedal of UNAIDS emphasizes, "It does not cost one cent to preach Sunday after Sunday that discrimination of people with HIV/AIDS is a sin and against the will of God."[10]

However, what communities of faith can do most effectively is to demonstrate theologically and practically to people and families living with HIV/AIDS that the church of Jesus Christ offers love, acceptance, forgiveness, and healing. Judgmental attitudes and shunning behavior have only prompted greater secrecy and shame, forcing people to hide their illness and keeping them from openly seeking prevention, treatment, and care. As Kofi Annan, secretary-general of the United Nations, declared on World AIDS Day 2002:

> The fear of stigma leads to silence, and when it comes to fighting AIDS, silence is death. It suppresses public discussion about AIDS, and deters people from finding out whether they are infected. It can cause people—whether a mother breastfeeding her child or a sexual partner reluctant to disclose their HIV status—to risk transmitting HIV rather than attract suspicion that they might be infected.[11]

People living with HIV/AIDS have repeatedly reported that the hardest part of having the disease is not the illness itself or facing the prospect of death and dying, but experiencing the fear and the reality of rejection from friends, family, church members, medical professionals, and even strangers.

In 1850, Nathaniel Hawthorne published a novel entitled *The Scarlet Letter,* in which a woman, Hester Prynne, was forced to wear a red letter *A* for "adulterer" in public. Her child was the result of a secret extramarital affair. Instead of forgiveness and grace, she faced a hostile, condemning community. Over the years, Hawthorne's book has served as a reminder that the sin of discrimination is far worse than the sin of adultery, for it labels people and treats them as "nonpersons" rather than as forgiven sinners in the family of God. Now the scarlet letter *A* seems to stand for "AIDS" and attempts are made to brand it into the spirit and soul of the 46 million people infected with HIV/AIDS in the world.

Stigma and discrimination are not only horrendous personal evils to inflict on individuals, but they are social evils that undermine and threaten collective public health efforts at prevention, care, support, and treatment.

In Botswana, where 40 percent of the adults are infected, Health Minister Joy Phumpaphi has pleaded that unless the barriers of stigma and discrimination are overcome, preventing others from becoming infected in southern Africa will become even very problematic. People hide their positive status if they think they are going to be ridiculed or suffer personal harm. If they fear their partners or families will abandon them, why would they risk telling their status? But if they do not share their status, and others expect them to engage in unprotected sex, the possibility for the disease to spread is quite high.

Since women in many cultures suffer discrimination because of their gender and often have little or no control over their sexual lives, they are doubly discriminated against. Though men are the main disseminators of the disease, the women are the ones who most often are blamed.[12]

In an extensive study of HIV/AIDS in India, Journalist Kalpana Jain confirms that the fear of stigmatization is widespread. Jain states unequivocally that most people do not fear so much the possibility of an early death but the world of stigma and shame thrust upon them.[13] The cultural environment becomes the greatest killer, forcing individuals and families to hide the disease. A young Indian pastor once told me that anyone diagnosed with HIV/AIDS in his rural community would fear for his life. With a trembling voice, he told how a long time ago his grandfather had contracted cholera, and the neighbors were so scared "that they locked my grandfather in his house and burned him alive. Today that would happen if I had AIDS."

People worry not only about the stigma and discrimination they will face, but what will be inflicted on their families and loved ones. Children suffer not only from their parent's illness, but from ugly taunts and exclusion from other children. Men and women lose their jobs and then cannot provide food and shelter for their families. When one Indian man, Anand (a pseudonym), went public with newspaper and television interviews in order to spread awareness and promote prevention, the negative public reaction was so great that his mother lost her teaching job, his sister's marriage was canceled, and his lawyer brother-in-law faced hostility from his colleagues. His own brother threw him out of the house, and he was forced to live with his grandmother, who treated him like a pariah. He was forced into silence and could no longer function as an advocate against AIDS in the public arena.[14]

Global AIDS provides a new frontier for Christian service, for active Christian love. Getting involved in any way provides Christians an opportunity help solve the greatest health challenge the world has faced in the last 700 years. As Oliver Wendell Holmes once said, "it is required of a [person] that he should share the passion and action of his time at peril of being judged not to have lived."

Make Personal Connections

Another powerful way to help people understand how the sin of stigmatization and discrimination is contrary to the will of God is for people to meet someone living with HIV/AIDS or to hear the stories of those who suffer from prejudicial attitudes and actions. Only the most hardhearted people will then resist the promptings of the Holy Spirit to greater compassion and care.

Albert "Fritz" Mutti, the United Methodist Bishop of Kansas, and his wife, Etta Mae, openly share their experiences of losing two of their three sons to AIDS. A number of times I have been privileged to hear them tell how their sons lived with the disease and encountered discrimination and stigmatization from the very denomination their parents faithfully served. We once journeyed to India where they served as speakers at a conference at United Theological College in Bangalore. Halfway through their joint presentation, I began to think that perhaps their stories were too remote and "American" for an audience in India. But then I turned and looked at the faces of the listeners. How wrong I was, as the Mutti's heartbreaking stories crossed the cultural and geographical barriers, and people in India identified with their incredible loss. Loving and losing two sons to AIDS was a powerful testimony that melted hearts and created a sense of outrage as well as compassion.

Some people are consumed with hate. Bishop and Mrs. Mutti live in Topeka, Kansas, where a particular pastor and church devote their entire ministry to attacking gay persons and those living with HIV/AIDS. They know no boundaries to their ugly misbehavior. They picket the funerals of people who die from AIDS. They journeyed to Laramie, Wyoming, to condemn Matthew Shepard, who had been brutally killed because he was gay. They followed Bishop and Mrs. Mutti around as they spoke about their sons' struggle with HIV/AIDS, hurling vile epithets and waving their placards saying, "FAG METHODIST CHURCH" and "FAG BISHOP MUTTI." Etta Mae is very candid about the pain it caused them:

> Abuse like that hurts. The adage "words can never hurt you" is not true. Hatred hurts. It stings to the core. . . . We know of very few people outside that one church who defend such shameful behavior. Yet over and over again we feel the same kind of hostility from otherwise upstanding church members. "It is the sin we hate," they say. "We love people with AIDS. We love homosexual persons. It is the sin we hate." The use of the word "hate" reveals the under-lying message. That certainly is the feeling we perceive. That word "hate" hides entirely the loving intention.[15]

At that same conference in India, I became acquainted with a courageous and winsome young Indian man, Ashok Pillai. A Hindu with a heart of love for all people, Ashok was the first in India to dare to be publicly identified as HIV-positive. He often talked about when he was in the Indian Navy and was diagnosed with HIV. A popular guy, he was suddenly shunned. No one would even sit at the table to eat with him. Kalpana Jain describes what happened when Ashok was all alone in a public place, facing rejection from his buddies:

> Tears welled up in Ashok's eyes. Each morsel he took seemed to choke him. But slowly and deliberately he fin-ished the rice and fish he had served himself. . . . Each movement, each action of his was under scrutiny. He wanted to run and get away from their gimlet stares. But better sense commanded him to stay; to behave as though he did not care. He had to live. He had to eat, even if he

was feeling nauseous. He finished every bit on his plate.
The whispers in the room were still alive—ringing in his
ears, weighing him down.[16]

With incredible fortitude, Ashok dared to be himself, ultimately
helping to form the Indian Network for People Living with
HIV/AIDS. He served as the organization's president and campaigned
tirelessly for a world without AIDS. He conquered his fears of rejection and spoke the truth to power, calling government, cultural, and
religious organizations to compassionate involvement. Though a
Hindu himself, he volunteered his time and energy to speak to any
Christian group that was willing to listen and learn. For me, he was a
Christ-like figure because he sought to love and save people, even
those who scorned and rejected him. His untimely and sudden death
in 2002 was a major loss to all who knew him and for millions he
sought to help. When persons come to know and care for real persons
living with HIV/AIDS, hearts are changed and sin resisted.

Walk in Another's Moccasins
An effective way to help Christians understand how devastating
stigmatization and discrimination are to a person's emotional and
physical well-being is to invite them to consider imaginatively how
they would feel and respond in similar situations. We can keep as our
guide the truism given to us in a traditional Lakota prayer: "Before I
judge another, let me walk in his moccasins for two long weeks; then
I shall understand, and not condemn."

At a conference addressing the global AIDS crisis, Elaine Blinn, a
medical social worker, challenged church leaders to individually
write their five most treasured values on single slips of paper. Each of
us quietly reflected for a moment and then privately wrote values like
God, family, lover, friends, job, church, sex, health, independence,
money, happiness, security. Nobody revealed to anybody else what
he or she wrote, so values could have included any of these items or
others. Then Blinn shocked us by asking us to rip up one of the sheets
of paper. An audible groan swept across the audience. After some hesitation, one could hear pieces of paper being torn. Each of us had to
make a choice of what we would give up, if forced to do so, and we
experienced some pain. Hardly had we finished doing that when she
told us to destroy another sheet of paper. This time the reaction was

even sharper, with a few participants registering vocal protests, saying they could not possibly tolerate sacrificing another value. Then in the poignant silence, we experienced the sounds of paper reluctantly being shredded.

Then Blinn asked us to turn to the person seated beside us and share our feelings. What a relief and comfort to talk with someone about how hard it had been for us to give up something we held so sacred. Life is a choice of values, but we are not used to being forced to surrender anything like friends or health or sex. At that point Blinn instructed each of us to hold up our three remaining values and let our neighbor blindly select one and destroy it without looking at it. By then the emotions of these sophisticated church leaders were raw, as they saw cherished values like God or church or family force-fully taken from them and trashed.

Of course, by this time Blinn's point was abundantly clear. People diagnosed with HIV often suddenly discover their life values tumbling out of their control. The person who tests positive for HIV fears that his or her world is collapsing and that the most intimate values—be they faith, family, friends, job, sex—are in dire jeopardy. And if it happens to that person, it can happen to any of us. As a young man in Tanzania said, "If you see someone being mistreated because they are HIV infected, it is obvious the same will happen to you when it is known you are HIV."

Theologian Gillian Paterson, in her essay "Church, AIDS and Stigma," vividly illustrates the experience of stigmatization with his story of Yupa, a Christian woman in Chiang Mai, Thailand. Yupa's husband was the leader of a local church and felt increasingly ill. Eventually their doctor suggested that both she and her husband have a blood test. Both proved to be HIV-positive. Yupa cared lovingly for her husband; in fact, he ultimately died in her arms.

Yupa, however, felt the full force of stigmatization and discrimination. Instead of being a respectable woman in the life of the church, she was treated as an outcast. She was no longer welcome in her church, and her husband's family rejected her. Paterson reports that she was told that "God was punishing her, and she should avoid the presence of God-fearing Christians. Her family received death threats, and people would look the other way if she met them in the street." Fortunately, Yupa eventually found a support group and became a volunteer helping other people living with HIV/AIDS. However, she says, "I am happy that my husband died before he learned the shallowness of his church's claim to be loving and compassionate."[17] Imagining, or empathizing with, another person's pain or situation helps to move us closer to our neighbor, prompting us to ponder what it would be like if faced with HIV/AIDS ourselves.

Protect the Human Rights of All People

Finally, Christians can fight the sins of stigmatization and discrimination by advocating and supporting laws that protect the human rights of people living with HIV/AIDS. Laws that insist on medical confidentiality, protect employment, ensure medical treatment, safeguard housing, and punish harassment help curtail prejudicial treatment.

In the African American community, it has been said, "Laws cannot make people love you, but they can keep them from lynching you." Likewise legislation aimed at protecting the human rights of people and families living with HIV will not necessarily transform hard-hearted people into compassionate friends, but it can restrain them from acts of cruelty and teach them the basics of human decency. In the process, it protects people from harm and may eventually help people understand that people living with HIV/AIDS are not a threat to them, their families, or the community.

The General Assembly of the United Nations forthrightly declared that nations should adopt laws that protect the human rights of people living with HIV/AIDS, eliminate discrimination, and ensure equal rights in education, employment, health care, and other services. Specifically, they called on countries to promote, protect, and respect the rights of people living with HIV/AIDS, and to "develop strategies to combat stigma and social exclusion connected with the pandemic."[18]

If HIV/AIDS is to be conquered, churches must join with others in urging that the rights of sexual minorities in every culture and country be protected. In too many places discrimination is not only permitted but also encouraged against gays, lesbians, bisexuals, and transgendered persons. Sexual minorities are subject to extortion, blackmail, illegal detention, and physical, verbal, and sexual abuse by police and others.[19] As long as society and states tolerate such violations of human rights, silence, and secrecy will prevail and hopes for a world without AIDS will evaporate.

AIDS Is Not a Dirty Word

The church will not provide the finances or scientific research that finds a cure or vaccine for HIV. The church will not likely match the contributions of many other non-governmental organizations, which have devoted themselves and their resources to creating a world without AIDS. What the church can do is relieve the stigma and discrimination by standing in solidarity with those living with HIV/AIDS and by speaking and acting out in every venue possible to encourage acceptance, understanding, love, compassion, care, and treatment.

The story of Ashok Pillai did not end with the initial episode of being rejected in the Navy dining hall. The next morning as he sat alone trying to eat his breakfast omelet and a piece of bread, another sailor, Ravindra Krishnarao Rahate, suddenly sat down beside him, touching his shoulder. Ravi reached over and plunged his fork into what remained of Ashok's egg omelet, thrusting it into his own mouth. To the shock of everyone in the dining hall, he announced his friendship and stood against the bigoted crowd. Ravi provided "a healing touch that no one else had. No gift, no gesture could have been greater than that for Ashok."[20] It is precisely this type of "healing touch" that Christians can offer to people living with HIV/AIDS, and, thereby, help to destroy stigmatization and discrimination.

The church's profession of human rights, however, will ring hollow if stigmatization and discrimination against people with HIV/AIDS are allowed to continue within the church. If laypeople and clergy diagnosed with HIV lose their positions of leadership within the church, then the church loses any authority it may have to speak for human rights in the broader society.

One notable exception to church stigmatization is Rev. Gideon Byamugisha of Uganda, who was the first practicing priest in Africa to declare publicly he was living with HIV/AIDS. Since being diagnosed, he has been promoted to a Canon in the Anglican Church and become an effective champion of the rights of people living with HIV/AIDS and a leader in motivating the church to combat global HIV/AIDS. In his book *Breaking the Silence on HIV/AIDS in Africa*, he writes:

AIDS does not just happen to "other people." AIDS can and does happen to any of us. . . . If those of us with HIV and AIDS can obtain help and compassionate support from those around us, we can live positively and constructively, and help our brothers and sisters to avoid our situation. If we face instead punishment, blame, or discrimination, our lives will be more miserable, and will hide the danger and the experience that could save our lives and the lives of others. Blame sustains denial, and denial fuels the spread of AIDS.[21]

In contrast, Episcopal Bishop John S. Spong spoke of his friend, Father Ray Roberts, who died of AIDS without ever really knowing acceptance and care from the church he loved and served. Spong emphasizes there are no outcasts in God's kingdom. He laments: "We Christians assert that we see the human face of this God in a Christ who reigns with outstretched arms of welcome from a cross to which humanity has nailed him. From that painful throne this Christ issues an invitation: 'Come to me all who travail and are heavy laden. I will give you rest.' It is a scandalous outrage that the church that claims to be the body of Christ cannot make good the inclusiveness of this invitation."[22]

As the Anglican archbishop Njongonkulu Ndungane of South Africa says, "We need to shout from the rooftops that AIDS is not God's punishment of the wicked. It is a virus and not a sin, and the stigma that society has created around the epidemic is causing people to die instead of living positively."[23] In the United States, one young man, Ryan White, suffered a high degree of stigmatization and intolerance as a teenager with HIV/AIDS. Despite being ostracized and denied public schooling, he and his mother courageously defied public prejudice and fought for acceptance and understanding of all people living with HIV. At his Indianapolis funeral in 1990, the Presbyterian pastor, Raymond Probasco, enunciated a goal for all Christians: "With God's help, and each of yours, we'll make AIDS a disease and not a dirty word."[24]

5

Women, Children, and HIV/AIDS

I was sick with AIDS and you did not visit me. You did not wash my wounds, nor did you give me medicine. . . . I was stigmatized, isolated, and rejected because of HIV/AIDS and you did not welcome me. I was hungry, thirsty, and naked, completely dispossessed. . . . and you did not give me food, water, or any clothing. I was a powerless woman exposed to the high risk of infection and carrying a huge burden of care, and you did not come to my rescue. I was a dispossessed widow and an orphan and you did not meet my needs. . . . The Lord will say to us, "Truly I tell you, as long as you did not do it to one of the least of these members of my family, you did not do it to me.[1]

—Musa W. Dube, Botswana

The world reserves the worst stigmatization and discrimination for women. In country after country, women are treated as practically nonpersons, relegated to second- and third-class citizenship, subjected to violence and abuse, treated as property, limited in educational and employment opportunities, and deprived of basic health care and reproductive information. In many a culture when a woman is diagnosed with HIV/AIDS, the stigmatization and bias is amplified and the person is disowned and even abandoned.

One illustration comes from a public AIDS hospital in a suburb of Chennai (Madras), India. Overcrowded, with people sleeping outside under trees waiting for care, the hospital cares for about six hundred patients. These people are poor and marginalized. Three wards serve children, men, and women. There are not enough beds; therefore, there is a rotation system by which the sickest get the beds until they feel better, after which they are transferred to mats on the floor at the foot of the bed. A visitor to the women's ward, filmmaker Robert Bilheimer, reported the following:

> The ward was immaculately clean, and quiet. For the most part, the women just stared off into space, their thoughts and emotions difficult to read. . . . When the woman is finally diagnosed with a deadly disease like AIDS, she is then shunned, and, for all intents and purposes, deemed to be worthless.
>
> "Do you notice anything different here?" the doctor asked me. I looked around, and then it struck me. There were no visitors. . . . Whereas the men and children have wives or grandmothers sitting by their bedsides, the women have no one. I asked the doctor if a husband had ever set foot in the ward. "Never. Not even one."
>
> So not only are Indian women dying of AIDS, in growing numbers, they are dying alone.[2]

An "Equal Opportunity" Disease

Around the world, women are becoming infected and are dying in escalating numbers. What was once viewed primarily as a gay man's malady has now become an "equal opportunity" disease, with almost half of the world's HIV/AIDS infections afflicting women, chiefly as a result of sexual intercourse with infected men.[3] Biologically, women are four times more susceptible than men to sexually transmitted diseases.[4]

In sub-Saharan Africa, women account for 58 percent of the infections and the numbers are rapidly rising. The infection rate for young African women between the ages of fifteen and nineteen is five to six times higher than for young men. Likewise, in countries like Great

Britain and Ireland, more than half of the new infections are the result of heterosexual sex.[5] In Argentina, between 1988 and 2001, the infection rate exploded exponentially, going from one woman to twenty men to one woman to every three men.[6]

Women are not only highly vulnerable to HIV/AIDS, but they are exploited and mistreated in culture after culture, religion after religion, and country after country. Limited progress in the global battle against AIDS will be registered until the social, economic, cultural, and religious status of women is upgraded. Deprived and subordinated women around the world are very susceptible to HIV infection and AIDS-related death. Ensuring the human rights and welfare of women around the globe is integral to any strategy of conquering HIV/AIDS.

The Patriarchy Problem

Christianity and other religions give lip service to honoring and caring for women, youth, and orphans. But reality rarely matches rhetoric so that, in truth, women, youth, and children are treated as second-class or lower citizens. The discrepancy between the idealism expressed and the reality experienced is painfully evident amid the global pandemic of AIDS.

Christianity and other world religions developed amid patriarchal societies in which women are treated as objects rather than persons. To this day, women have neither been accorded equal rights within the society nor equal rights within religious communities. The male, in most instances, has been granted authority and power over women, especially wives, and this has led to devastating consequences for women and their health and well-being.

Women, for example, have far too little control or autonomy over their sexual lives and are often forced to submit to the erotic wishes and whims of men. This behavior has often been overtly endorsed by theologies that proclaim the husband as the "head" of the family and relegate women to secondary roles within the church and culture.

This hierarchical ordering is often justified by arguing that men are called to sacrifice themselves in love to protect and care for their wives and children. Clearly, however, this is more myth than fact, as women everywhere suffer from severe violations of their human rights and endure great violence.

An Ethical Response

Improving the status of women is not only a matter of health and survival, but is fundamental to practicing Christian ethics. The church cannot tolerate the injustice of sexism and the widespread assault aimed at women and young girls. What follows are six commitments Christians must make to help upgrade the status of women in the world and protect the well-being of youth and children. Obviously this list is illustrative, not exhaustive, and other steps or approaches can and must be added.

Challenge Men's Unsafe Sexual Practices

The AIDS calamity has confirmed that the sexual practices of many men must be challenged, since it is clear that their behavior enhances the risks of infection for women. Practices such as having multiple partners and engaging sex workers (prostitutes) are more widespread than previously acknowledged. Unwillingness to use condoms only increases the risk of infection for women. When women ask their male partners to use condoms, they sometimes refuse and angrily accuse women of being unfaithful. For example, after Cecelia Mtembu's husband died in South Africa, she chose to be tested and was diagnosed as HIV-positive. A faithful wife, she says, "I was so angry at my husband, because sometimes I tried to get him to use a condom but he always said no."[7]

The most endangered people on earth are married women because they are the most lacking in power over their own sexual lives. Some AIDS activists say that getting married is the riskiest sexual behavior an African woman can engage in! There was a shocking discovery in Tanzania: sex workers often were more effective at protecting themselves from HIV than housewives, because they had more power to insist on safer sexual practices.[8]

Women's subordination worldwide results in similar situations elsewhere. For example, in Cambodia, reports indicate that "it is common for men to visit a prostitute before going home to their wives. . . . One characteristic of the epidemic is that women who have been infected by their husbands are now dying, often along with their children."[9]

It is also clear that younger unmarried women are also exceptionally endangered because of various cultural myths and practices. For example, it has been widely reported, that in some cultures men who are HIV-positive believe that by having sex with a young virgin they will be cured. As a result, rape increases and infections spread. One-third of the pregnant teenagers interviewed at a clinic in Cape Town, South Africa, claimed their first intercourse was coerced.[10] The church cannot tolerate sexual abuse in any form.

What sociologists call "cross-generational sex"—older men using teenage girls as casual sexual partners—is an astonishingly common practice in sub-Saharan Africa. In return for sexual relationships the young women get gifts like clothes, school tuition, food, cheap plastic shoes—and the "gift" of HIV. In this region, teenage women between the ages of fifteen and nineteen have an infection rate six times higher than young men their age. Cross-generational sex is a form of polygamy without legal blessing.[11]

The actual tradition of polygamy and multiple partners complicates AIDS prevention and control in Africa. King Mswati III, the thirty-five-year-old leader of Swaziland, has nine wives and two fiancées and advocates polygamy for others, saying it does not contribute to the spread of HIV/AIDS. Women's empowerment groups and health advocates, however, publicly dispute his assertions, noting that multiple sex partners contribute to AIDS and that the king should urge the men of his country, "his warriors," to "cut down on girlfriends" because polygamy is spreading AIDS in a country where nearly 40 percent of the Swazis are HIV-positive.[12]

Provide Proactive Education
Curbing the AIDS pandemic requires more than condemning unsafe male sexual practices. Proactive educational programs are also needed to enlighten men of all ages about prevention and appropriate ways of treating their partners. Harmful concepts of masculinity must be exposed and other models of masculinity must be shared. New ways of positively relating to women must be introduced. Men must be viewed not simply as part of the problem, but critical to the solution. By getting men more fully involved in the fight against AIDS, they can contribute significantly to their own health and well-being as well as that of their sexual partners.

Having studied the statistics on women, and after visiting women in AIDS hospitals and hospices, I find myself outraged and embarrassed by male behavior. It is unconscionable and unacceptable. However, when I actually meet some of the infected men themselves, I am often overwhelmed by their circumstances.

They are not preppy young college guys or even sophisticated male businessmen tourists. Instead, I have met with illiterate rickshaw pullers who live far from home in crowded shanties. Or I visit with male migrant workers or lorry drivers who spend months and months away from their families and who have no clue how HIV is transmitted or how to use a condom. Their lives are wretched; they have little or no access to health care or education as they struggle for their existence. After spending hours in an AIDS hospital in India, I was impressed how all of the men and women were essentially good people, but the "misery-go-round" of poverty, illiteracy, racism, and disease has robbed them of health, life, and even hope.

Ignorance is widespread and lethal. A high percentage of both young men and women have no knowledge of how to protect themselves. UNICEF studies reveal that in Tanzania 51 percent of the girls and 35 percent of the boys lack information, while in Bangladesh the numbers are even higher: 96 percent of the girls and 88 percent of the boys are uninformed. Additionally, lack of education about sexuality and HIV/AIDS in particular means that young people believe that if a person looks healthy then there is no danger. UNICEF reports that in Nepal 80 percent of the girls don't know that healthy-looking men can transmit the disease, and more than half the girls of South Africa and Lesotho are deceived by looks.[13]

Columnist Ann Landers once remarked that if you thought education was expensive, try ignorance. Though it is not easy or inexpensive, the positive news is that men can change their behaviors and women can protect themselves if intensive efforts at education are undertaken. Peter Piot, executive director of UNAIDS, reports that it has already been demonstrated that

> in parts of Africa, Central America, and Asia, long distance truck drivers have been encouraged to reduce their number of sexual partners and more consistently practice safe sex. In Thailand, there have been successful programmes for prevention among army recruits. In many countries, including the United States, college students are beginning to delay the onset of sex and are using condoms more consistently.[14]

The church in every place needs to be a part of an education program that aims for behavioral change. But first Christians must change their own behavior and get involved in open, honest discussions of sexuality and HIV/AIDS.

Reach Out to Impoverished Women

The church must make it a priority to reach out to the most impoverished women of the world. Poverty-stricken women are exploited at every point. When women experience low social, economic, and cultural status, they are more likely to become infected with HIV and pass the virus on to others.

This is clearly the case for women employed in the commercial sex industry. Millions of women are forced into prostitution by illiteracy, exploitation, and economic necessity. Some women enter the world's oldest profession as a matter of choice, but for the overwhelming majority it is a life-and-death matter for them and their children. As one Zambian widowed mother asked, "How else do I feed my children except by having sex with men?"[15]

Sex networks exist throughout the world. Accurate counts are impossible; few governments attempt accurate statistics. Estimating the number of prostitutes in a city or country has proven more difficult than estimating the number of fish in the sea. Some estimates report that 200,000 Nepali girls have been sold into sexual slavery in Indian brothels. Probably 60,000 children work as prostitutes in the Philippine sex industry, and perhaps as many as 200,000 in Thailand.[16] Those engaged in sex work may have no religious faith or be quite religious. Writing from India, Journalist Kalpana Jain provides this shocking eyewitness account:

> It was a Good Friday when I traveled on the highway that connects Kathipudi to Annavaram in Andhra Pradesh. I saw sex workers all along this route, risking their lives, as strange, perhaps drunken, men picked them up, and driving recklessly took them to God knows where. These were all courageous, self-respecting women; some of those I talked to were fasting as it was Good Friday, yet they were all looking for clients so that they could feed their children at home. . . . To take home 100 rupees[US$2], they

would need to have at least five customers. Some of the women could get cheated and be thrown out on the highway. There was no madam from the brothel to protect them. A high percentage of these women suffered from sexually transmitted diseases and HIV infection.[17]

While attending an ecumenical church conference on AIDS in Mumbai (Bombay), India, some of us went into the famous red-light district of Bombay during the daytime to visit with our "sisters," the term the Salvation Army instructed us to use. The plight of these women and their little children can hardly be described. An estimated 500,000 women exist in small, squalid, and stinking quarters, being paid a pittance in exchange for sexual favors. Controlled by pimps and madams, they have little likelihood for a better life. Disease and crime are rampant.

In that place, however, were a few dedicated church workers from the Salvation Army and the Orthodox Church. Working out of limited quarters, they offer health care, prevention education for HIV/AIDS, and treatment for sexually transmitted diseases. They are forced to work with care and courage, since openly "rescuing" or "rehabilitating" women is to threaten the economics of the crime lords of the area. Yet they are seeking to reach out to the most impoverished women in the world in Christ's name.

A more controversial, but some say more successful, approach is the Sonagachi Project in Calcutta, India. This approach does not try to "rescue" or "rehabilitate" sex workers, but to protect, educate, and guard their health. Recognizing sex work as a valid profession, the sex workers are unionized, and they openly campaign for their civil rights. The claim is made that the rate of HIV infection is ten times higher in Bombay's red-light district than in Calcutta.

Professor Elizabeth Ngugi has successfully rehabilitated sex workers in Nigeria. Besides offering HIV/AIDS education and health care, she seeks to create economic alternatives for women trapped in prostitution. Former President Jimmy Carter was welcomed by sex workers in the dirt-floor building in Abuja, Nigeria, that serves as Ngugi's HIV-training center by day and a bar by night. One woman, Angela, told Carter that she was married at the age of fifteen to a man who beat her. With no other choices, she became a prostitute in order to support herself. Now she is a peer educator, training other Nigerian prostitutes how to protect themselves by using condoms. Far from being scandalized, the famous Sunday school teacher, Jimmy Carter, writes that "most see commercial sex workers as a problem in the spread of the epidemic. The women we met today see themselves as part of the solution. And they are right."[18]

Christians typically judge these impoverished sex workers, whom we label with the negative term "prostitute" and view as the worst of sinners. A new theology is needed, however, for truthfully they are far more "sinned against" than sinful. If Jesus were to speak today, he might say to a wealthy church apathetic about global AIDS: "It will be easier for a sex worker to enter the kingdom of heaven than for a rich person."

Reject Patriarchal Structures

To help women and children, the church must reject patriarchal structures of church and society. Too often the church has openly or covertly supported patriarchal societies in which women have been treated as objects rather than subjects. In such societies, women are more easily exposed to the HIV virus. Men refuse to be tested for HIV or withhold knowledge of their status from their partners. Such attitudes contribute to the diminishment of autonomy for women, often curtail educational opportunities, and frequently prevent the use of condoms for prevention's sake.

Attitudes like this have contributed to the spread of HIV/AIDS, for example, in Latin America. In São Paulo, Brazil, AIDS is the leading cause of death among women aged twenty to thirty-five. These women have lower incomes and less education than men. Honduras has been the Central American nation hardest hit by the AIDS epidemic and the country may be suffering from a particularly potent strain of HIV that is typically dangerous to women.[19] A common notion in the Caribbean is that if you use a condom with your mistress or a prostitute, it is considered equivalent to being faithful to your wife. Antonio de Moya, a Dominican Republic epidemiologist, says: "The paradox of our culture is we have resolved Hamlet's dilemma. For us it is to be and not to be. The culture is disjointed. We should be talking about fidelity or prostitution, not both."[20]

Traditional patriarchal culture in Africa undergirds the legal system, governance structures, and values that uphold the unequal treatment of women and girls. Several traditional practices contribute directly to the spread of HIV/AIDS: female and male circumcision using the same knives, wife sharing, polygamy, dowries, widow inheritance, and widow cleansing. The latter practices of widow inheritance and widow cleansing prescribe that a widow should be "cleansed" by having sexual intercourse with a stranger three days after her husband is buried so she can be "inherited" by one of her husband's relatives. Besides dehumanizing the grieving woman, the tradition exposes her to HIV. Kenyan authorities believe it contributes to the high incidence of AIDS among the Luo people of Western Kenya. Christian opposition to this tradition has made a difference, saving some widows from indignity and protecting their health in a populous province where one in every five people is infected.[21]

Compounding the plight of women are widespread beliefs in witchcraft. Old widows in rural Zimbabwe are accused of bewitching people with AIDS. Witch-hunters either banish the widows from the community or, worse yet, torture them with bizarre exorcism ceremonies. Superstitions combine with ignorance as villagers see young people dying of AIDS, and they seek someone to blame, believing that such a pandemic is unnatural. One woman, Nkosana, who lost her husband and her only two children to AIDS, reports that her in-laws gave her only one hour to leave her village, and she was not allowed to take any of her possessions. Another woman, Ntombama Mlalazi, was branded a witch and subjected to rituals that left her face and right arm permanently disfigured.[22]

Changing the culture and initiating legislation to stop these traditional practices is a great challenge since the political will is missing and male-dominated parliaments prevail. Yet Christians are called to speak and act for women's liberation.

Champion Human Rights Legislation

The church must champion human rights legislation, thus condemning sexism and working to implement laws that eradicate gender inequalities. As discussed in chapter 4, such steps are essential if the AIDS pandemic is to be brought under control and eventually ended.

The 1994 International Conference on Population and Development in Cairo, Egypt, and the 1995 United Nations (UN) Fourth World Conference on Women in Beijing, China, endorsed a variety of goals aimed at eliminating gender inequalities and ensuring equal rights. Embraced by 179 countries, these goals face constant criticism by some within the religious community and are endangered by conservative political forces that seek to roll back the progress made in Cairo. An Argentinian epidemiologist, Mabel Bianco, MD, charges that the current Bush administration, for example, is seeking:

> to withhold information from adolescent girls about how they can protect themselves, replacing it with the directive that they abstain from sexual intercourse. This strategy is simply not sufficient to protect the millions of women and girls who contract the disease through violence, coercion and the sexual habits of their partners, over which they have no control. . . . Unless societies oppose these conservative forces and instead move forward on the agreements established at Cairo, the epidemic will defeat us. . . . Only when we stop letting discrimination dictate our policies, and allow women to make decisions about their own sexual health, will our combined efforts to stem HIV/AIDS stand a chance.[23]

Jennifer Butler of the Presbyterian UN Office claims President Bush joined an "unholy alliance" of conservative U.S. right-wing groups to work against women's rights alongside conservative Catholic and Muslim nations, including Iran and Iraq—neither of which is noted for progressive rights for women. Butler notes that the United States "bowed to pressure from the Religious Right, blocking progress on measures that would prevent the spread of HIV/AIDS and lower the number of unwanted and early pregnancies among adolescent children."[24]

This climate of fear and opposition to women's rights is evident in many ways. For example, after the South African version of "Sesame Street" introduced an orphaned female HIV-positive character to help educate children about AIDS, six male U.S. Republican lawmakers wrote a threatening letter to the Public Broadcasting System, expressing their concern that such an approach might be used in the United States.[25]

In contrast to American hesitation and opposition, the voices of African women are rising in support of their human rights. At the

2003 African Women's Sexual and Reproductive Health and Rights Conference, they expressed support for the Cairo resolutions and called the governments of the African continent to meet the following commitments:

- Ensure universal access to sexual and reproductive health services in the context of "health for all" at all ages, . . .
- Modify HIV/AIDS policies, programmes, and budgetary allocations such that they are designed to reduce the vulnerability of women and girls . . .
- Support actions to end all forms of violence against women and girls, including practices such as child marriage and FGM [female genital mutilation], marital rape and other sexual coercion, . . .
- Invest in comprehensive sexuality education, reproductive and sexual health services, and life management skills training, for all adolescents.[26]

Provide Protection and Health Care for Women
The church must be in the forefront of enabling women to protect themselves against HIV/AIDS and receive proper health care. The church does not have the resources or the expertise to develop such products or services, but it can lend its voice in support of their development and use. Above all, it can ensure that the church is not itself a stumbling block that would create new stigmas or obstruct product distribution and services to women.

Urgently needed are ways women can be in control of their own bodies to prevent infection. In an ideal world women can simply say no to unwanted or dangerous sexual experiences. But in the real world where most females live, women are ensnared by cultural and religious taboos that force them to comply with male wishes and coercion, even when injurious or dangerous to a woman's health.

Needed, therefore, are woman-controlled prevention devices in sexual situations such as female condoms, diaphragms, or microbicides. Researchers at the Women's Global Health Imperative hope diaphragms will help prevent HIV and other sexually transmitted diseases because the cervix is very susceptible. Cervical tissue is more fragile than the vagina, subject to easy damage and inflammation. It also has more HIV-receptor cells than the vagina.

The Bill and Melinda Gates Foundation is leading the way in efforts to determine if diaphragms will safeguard millions of women who currently lack any means of protection. The foundation, in fact, has funded a $28 million study that involves about 4,500 women in two sites in South Africa and one in Zimbabwe. Additionally, they have launched extensive research on low-cost microbicides (sometimes called "chemical condoms") such as vaginal creams, gels, and capsules that would destroy harmful microbes, including HIV.[27]

Women are at greater risk than men for HIV. Scientists claim that the virus is transmitted more "efficiently" from men to women than from women to men. Journalist Stacie Stukin notes that "a single unprotected sex act is eight times more likely to infect a woman than a man."[28] In Thailand, research indicated that 76 percent of women with HIV reported their only sexual contact had been with their husbands.[29] The irony is that the public primarily blames women for the spread of the disease. Female sex workers are more frequently targeted for liability rather than the men who frequent them.

In the United States, African American women are more endangered than white women. According to the Centers for Disease Control and Prevention, approximately one in 160 African American women are infected compared to one in 3,000 white women. AIDS mortality rates are nearly ten times higher for African Americans than for whites due to various factors, including lack of prevention education and proper medical care.

Eliminating mother-to-child transmission of HIV is critical. Medical procedures and medications are now available that significantly reduce transmission potential. In some places, women are urged to have abortions or are forced into sterilizations. In much of the Two-Thirds World (non-industrialized countries that comprise a majority of the world), there is no access to treatment with a drug that blocks transmission.

For example, in the popular tourist resort city of Puerto Plata, Dominican Republic, doctors complain they do not have the necessary medicine to prevent mother-to-child transmission. While AIDS tests for pregnant women are mandatory, results often are devastating for women because of the stigma attached to the illness by their employers, families, and communities. Many doctors, fearful of infecting themselves and their nursing staff, refuse to perform Cae-

sarean sections on HIV-positive women, even though this proce-
dure is crucial in reducing the risk of transmission of HIV to the
child.[30]

In contrast, Dr. N. M. Samuel operates a rural clinic in Namakkal,
India, where holistic efforts are under way to deal with these issues.
Namakkal, along a busy highway frequented by many trucks and
truckers, has the highest infection rate in India, especially among
pregnant mothers. Not only is medication available to block the
transmission of HIV/AIDS, but a program of prevention is also vigor-
ously pursued within the community. Thanks to support from United
Methodists in Colorado, two HIV-positive mothers are currently
working as community caregivers. Both have lost their husbands and
babies to AIDS. They live in the neighborhood and provide a connection between the clinic and the community where people live. An
expanded outreach program employing HIV-positive men and home
orphanages to care for the escalating number of children left without
parents is planned.

Protect Children and Youth

The church must also be conscientiously compelled to protect the
well-being of youth and children. The world currently has an estimated 14 million orphans because of AIDS. Every fourteen seconds
an African child loses a parent to AIDS, and the number is expected
to escalate in every part of the world. Zimbabwe alone is estimated to
have 800,000 orphans, and by the year 2005 it will have 1.1million.[31]

The words of Jesus should ring loud and clear in every Christian
heart: "Let the little children come to me, and do not stop them; for
it is to such as these that the kingdom of heaven belongs" (Matthew
19:14). The plight of children suffering from HIV/AIDS has probably
been underreported. If Christians fully understood the horrendous
healthcare conditions in the Two-Thirds World, it is hard to imagine
they would not respond more generously to AIDS mission efforts and
become more politically active to press for greater national and international efforts. This graphic description from Stephen Lewis, the UN
secretary-general's special envoy for HIV/AIDS in Africa, after his visit
to Lusaka, Zambia, ought to be published in every church bulletin
and newsletter:

The infants were clustered, stick-thin, three and four to a
bed, most so weakened by hunger and ravaged by AIDS
that they really had no chance. We were there for forty-
five minutes. Every fifteen minutes, another child died,
awkwardly covered with a sheet, then removed by a nurse,
while the ward was filled with the anguished weeping of
mothers. A scene from hell.[32]

Lewis also emphasizes that there is a growing rate of sexual abuse
of children and adolescents. Sexual assault of children is reaching
"shocking proportions," with orphans being the most vulnerable to
abuse and infection of HIV. Lewis says, "There's something deeply,
deeply wrong when children are the frequent victims of adult sexual
violence."[33] He notes that the world has not developed any evident
solution, as never before in history has there been such a mass of
orphans. The numbers overwhelm the ability of extended families to
handle all the children and responsibility.

Children also suffer discrimination because of their parents' illness
or deaths. For example, thirteen-year-old Claris Akinyi doesn't skip
on the African playground with her classmates anymore. Because her
father died with AIDS, the children do not play with her. Of course,
she does not have much time for recreation since she now cares for
her mother, who is dying with AIDS, and her four younger siblings.
She supports them on the dollar a day she earns by selling corn.[34]
One has to wonder what will happen to her if she doesn't get help
from some church or government agency. If I were a young girl and
faced with such a situation, the temptation to sell my body would be
very great.

While the vast majority of orphans are in the Two-Thirds World,
the increasing number of parentless children in the United States
should not be overlooked. About 50 percent of the women with HIV
in the United States have at least one child under the age of five.
Thanks to anti-retroviral therapies, the death rate has been lowered
in the United States, but the overall AIDS-related death rate for
women is increasing.[35]

In Malawi (southeast Africa), some 25 percent to 50 percent of the
men and women in their military are expected to die by the year 2005.
Aside from the impact this has on the individuals involved and the
security of the nation, it is anticipated to greatly increase the number

of orphans. In a recent year, for example, 135 soldiers died, leaving over 500 children orphaned, one quarter of them infected by HIV.[36]

Historically, in almost every culture women have been the primary caregivers for children. In culture after culture men have opted out of—or been kept away from—their responsibilities in this area. Now with the onslaught of AIDS, many children are losing one or both parents to the disease. In Africa it is said there are some villages composed only of children! Famous rock musician Bono says, "A 'Lord of the Flies' syndrome is emerging: children bringing up children."[37] Stephen Lewis describes what this means:

> The result is the present and escalating reality of orphan street children, of orphan gangs, of orphan delinquency, as hordes of kids, torn from their familial roots, wander the continent, bewildered, lonely, disenfranchised from reality, angry, acting out, unable to relate to normal life. Some have already reached adulthood; they've had no love, no nurturing . . . how do they bring up their own children? And in the meantime, they can be a high risk group, posing a collective threat to social stability.[38]

If the church of Jesus Christ is to effectively engage in combating the stigmatization and discrimination of HIV/AIDS and in preventing future infections, the well-being of women, youth, and children must be a high priority. In summary, our understanding of mission and ministry commits Christians to:

- Challenge the sexual practices of men
- Provide behavorial change education to men and women
- Reach out to the most impoverished women of the world
- Reject patriarchal structures of church and society
- Champion human rights legislation and eradicate gender inequalities
- Enable women to protect themselves against HIV/AIDS and receive proper health care
- Protect the well being of children and youth

Hearing and Heeding Women's Voices

Amid the AIDS crisis, several clear, prophetic voices are emerging from women theologians of the Two-Thirds World, particularly Africa. They are attempting to reform both traditional patriarchal African culture and liberate Christian thinking from its narrow, male-dominated theology—and all this against incredible odds. Though they speak in a particular context, their voices and views have global implications and need to be both heard and heeded.

New Testament professor Musa W. Dube of Botswana calls on the church to repent of its theological mediocrity. Blanket claims that God is punishing the infected for their sins mistakenly lead us to fighting the sick rather than HIV/AIDS. Associating immorality with AIDS fails to account for the complexity of the AIDS crisis, such as

> the children who are born with HIV/AIDS infection. Neither does it sufficiently confront the problem of married women who are married to unfaithful partners. It cannot address the situation of those women and girls who are raped in their homes, on the roads, in the offices and in their churches. This theological understanding does not cater for the sex workers, who have to choose between dying of hunger and selling sex. Neither does it address the question of loving mothers and old women in the rural areas, the nurses who get infected in the process of caring for the sick. Is God punishing these groups of people, have they sinned?[39]

Instead, Dube insists, we need to understand that "HIV/AIDS is violating the kingdom of God and it is not, and cannot be, sent by God." Jesus did not go around asking people how they got ill, but rather sought to restore their health. Our theological focus should emphasize that God wills health for all people and should "concentrate on the healing of God's people without judgments."[40]

Old Testament professor Madipoane Masenya of the University of South Africa laments that the forces of death are currently more victorious than the forces of life and that women biologically and culturally are more susceptible to HIV. She notes that "in African women, we witness the intersection of different oppressive forces weighing women down to the very bottom of the patriarchal ladder: sexism, classism, racism and the HIV/AIDS epidemic."

Even more disturbing for Masenya is that the status of Christian women is only aggravated by prevailing narrow male interpretations of the Christian faith and the biblical canon. For example, limited literalistic interpretations of Ephesians 5:22 ("Wives, be subject to your husbands as you are to the Lord") and 1 Corinthians 7:5 ("Do not deprive one another . . .") reinforce cultural expectations that the man controls the body of a woman.[41] As Anna Mary Mukaamwezi Kayonga notes:

> Many women are becoming victims of AIDS due to unfaithful men and husbands that spread it by moving from one woman to the other. Christian marriages are being threatened. Women feel that they are bound to this particular man even when he is unfaithful; on the other hand, they are scared in case the husband is already infected. This in particular is a problem in rural areas where most of the women try to be faithful to the husbands who are working in urban areas. They come home and wives are unsure.[42]

Both Masenya and Dube want women to have control over their own sexuality and bodies—that they "condomize" (that is, insist on the use of condoms). Dube, with her gift of paraphrasing scriptural language, proposes that the church needs a prophet willing to unabashedly declare:

> You have heard that you must abstain, but I say to you, avoid all relationships that deny the human dignity of all people. . . .
> You have heard that you must be faithful, but I say to you, be honest to confront and do away with all the inbuilt oppressive relationships of men and women in marriage, in church leadership and all other social relationships.
> You have heard that you must condomize, but I say to

you "confront" all facts that destroy human life and creation as acts of your worship.

You have heard that you must abstain and be faithful,
but I say to you, whenever you have sex condomize.[43]

In this time of global crisis, Masenya calls on the church to raise its
"prophetic voice against the injustices done of humanity." She
declares: "This is a moment to speak the mind of God, a mind geared
at giving life to the sick and dying. . . . If this one who has been called
to be the light of the world decides to put the light under the bushel,
who is expected to do it? This is the moment for the church to heed
to the call: 'Let the Church be the Church!'"[44]

6

The ABCs of Prevention

The greatest weapon of mass destruc-
tion in the world right now is AIDS.[1]

—Richard Stearns

To borrow a line from a popular Hollywood movie, *Two Weeks Notice:* "As long as people can change, the world can change." Hope exists. A world without AIDS is possible because AIDS is preventable. Unlike many diseases—cancer, sickle cell anemia, or multiple sclerosis— medical scientists know how to keep people from becoming infected by HIV. Prevention is a vital part of the comprehensive response to this pandemic. Prevention offers tangible hope that one day this global pandemic will not only be controlled but also eventually ended.

Responsible strategies of protection recognize that basically only three body fluids are sufficiently concentrated with HIV to cause significant risk for the transmission of the virus: blood, semen, and vaginal fluids. Saliva, urine, and feces in the absence of blood do not carry sufficient concentrations of HIV to cause transmission. Therefore, high-risk sexual behaviors are vaginal and anal intercourse, and any activity that exposes a person to HIV-contaminated blood.[2] The risks of oral sex are debated, but appear to be quite low, unless there are mouth sores or bleeding gums.[3]

Prevention, however, is not simple or easy. In fact, prevention seems to run contrary to many impulses and traits of human nature. As the philosopher Santanya has noted, sex is nature's categorical imperative. Under the pressure of that drive, people take enormous risks with their own health and that of others.[4] Prevention requires behavioral change that is difficult and demanding. Changing sexual behaviors for the long term are particularly problematic since they are very complex psychologically and physically. However, until at some future date a vaccine or cure is discovered, no alternative exists to behavioral change.

The Christian church must be in the forefront of efforts at prevention, neither blinking with embarrassment about sexual matters nor hiding lifesaving information. Jesus said, "I came that they might have life, and have it abundantly" (John 10:10). As Christians we are called to be ambassadors of life, not missionaries of death.

The sobering results of a recent global survey of prevention efforts, however, indicate that known prevention methods are not available to most people. Specifically:

> Only 5 percent of women have access to drugs to prevent mother-to-child transmission. Just 12 percent of people have access to voluntary HIV counseling and testing. Of those at high risk, 24 percent, have access to AIDS education. Only 42 percent of people in need have access to condoms.[5]

The Bill and Melinda Gates Foundation is quite clear in its life-giving mission. On their Web site they state:

> Aggressive prevention efforts are needed to prevent the 45 million new HIV infections projected by the end of the decade. By scaling up existing prevention strategies, we can avert nearly 28 million (63 percent) of these new infections. We know what it takes—and these proven tools are available today.[6]

Why can't the ecumenical and evangelical wings of the Christian church be as mission-specific and committed to preventing a high percentage of the likely 45 million new HIV infections? How much human suffering and how many deaths is the church willing to prevent? Can a new catechism be introduced that includes the ABCs of HIV/AIDS prevention? By emphasizing this alphabet for life, the church can make a significant contribution to slowing the growth of global AIDS and saving innumerable lives.

A Is for Abstinence

Fundamental and frequent teaching of the Christian church over the centuries has focused on advocating the practice of abstinence from sexual intercourse. This has taken many forms, from sects abandoning sex completely, to priests and monks embracing vows of chastity, to contemporary mantras like "celibacy in singleness and faithfulness in marriage." The teaching has included theologies ranging from those that condemn sexual pleasure as sinful to those that celebrate sex as God's good gift to humanity when expressed in responsible and caring relationships.

Without a doubt, abstinence from sexual relationships is a primary method of preventing HIV/AIDS. By not having sexual intercourse, a person avoids the possibility of HIV through the exchange of infected semen or vaginal fluids. By abstaining from intravenous illegal drugs or using "dirty" needles, prevention is possible.

Advocating abstinence from sexual activity, of course, has a long tradition in many world religions. Church, and even government, programs emphasizing abstinence have received increased attention in the United States, thanks especially to more theologically conservative Christians. Not only have they introduced them in their churches, but they have used their political muscle to influence elected officials to fund such programs more generously in the public schools and other settings.

President George W. Bush, in his 2003 State of the Union address, dramatically proposed tripling American financial aid for combating global AIDS. In the legislative fight for the $15 billion, Republican legislators, with Bush's support, inserted amendments putting a greater emphasis on faith-based groups and sexual abstinence programs. Early reports suggested that one-third of the $15 billion was to be devoted to abstinence efforts, but later analysis showed that the one-third set aside was for specific "abstinence until marriage" programs, which would mean $1 billion over ten years rather than $5 billion as first projected.[7] Congressman Mike Pence of Indiana celebrated the emphasis on abstinence, saying, "It's important that we not just send them money, but we send them values that work."[8]

There is a similar gap between church teaching and actual human sexual behavior and how politicians talk and how they behave. Rhetoric and reality often stand in startling juxtaposition. A recent article in the *Denver Post*, for example, blithely devotes nearly a whole page to how many sexual partners young heterosexual adults should acknowledge to people they are dating. Individuals openly give their names and comments. One man says, "I like a woman with morals. I guess up to six [previous sexual partners] is OK, but if it's more than that, she's someone I'll stay away from." It is suggested that women will tolerate up to fifty past partners. Nowhere in the article is AIDS mentioned as a threat.[9] This "lifestyles" story prompted no editorial controversy, even though church and state continue to give lip service to abstinence before marriage.

You can't export what you don't have! But that doesn't seem to stop the U.S. government from insisting on funding abstinence programs in other countries. Poverty-stricken lorry drivers, wandering migrant men, illiterate rickshaw pullers, and women struggling to find food to feed their children would probably be bewildered by the inconsistency and incongruity of our ethics.

Citing this dilemma does not mean that abstinence messages are invalid, but perhaps it should make churchgoers and politicians a bit more humble when encouraging remedies for the world epidemic.

B Is for Be Faithful

Fundamental to HIV prevention is faithful sexual relationships. Basic to Christian ethics is the commitment to promise keeping; it is the essence of trust. Christians believe the promises of God as expressed in Scripture and trust deeply in the words of Jesus, such as "Remember, I am with you always, to the end of the age" (Matthew 28:20). Without such confidence in biblical promises, Christians might be overwhelmed by the suffering, injustice, and tragedy of all the Good Fridays of this world. Instead, even in the age of global AIDS, we can be an Easter people, full not of optimism, but of hope.

Helping people understand and avoid the hazards of engaging in sex outside of marriage and other committed relationships is an important prevention strategy. The slogan of "no sex before marriage and none outside of marriage" works if both partners have truly been faithful to this commitment all their lives. However, as soon as either person in a previously exclusive sexual relationship takes another sexual partner, the risk for HIV occurs. Anne Bayley dramatically illustrates the risks of sexual networks when she writes:

> It is very important to recognize that in any sexual relationship each partner is in indirect physical contact with every current or past sexual partner of the other person. For example, if a young man pays to sleep with a woman who sells sex, and if she has slept with eight or ten new men every month for five years, then that man (even though he may be having sexual relations for the first time) is indirectly in contact with at least six hundred other men, any one of whom may be HIV-infected. He is *also* in indirect contact with all the previous partners of every one of those 600 men; sexual networks soon become very large.[10]

Professor Edward C. Green of the Harvard Center for Population and Development Studies is a strong proponent of the "be faithful" dimension of prevention. He fears it often gets overlooked in the debate between advocates of abstinence and champions of condoms. Based on research in Africa, he points particularly to Uganda where partner reduction (mostly in the form of mutual monogamy) "was probably the single most important behavior change" in helping to reduce the rate of HIV infection. Uganda's main message about "zero grazing," or sticking to one's partner, helped Uganda achieve a "miracle" in reducing the percentage of people infected in that nation.[11]

Green believes condom use should be promoted but thinks there has been an overemphasis on condoms as prevention. He contends that delaying sexual initiation is critical in reducing the incidence of HIV. Delaying the time young women are married or begin their sexual activity is crucial. In his view, if far more money and efforts were invested in programs focused on abstinence, partner delay, and faith-fulness, more significant behavioral change would occur in the world. He strongly advocates that "religious organizations ought to be given more support in doing what they do best, namely promot-ing fidelity and abstinence. If FBOs [faith-based organizations] also want to promote condom use, so much the better."[12]

President Museveni of Uganda organized a full-scale political and cultural effort to conquer AIDS. As a result, HIV prevalence declined from 21.1 percent to 6.1 percent among pregnant women between 1991 and 2002. He encouraged faith-based organizations, both Chris-tian and Muslim, to emphasize both abstinence and faithfulness. He emphasized "a return to our time-tested cultural practices that emphasized fidelity and condemned premarital and extramarital sex." He did not oppose condoms, but he claimed that "the best response to the threat of AIDS and other STDs is to reaffirm publicly and forthrightly the respect and responsibility every person owes to his or her neighbor."[13]

In Tanzania, a group of young journalists in their twenties and thir-ties have created an association to encourage "people to abstain from wanton and unsafe sex."[14] They are seeking to emphasize the impor-tance of being faithful and reducing the number of sexual partners.

C Is for Condoms

C is for using condoms, but it could also stand for controversy, since Christians seem hopelessly split on the subject. This third strategy—the use of condoms—is the method most public health leaders and governments promote as the most realistic and effective prevention method. Yet conflict and controversy rage around the world among religious people regarding this simple, latex, low-tech, underutilized, highly effective device. People who do not choose abstinence as their way of life, or who may face risk from sexual networks (either because they have sex with someone other than their partner or their partners possibly do), should be encouraged to use condoms.

At the 14th International AIDS Conference in Barcelona, Spain, it was noted that millions of dollars are spent searching for high-tech remedies and vaccines that may or may not prove to be effective, while the mechanism of condoms is greatly underfunded. No patent barriers exist and condoms are relatively inexpensive, yet a United Nations (UN) report found a shortage of 2 billion condoms a month in Africa alone. Worldwide, 8 to 10 billion condoms are needed yearly to help stem the AIDS crisis, but Africa receives less than 1 billion, and government donations for this purpose are decreasing. In 1990 the United States gave 800 million condoms to the Two-Thirds World, or non-industrialized countries, but only 360 million in 2000.[15] The former head of the Centers for Disease Control, James Curran, asked the obvious: Why not "provide free condoms worldwide?"[16]

Unfortunately, many men, especially in Africa, refuse to use condoms. Reasons for their reluctance include believing that condoms reduce sexual pleasure and are unmanly. Some complain that it is like eating "a banana with its skin on" or "candy within a wrapper."[17] Others allege there is a conspiracy of white people trying to keep persons of color from having children. Women who try to insist that men wear condoms may be met by responses such as one given by a male school teacher. He said that in Zulu custom, "the woman has no power with the man. Because I paid eleven cows for her, she is supposed to do everything I say."[18]

Distrust and cynicism about condoms are widespread, for example, in places like South Africa. Slipshod testing practices, for example, have made southern Africa a dumping ground for substandard foreign condoms, and many report breakage. Further, Denver psychotherapist, Paula J. Murphy, questions whether male African prophylactic usage might increase if condoms were not always white latex but were readily available in different colors. Christoph Benn, representing the World Council of Churches (WCC) at the UN General Assembly Special Session on HIV/AIDS, sought to dismiss the "widespread myth" that all churches and religious organizations were against the use of condoms. He noted that the WCC, with some three-hundred member churches around the world, has endorsed the use of condoms for the prevention of HIV transmission.[19]

However, many Evangelical Protestant Christians are either opposed to using condoms or very hesitant about endorsing or promoting their use. They believe condoms (1) encourage early sex activity, (2) promote promiscuous sexual behavior among multiple partners, (3) are highly unreliable, and (4) cost more than poor people can afford. Their opposition or condemnation fails to deal with issues such as how people with HIV continue their sexual lives, and how people in a marriage or relationship who are not infected should protect themselves.

Advocating condoms proves difficult for many religious leaders, as previously noted, since some faith communities oppose their use altogether, while many others are simply uncomfortable discussing intimate sexual matters. Yet, in light of the limited options and the potential health benefits, it is imperative to articulate and promote an ethic of responsible sex and the distribution of condoms as a higher ethical and theological good. If, realistically, people are not refraining from dangerous sexual activity, then those concerned to address this global emergency must join with others in promoting prevention in every way possible (including condom distribution), lest people suffer, lives be lost, children become orphaned, and societies crumble under staggering health care and other economic costs.

The Roman Catholic Church, particularly in Africa and Latin America, probably offers more hospices, hospitals, orphanages, and parish programs providing care for people with AIDS and their families than any other religious organization. The Vatican speaks out for increased international spending on AIDS care and treatment. Pope John Paul II has attacked the international pharmaceutical companies for excessive and sometimes even exorbitant costs of AIDS drugs.

However, Roman Catholics consistently denounce the use of condoms. In Honduras, where the incidence of HIV is exceptionally high, the Catholic Church used its influence to stop a campaign involving the distribution of a million free condoms.[20] This was dramatically underscored in July 2001, when the Roman Catholic bishops of southern Africa (South Africa, Botswana, and Swaziland) met in Pretoria, South Africa. Standing in the heart of the global AIDS pandemic, they pronounced the "widespread and indiscriminate promotion of condoms . . . an immoral and misguided weapon in our battle against HIV/AIDS." By undermining abstinence and marital fidelity, they said, "condoms may even be one of the main reasons for the spread of HIV/AIDS."[21]

One commentator, Mindy Cameron, called this "logic that is both convoluted and deadly." Others have called the church "missionaries of death, not life." One African bishop suggested that without a "theology of condoms," one ends up with a "theology of coffins."

Unfortunately, Roman Catholic leaders are not alone. While most Protestants do not publicly condemn condom use, they certainly hesitate to publicly promote and distribute them, and find themselves tongue-tied when offering realistic sex education. Condom promotion and AIDS-related sex education have also been condemned by a range of religious leaders from Islamic leaders in Pakistan to Evangelical Protestants in Jamaica. The Council of Islamic Clerics in Nigeria earlier this year condemned a planned seminar on HIV/AIDS as violating Islamic law, calling it a Western "gimmick to spread immorality in our society."

Pentecostal preachers and churches often compound the dilemmas faced by health workers by their promises of miraculous healing, thereby unintentionally encouraging risky sexual behavior. Convinced they have been "cured," people have sex with their loved ones or others, and the virus spreads.

Fortunately, some religious leaders and organizations have taken a different stance. Uganda's Islamic Medical Association promoted a prevention campaign. In Senegal, where more than 90 percent of the population is Muslim, the spread of HIV slowed significantly after Islamic and Christian leaders joined a government prevention campaign that advocated condoms, abstinence, and fidelity. South Africa's Anglican archbishop Njongonkulu Ndungane has been a leader in promoting prevention including condom use, and officially the World Council of Churches has been an outspoken advocate of all forms of prevention.[22]

Around the world, some Roman Catholic theologians and many social justice activists are challenging Vatican dogma. Some, like Bishop Eugenio Rixen in Brazil, have called condom use "a lesser evil." For example, if an HIV-positive husband uses condoms to avoid infecting his wife, this would be acceptable. Giving permission in this case would not mean accepting the man's possible previous infidelity, but it would protect life. Recently, even the bishops of South Africa have been inching toward this position, suggesting in a pastoral statement that condoms might be appropriate in marriages where one partner is HIV-positive.

Methods of preventing death from HIV/AIDS should not be condemned simply because they also have the potential to prevent pregnancy. The "doctrine of double effect" in Christian ethics assumes that an object used for a function different than its original purpose becomes the nature for which it is used. A pencil used for writing, but used to stab or kill someone, becomes a weapon. Pope Paul VI applied this doctrine in relation to contraceptives in his 1968 encyclical *Humane Vitae*. He banned contraceptives but authorized the birth control pill when used to manage irregular menstrual cycles.[23]

Ethicist Richard A. McCormick, in a collection of essays titled "Catholic Ethicists on HIV/AIDS Prevention," illustrated the "lesser evil" principle by referring to drunk driving. McCormick argued: "We say, 'Don't drive while drunk; let someone else drive.' But supporting the designated driver doesn't mean we support over-drinking. It simply means that we don't want the irresponsibility doubled."[24] Young people on a TV music channel questioned United States secretary of state Colin Powell about condoms. His answer infuriated some religious leaders, but he was quite explicit: "I certainly respect the view of the Holy Father and the Catholic Church. In my own judgment, condoms are a way to prevent infection. Therefore, I not only support their use, I encourage their use among people who are sexually active and need to protect themselves."[25]

Condoms allow for "safer" sex but do not guarantee "safe" sex. There is no 100 percent guarantee they will protect HIV transmission, since condoms sometimes fail or break or are used improperly. Safe sex requires that both partners agree to be with only one partner for life. Yet, while condoms are not perfect, statistically their widespread use can reduce HIV incidence.

Other Letters in the Alphabet of Life

Stopping with the letter *C* too often characterizes the discussion of the ABCs of prevention. Other steps or strategies are also important.

D Is for Drugs

Four types of drugs hold promise for preventing HIV/AIDS now or in the future: vaccines, vaginal microbicides, drugs to prevent mother-child transmission, and anti-retroviral (ARV) treatment.

Vaccines. A vaccine that would immunize people from infection is the great future hope of worldwide prevention. Shortly after the AIDS epidemic began in the United States, the secretary of health and education in President Ronald Reagan's cabinet predicted publicly that a vaccine would be found in two years. Unfortunately, her wildly optimistic projection did not come close to being realized, and prospects for a workable vaccine remain yet a distant dream. Vigorous research and trials are in progress, but HIV viruses have proved hard to kill. And there are many different strains of the HIV virus. It appears one vaccine is unlikely to work to prevent all these various strains of the virus.

Ethical questions abound regarding the human trials that will be necessary to determine the efficacy of a vaccine. Scientists will have to compare thousands of people who receive the new drug with thousands who are given a placebo. The poor of Africa and Asia are the most likely people recruits. Will these people know enough and be told enough so that they can freely give informed consent? And will volunteers in such trials receive the very best treatment available? Michael Specter asks: "Will people used as subjects benefit from the research? (Africans served as essential participants in trials for the principal vaccine now used against hepatitis B; yet when the vaccine finally arrived they could not afford it.)"[26]

Once a vaccine or vaccines are discovered, many ethical and practical issues will emerge. Primarily, how will health agencies and governments handle the required vast immunization program? Vaccines have been available for fifty years for polio, but only recently have they been available to the poorest of the poor in the world. Eradication of polio is now on the horizon, thanks to the dedicated efforts of the UN, national governments, and non-governmental organizations like Rotary International. But medication for malaria, which kills millions every year, is still unavailable to most poor people. Likewise, treatment for tuberculosis still is not provided for the masses that suffer and die every year around the world.

Immunization is no panacea. By the time a vaccine is discovered and distributed, many hundreds of millions will already be infected. Therefore, until a vaccine or cure is readily available, the mantra of Christians will need to be "prevention, not vaccination." It is the only viable strategy to cope with the escalating pandemic that engulfs humanity. Once immunization is possible, the church should emphasize both prevention and vaccination, since the ABCs will still be theologically and medically viable approaches to a healthy life.

Microbicides. Scientists seek to create effective vaginal microbicides for women in a variety of gels, creams, and tablets. Women are especially vulnerable to HIV, and new medicine is urgently needed.

Female condoms exist, but they are expensive and not read-ily available. Worldwide sales peaked at $6 million annually, com-pared to $295 million for male condoms in the United States alone. Cultural and personal taboos make their use problematic in many situations. Men often object to women using protection. When a woman chooses to use a condom, she often is accused of being immoral or infected or both. A vaginal microbicide could be used with or without a partner's knowledge or consent. It would create needed autonomy for women that is now seriously missing in the world.

Pharmaceutical companies have shown less interest in this prod-uct because they do not see profitable results from their investment. It has to be cheap—say thirty-five cents a dose—if it is to be effective in the Two-Thirds World. The Rockefeller Foundation estimates that microbicides would produce $18 billion in worldwide revenues and prevent 2.5 million infections over three years. This figure is not con-sidered sufficient for the pharmaceutical companies, so research is primarily funded through governments and foundations.[27] The Bill and Melinda Gates Foundation has donated more than $50 million to microbicide research.

Many scientific problems still need to be resolved before an effec-tive microbicide is on the market. But journalist Stacie Stukin predicts that "a sleek strawberry-flavored microbicide in a lipstick-like case would be the must-have purse item of the coming decade."[28]

Transmission inhibitors/Anti-retrovirals. More than 600,000 infants each year become infected with HIV/AIDS. Most are in the Two-Thirds World, since effective treatment in the so-called First World (comprised of industrialized countries) has significantly reduced the transmission of HIV. Of the 5.1 million children worldwide who have been infected with HIV, 90 percent come from mother-to-child trans-mission. Two-thirds of transmission happens during pregnancy and delivery and one-third through breastfeeding.

Considerable research globally has concluded that anti-retroviral (ARV) regimens are safe and effective in preventing HIV transmission from mother to child. For example, South African Maria Hadebe expe-rienced the painful AIDS-related death of her two-year-old daughter, Maphaladi, in the Johannesburg Hospital. Later, when she realized she was pregnant again, she was terrified for the future of her next child. Thanks to a court case forcing the South African government to make the anti-AIDS drug Nevirapine available to HIV-positive mothers, she was able to get the treatment. She carried the drug with her everywhere she went, since a single dose is given to the mother at the onset of labor, followed by a few drops to the baby afterward. She was so grateful that she wanted to name her son Nevirapine, but nurses and her mother warned against it, saying the child would later face discrimination because people would know that her mother had HIV/AIDS. Little Lebo seemed healthy at eight months, but until he is tested sometime after his first birthday, there are no absolute assurances that he is free of the virus.[29]

Therefore, preventing mother-to-child transmission involves more than providing medicine: it requires counseling and testing; providing support for mothers, fathers, and children; and assistance on appropriate infant feeding programs. One such program exists along a major truck route in Namakkal, a rural region that has one of the highest rates of HIV infection in southern India. There in Namakkal, I visited a clinic supervised by Dr. N. M. Samuel. A remarkable team of doctors, nurses, and people living with AIDS worked together to combat mother-to-child transmission. Any success of stopping the transmission to an infant was tempered by the realization that the mother herself probably would die soon, since the cost of anti-retroviral treatments are beyond the scope of the clinic's budget. Even so, their work is laudable.

Surprisingly, anti-retroviral (ARV) treatment also contributes to prevention strategies. Effective, life-giving treatment encourages people to get tested and to take steps to prevent the spread of the disease. Former South African president Nelson Mandela has argued persuasively that if persons think they have no hope for treatment, then they are less likely to want to find out if they have the disease. The insight that "without a vision, the people perish," applies to AIDS prevention. If people can hope to get help through counseling and treatment, they are much more likely to get tested and work to avoid spreading the virus to others.

The high cost of drug treatment prohibits their widespread use. The global genocide that is occurring could be avoided if the price of the drugs was dropped dramatically and the world's governments were committed to the priority of making treatment universal. Instead, in 2003 only about 50,000 of 30 million infected people in the Two-Thirds World were getting treatment.

Excruciating ethical choices are before us. Dr. Samuel, for example, counseled a young man in India who wanted treatment for both of his parents who were infected. However, he could only come up with sufficient funds to treat one of his parents. How was he to choose? Should he save his mother or his father?

E Is for Education

Religious leaders and communities have many opportunities and resources for engaging in education for prevention's sake. If we want to be constructively engaged, then a creative use of the teaching occasions that arise in congregations, schools, seminaries, and other places can be made to educate members and the public about how to prevent HIV/AIDS.

Honest, forthright discussions can be encouraged and the veils of secrecy and shame can be lifted so that people will understand the dangers and dilemmas of the disease and how it impacts health and well-being. Misunderstandings and misplaced fears can be overcome and people can better understand how the disease is transmitted and avoided.

In the absence of a cure or a vaccine, education is essential, but disagreement about the nature of that education is ubiquitous. We need to rise above the disagreements and move to the forefront of efforts to promote factual sex education. Churches around the world, however, have historically been very shy about offering realistic sex education. Even the term "sex education" seems so loaded with negative connotations that sometimes euphemisms such as "education for human loving" are utilized.

Brenda Almond, a philosophy professor, underscores the importance of an educational program that embraces the reality of sexuality, not just romantic or idealized versions:

> This means not only the forms of sexuality that furnish ideals for literature, poetry and religion, but also sexuality for money, sexuality for release, sexuality for one, sexuality for same-sex partners. Some will find this repugnant, but they will have to ask themselves whether they can take responsibility for the safety of their own young in a world overlaid by the invisible menace of the AIDS virus.[30]

"Education for human loving" is not made easier by the fact that people are often less than truthful about their personal sexual lives. Only with the global AIDS pandemic has there been a realization of how widespread and frequent are unsafe sexual practices. An Episcopal priest, William Henry Barcus III, met with 150 parents and 50 teenagers and asked how many teens were having sex. No hands went up. When meeting with the youth alone, all the hands went up![31] Somewhere between denial and exaggeration rests the truth—and the challenge for educators.

F Is for Fighting Dirty Needles

Many HIV infections are caused by intravenous injections of usually illegal drugs. The HIV virus is spreading rapidly in certain areas of Eastern Europe and Asia because of the high use of intravenous drugs. For example, the rate of use in Russian prisons among young men is reportedly very high. After they are released, the virus is spread into local communities both by continued intravenous drug use and heterosexual sexual relations.

A highly controversial prevention method utilized in the United States, Europe, and elsewhere is to ensure that people who are using intravenous drugs have access to clean needles. Critics say needle exchange programs simply encourage illegal drug use, and, therefore, are unacceptable and immoral. Others, like Massimo Barra, MD, creator of an Italian Red Cross foundation, contend "this approach not only helps to significantly reduce HIV infection among injecting drug users, but also opens a way to reduce drug addiction."[32]

G Is for the "Good" Practice of Medicine

Good practice takes many forms, including: ensuring a safe blood supply, halting unsafe injections, treating sexually transmitted diseases, combating malaria and tuberculosis, and, possibly, encouraging male circumcision.

Safe blood supply. Ensuring a safe blood supply has been a significant step forward in preventing HIV/AIDS. Spread of the HIV virus through blood transfusions has been a common phenomenon, especially in early stages of the pandemic. In the United States, many hemophiliacs were infected because they were so dependent on transfusions. It still remains a concern, but good practices have been instituted to monitor the blood supply in the United States and in nations with a well-developed medical structure. However, in many poorer nations in Africa, Asia, and Eastern Europe, the problem persists.

Halting unsafe injections. The reuse of needles in medical settings has caused the spread of HIV. Unsafe injections are preventable but are far too common in poverty-stricken countries around the world. The World Health Organization estimated that 2.5 percent of all HIV cases are caused by unsafe injections. Some 16.7 billion injections are given annually throughout the world. In sub-Saharan Africa, some 17 to 19 percent of all injections are given with reused equipment. The World Health Organization (WHO) estimated in 1999 that 50,000 to 100,000 new HIV cases in sub-Saharan Africa were caused by unsafe injections.[33]

Treatment of all sexually transmitted diseases. The aggressive treatment of sexually transmitted diseases (STDs) can reduce HIV transmission. Diseases like gonorrhea, syphilis, herpes, and genital warts are often associated with HIV infection. Venereal diseases create sores that open the way for the HIV virus. Also these STDs are indicators of unsafe and unprotected sexual behaviors that are known to transmit HIV.[34]

Treatment of other diseases. Malaria and tuberculosis do not cause HIV/AIDS, but they weaken the immune system, making a person more susceptible to HIV. Programs that combat malaria and tuberculosis, therefore, are critical components of an overall strategy to create a world without AIDS.

Circumcision. Removing the male foreskin—that is, circumcision—may prove to be important in prevention. Practiced by at least one-third of human cultures around the world, circumcision is a practice developed thousands of years ago. Preliminary results by Canadian researchers in Africa have concluded that, on average, men in Africa who have been circumcised have "a 50 percent lower risk of contracting HIV."[35] Other research, however, suggests this may not be a significant factor in the prevention of the disease. *Since circumcised men do get HIV,* the danger is that a false message will be sent suggesting people who get circumcised will not get HIV/AIDS.[36]

Clinical research is under way to verify or disprove this finding regarding risk factors and circumcision. For example, the Luo tribe of Kisumu, Kenya, does not traditionally practice male circumcision. HIV-negative male volunteers between the ages of eighteen and twenty-four will be circumcised and then studied to see if they are less likely to get HIV than those uncircumcised. Scientists do not know whether the difference between circumcised or uncircumcised is biologically based or the result of unrelated behaviors.

Good practices in medicine include many more dimensions, but the five mentioned highlight the importance of not only finding "miracle" drugs but also for ensuring a medical infrastructure that can consistently deliver good medical prevention and care.

Ethics in a New Key

Theologian Robert McAfee Brown emphasized years ago that Christian theology must be sung in a new key. His musical scale of *A* to *G* emphasized that the old harmonies of the Western world are fading, and the theological melodies of the poor, the marginalized, and the suffering need to be heard.[37]

Our *A* to *G* alphabet of life provided above stresses that people and families living with HIV/AIDS are teaching us a new tune about Christian sexual ethics, and church leaders need to listen, learn, and join them in articulating a responsible sexual ethic of prevention.

Christian attitudes toward prevention must change and are changing. Theological sexual guidelines developed 2000 years ago—or 200 years ago—or even 20 years ago are generally not sufficient to stem the AIDS pandemic. Principles based on abstinence and faithfulness need not be abandoned, but a more realistic and responsible sexual ethic must emerge. Failure to share vital lifesaving information about prevention has caused critical observers of the global scene, like David Patient, to conclude, "many churches have the blood of their parishioners on their hands, and their approach toward condoms and human sexuality is not helping to [keep] the rank and file of the Church. . . . [It] is driving people away from God, not towards him. Many leaders in the religious community are as guilty of killing their flock as the virus itself."[38]

On one World AIDS Day, Catholics for a Free Choice purchased newspaper advertisements criticizing the Catholic hierarchy for lobbying the UN and governments everywhere to restrict access to condoms. They contend that "Catholic bishops preach sanctity of life. But their ban on condoms contributes to millions of people around the world dying."[39]

However, the ethical and evangelical breakthroughs on a pastoral sexual theology appropriate in the age of AIDS are not likely to emerge from Vatican pronouncements, World Council of Churches proclamations, or even prophetic liberal academic voices. Rather, it is arising from the context where people are living and dying with HIV/AIDS. It is coming from Roman Catholic priests and nuns who labor in love at the grassroots of societies and sanction condoms because they know the nonsense of sexual restrictions that lead to death, not life. This new ethics will come from Protestant laity and pastors in places like Zambia that tire of setting aside every Saturday for nonstop funerals. New words and theology will tumble from the lips of religious leaders who seek to be good shepherds of their flock, unwilling to lead them to the slaughter of AIDS.

All the voices and viewpoints will not be the same and probably will not be orchestrated in perfect harmony. For example, United Methodist Bishop Joseph Humper of Sierra Leone, West Africa, contends it is not so much HIV/AIDS, but the culture of silence around the pandemic that is killing Africa's future leadership. He condemns beliefs that HIV/AIDS is God's curse or that it is contracted through witchcraft. He encourages sexual abstinence before marriage and advocates that "both our polygamous and monogamous community members must be taught to remain faithful to their spouses."[40]

Archbishop Bonifatius Haushiku of Namibia provides leadership for a country where every fourth person is a Catholic and every fifth adult is HIV-positive. In launching Catholic AIDS Action, he declared that "AIDS is a disease, not a sin." In the face of this overwhelming disease, Lucy Y. Steinitz, national coordinator of Catholic AIDS Action in Namibia, reports that grassroots Catholics are realistic in addressing issues of sexuality and sexual expression. For them the alphabet of life is:

A is for Abstinence before marriage.
B stands for Be faithful in marriage. This is the Christian way, and it guarantees life. But if you find that you cannot follow this teaching, then choose
C for Condom, because the alternative is
D for Death.[41]

Out of Maputo, Mozambique, a story has emerged of one bishop who is thinking and talking differently than traditional Christian leaders. During a church conference designed to educate parishioners about the dangers of HIV/AIDS and how they could get involved in issues of education, prevention, home-based care, and the plight of orphans, the bishop offered to share the church's position on condoms. He began by saying, "God clearly tells us that we must protect life at all costs. To not do so is committing a serious sin against God."

Continuing, he spelled out his understanding of the meaning of that broad theological precept:

> It means that A is for abstinence, and looking around at all of you today, many of you cannot live by this advice. Let us be realistic, few if any of you can abstain. Which brings us to B, be faithful . . . many of you are not. So that leaves us with C . . . condoms. Now many of you believe that condoms are a crime against God . . . that wasted semen is a sin, and I am here today to tell you otherwise. You see, if you are HIV-positive and have unprotected sex and you infect someone, you have, in the eyes of God, committed murder. Or if you are HIV-negative and you have unprotected sex with someone who is infected, and they infect you, you have, in the eyes of God, committed suicide. So my children, wearing a condom is not a sin . . . not wearing one IS![42]

Reportedly, now Sunday church services are no longer the same—part of the celebration is the blessing of condoms!

What this new practical and pastoral sexual ethic will look like in terms of prevention is yet to be determined. Of course, we must take a comprehensive approach to HIV/AIDS prevention. David Serwadda, head of Uganda's Institute of Public Health, worries that abstinence has been overemphasized as the secret of his country's success at reducing the rate of HIV infections. He emphasizes, "It's time to stop looking for a magic bullet and use every weapon we've got."[43] Harvard's Edward C. Green warns against a "condom versus abstinence" strategy that forgets that the lesson learned in Uganda is that "a balanced, integrated approach that provides a range of behavior options is what works best."[44]

The prevention of HIV/AIDS requires both an emphasis on risk reduction and risk avoidance. Risk reduction (or remedies) emphasizes the use of condoms, treating sexually transmitted diseases, clean needles, reducing partners, and hope for a future vaccine. Risk avoidance accents behavioral change including an emphasis on abstinence, faithfulness of both partners (mutual monogamy), and saying no to injecting drugs.[45] Effective prevention requires that the entire alphabet of life—from *A* to *G*—be implemented.

Controlling and stopping this pandemic requires a creative response from all Christians—there is more work to do in education, prevention, care, and treatment than any one of us can do. If my more conservative friends are uncomfortable talking about condoms, much less distributing them, I support them in their focused efforts of promoting abstinence and faithfulness. If people do not want to talk about sex at all, then there is plenty to do in caring for the widows and the orphans. Using power or influence to restrict others who believe risk-reduction strategies are imperative leads inevitably to countless deaths. We do not all have to be in agreement or doing the same thing. We just need to be good shepherds preventively caring for our flocks and Good Samaritans caring for our wounded. We are called to this mission and ministry.

7

A World without AIDS

The HIV/AIDS crisis is not a crisis of lack of resources. It is a crisis of lack of conscience. It is the obscene gap between the haves and the have-nots that is driving this holocaust.[1]

—People living with HIV/AIDS,
Lusaka, Zambia

A world without AIDS requires more than the ABCs of prevention. Abstinence, faithfulness, and condoms are not enough to rid the globe of the scourge of HIV/AIDS. Attention must also focus on the structural dimensions of society, culture, and religion that aid and abet the spread of this disease. Christians and other people of faith eager to end AIDS must go beyond the personal questions and face the political issues that underlie this global catastrophe.

An AIDS theology focused only on personal sin is inadequate to deal with the complexity of those "sinned against"—people imprisoned by poverty, discrimination, racism, and cultural/societal structures over which they have no control. Christians need to sing every Sunday, just before they leave worship and go out in the world to serve, a benediction underscoring the prophetic words of Micah: "What does the Lord require of you but to do justice, and to love kindness, and to walk humbly with your God"(6:8).

An Unexpected, Unwelcome Banquet Guest

An unexpected and unwelcome guest has appeared at the banquet table of the "new world order," our post–cold war world situation. Just when the highly industrialized and militarized nations of the world began to celebrate the end of the cold war, the easing of tension between East and West, the triumph of capitalism, and the prospects of perpetual prosperity in their so-called First World, a stranger arrived to disturb the party.

The unwanted guest goes by many names and wears many faces. In certain parts of the world, "Mr. Cholera" has emerged, upsetting the banquet table, infecting millions and killing thousands. Cholera is the fruit of structural poverty—an illness that respects the sanitized rich and spreads primarily among the malnourished and the poor. This malnutrition lurks in the shadows of many heavily populated nations. Worldwide, 40,000 children die of hunger and associated diseases each day, because those in power in this new world order won't invest an additional $2.5 billion for their well-being. The entire world spends the equivalent of $2.5 billion on the military every day—and United States companies spend this much each year just to advertise cigarettes.

"Ms. Malaria" and "Ms. Tuberculosis" travel unhindered through the corridors of human life. Forty percent of the world's population is at risk from malaria, 90 percent of them children. It causes 1 to 2 million deaths per year. Worldwide, 2 billion people reportedly are infected by tuberculosis. Tuberculosis treatment is relatively inexpensive, costing as little as twenty U.S. dollars for the entire six-month course of daily drugs. Twenty-five million tuberculosis deaths over the next twenty years could be prevented. "Ms. Malaria" and "Ms. Tuberculosis" both could be brought under control in five years if First World nations contributed an additional $400 million to the task.

Throughout the world, "Mr. and Mrs. AIDS" threaten the future of humanity. For decades, demographers predicted a world population explosion, but in 2002 the United Nations Population Division revised its projections downward in part because it anticipates "a more serious and prolonged impact of the HIV/AIDS epidemic" than earlier forecasts. By projecting both fertility and life expectancy rates, demographers anticipate the world population to grow to 8.9 billion in the year 2050, but some countries will see population decline due to HIV/AIDS. For example, the population of Botswana in 2050 is estimated to be 1.4 million, 20 percent lower than it was in 2000. Disguised in these population statistics is the dire drama of human suffering and pain, hidden among calculations that during the current decade, "the number of excess deaths because of AIDS among the fifty-three most affected countries is estimated at 46 million, and that figure is projected to ascend to 278 million by 2050."[2]

Unexpected and unwanted guests are not newcomers at the feast of life. Jesus made several references to them in his teaching and preaching. Jesus himself suddenly surprised Zacchaeus up in a tree, telling him that he planned to visit his house. When invited guests failed to appear at a banquet, Jesus suggested scouting the streets and bringing in the uninvited

The banquet table of life has been set, but most of the world has been excluded. A hungry young street child wandered into a church in Brazil while communion was being served. As the bread was broken, he asked, "Is there enough for me?"

The most memorable unexpected and unwanted visitor appears in Jesus' parable of Lazarus, the poor beggar who sat outside rich man Dives's door. What makes this story troublesome is Jesus' suggestion that God judges us for our indifference to the poor and the marginalized. Our lack of justice and mercy has implications beyond the present life that should prompt us to reconsider our lifestyle and level of compassion. This story prompted Albert Schweitzer to become a missionary doctor in Africa.[3]

Pope John Paul II, speaking at Yankee Stadium in New York City, compared the rich nations of the world with Dives and the Two-Thirds World with Lazarus. He called on us to repent and to find new ways of redistributing the world's resources and wealth.

Dives would never have considered having Lazarus share the dinner table with him. What made Jesus profoundly different was his caring capacity for inclusivity, for having table fellowship with those whom others would exclude. Jesus epitomized the scandal of inclusivity. As theologian Sallie McFague has noted: "Jesus offended by inviting the outsiders to come in, to join with him not merely as needy outcasts but as his friends in joyful feasting. The central symbol of the new vision of life, the kingdom of God, is a community joined together in a festive meal where the bread that sustains life and the joy that sustains the spirit are shared with all."[4]

Christians are compelled to act in this inclusive spirit as we seek social justice for all our sisters and brothers in the world.

Love in a Time of AIDS

Readers of popular contemporary novels will know I have paraphrased the title of this section from Gabriel Garcia Marquez's book *Love in a Time of Cholera*.[5] One can do a play on words in Spanish, since the word "cholera" refers both to the epidemic disease and to rage or extreme anger. What does Christian love mean in a time of global AIDS and increasing global rage?

While many global tensions between East and West have lessened, the conflict between North and South has intensified. The extreme polarization of the world between the rich and poor has never been greater, with more than a billion people surviving with less than the U.S. equivalent of $370 of annual income. The disparity is especially highlighted in relation to matters of disease and health—with the poor suffering disproportionately not only from HIV/AIDS but from cholera, tuberculosis, malaria, Ebola, SARS, and various illnesses directly associated with malnutrition.[6]

Persons living with HIV/AIDS are expressing increasing anger and rage around the globe. Most of the world's money now devoted to HIV/AIDS is spent on vaccine and drug research, but the most impoverished regions of the world have no access whatsoever to what has been developed. Experts of this pandemic call for increased funding and a redirection of spending toward prevention, care, and treatment for people in the Two-Thirds World, but to date there have been limited results. Only 10 percent of the global HIV/AIDS budget is spent in poor countries, although 92 percent of all HIV infections have occurred there.[7]

Christians proclaim self-giving *agape* love as integral to our faith, but the great discrepancy between what Christians and the church profess in the affluent First World and what we share to combat HIV/AIDS and other diseases is embarrassingly minimal. Christian love appears anemic in light of the global health emergency. Our words are not matched by our deeds, our sermons not synchronized with any sacrifice.

Christian love in the context of global AIDS includes many challenges. It involves the imperative of prophetically denouncing injustice and protesting against the outrageous and systemic violation of human rights and the naked oppression of people wherever it occurs. It requires Christian solidarity with those who are treated as nonpersons, whoever they are. It presses us to struggle for new economic and political arrangements that correct the vast disparity in power and living standards that separate God's people between and within the "rich" and the "poor" nations. Christian love demands that we seek to switch swords into plowshares by drastically reducing militarization in all countries and repudiating the United States' arrogant imposition of military might and violation of national sovereignty of other nations. It calls us to share God's love in Jesus Christ through ministries of care and compassion that address the urgent health, education, social welfare, and hunger needs of the poor and marginalized. Where do we begin in creating a more socially just world?

Controlling Malaria and Tuberculosis
Demonstrating Christian love in a time of AIDS means targeting diseases such as malaria and tuberculosis for control, if not eradication. As mentioned above, the World Health Organization (WHO) claims both diseases could be brought under control within five years, if only $400 million more dollars were dedicated to the effort.

With 40 percent of the world's population at risk from malaria, and some 1 to 2 million deaths occurring every year, efforts to control the disease ought to be on every social justice agenda. Because of environmental devastation in various parts of the world, mosquitoes have proliferated and malaria has now increased. Nearly eradicated in the 1950s and 1960s in Asia and Latin America, malaria is now particularly prevalent in Africa, where it is often treated with the wrong drugs. Of the 1 million who die from malaria in Africa each year, some 90 percent are children under age five. Giving pregnant women hefty doses of anti-malarial drugs has helped reduce the infection rate. A vaccine against malaria is needed, but profit-driven pharmaceutical companies have demonstrated little interest. Fortunately, organizations such as the Bill and Melinda Gates Foundation have sponsored encouraging results, which may result in a vaccine by 2011.[8]

HIV/AIDS and malaria are linked. Malaria increases the severity of HIV/AIDS manifestation. HIV/AIDS undermines the body's defenses against malaria. The interrelationship of the illnesses makes for confusing statistics. But as one African observer writes: "In Zimbabwe, more than 2000 people are dying every week due to HIV/AIDS and HIV related complications. For those who are conservative with statistics, I advise them to visit our cemeteries!"[9]

Two billion people worldwide reportedly are infected by tuberculosis. As noted previously, tuberculosis treatment is relatively inexpensive and 25 million tuberculosis deaths over the next twenty years could be prevented. About one-third of people with HIV/AIDS in the developing world also have tuberculosis. It is the first manifestation of HIV/AIDS in 50 percent of the cases in developing countries.

The United Nations (UN) emphasizes the connection between these diseases through the Global Fund to Fight HIV/AIDS, Tuberculosis, and Malaria. Some evangelical Christians, by linking HIV/AIDS, malaria, and tuberculosis together in church programs, are starting to overcome some of the resistance and reticence toward AIDS that has accumulated during the past twenty years. Certain Christian denominations, such as the Presbyterian Church, U.S.A., are taking aggressive efforts in these areas by mobilizing local congregations not only to advocate social justice but also to sew mosquito nets and put together malaria packets for educational purposes. Bed nets treated with insecticide cut malaria infection rates by half, but fewer than one vulnerable child in twenty has the chance to sleep beneath one.[10]

A Denver surgeon, Pius K. Kamau, MD, has sought to mobilize the medical community to address the global issues of malaria, tuberculosis, and HIV/AIDS. What he says about his colleagues in medicine applies to most Christians in the pew. He notes that most physicians are like most Americans—they view the world through an American prism that says, "Our prosperity is all that matters." He suggests that our "circumstances of comfort" are so great that we have become indifferent to the world's suffering. He says that while he and thousands of his medical colleagues were absent from the world's medical battlefield, "millions in Africa succumbed to AIDS—20 million at the last count, and 68 million in a decade, if my peers and I do nothing." He insists that we have a responsibility for the sick of the world: "And as long as we serve a greater good—greater than good incomes, good standard of living, and a great country—and as long as we aspire to the Hippocratic principles, we must think and act as if the world's ill are our patients also. To 'above all, do no harm,' doesn't translate to doing nothing."[11]

Debt Relief for the Poorest Nations

Demonstrating Christian love in a time of AIDS means advocating debt relief for the poorest nations of the world. Many nations are paying more on debt repayment than on health care and education. One in three persons infected with HIV—some 13 million people—live in countries classified by the International Monetary Fund and World Bank as heavily indebted. Until there is substantial relief, little or no progress will be made in these countries in the struggle against HIV/AIDS.

This debt was accumulated over the years by impoverished nations. Much was wasted, either through political corruption or misguided projects. Very little actually was spent to help the ordinary people. Now people are suffering from debt incurred long before many of them were ever born. In Zambia, where one in five children dies before age five and life expectancy has been reduced to forty years because of HIV/AIDS, some 25 percent of the country's budget goes to pay off debt. This is larger than the amount spent for health care. In Niger, where 86 percent of the population is illiterate and one in four children dies before age five, over 25 percent of the national budget goes to debt relief. Overall, Africa spends more than four times on debt repayments than on health care.[12]

Twenty-six countries have qualified for debt relief of $53 billion out of an initial total debt of $74 billion. Half of these countries still spend 15 percent or more of their government revenue on debt repayment, more than they spend on health care. Twenty other countries have been identified as needing debt relief but have not yet qualified.

Continued advocacy of various petitions and policies that enact debt relief needs to be a part of the church's portfolio of social justice concerns. The rock star Bono has provided leadership on this issue. He has successfully lobbied right-wing conservatives like Senator Rick Santorum of Pennsylvania and former Senator Jesse Helms of North Carolina. He has spent weeks speaking in mainline Protestant churches in the heartland of America, pleading for better understanding of the relationship of Third World debt reduction to attacking HIV/AIDS. He explicitly told a group of evangelical Christians, "I'm a believer and I have faith in Christ." He translates that faith into challenging Christians to address debt relief and fight HIV/AIDS.[13]

Debt relief does make a difference. In Uganda, twice as many children are now going to school because debt has been reduced. One-half million children in Mozambique now get immunizations against diphtheria, tetanus, and whooping cough; debt relief has allowed them to allocate more for health care.

The following Web sites provide more information on the debt relief movement:

> www.jubilee2000uk.org
> www.oxfam.org.uk
> www.christian-aid.org
> www.dropthedebt.org

Access to Anti-AIDS Treatment

Demonstrating Christian love in a time of AIDS means championing access to anti-AIDS treatment in the Two-Thirds World. People living with HIV/AIDS have a right to these life-prolonging medicines, and governments have a responsibility to ensure their delivery.

The medicine that has made HIV/AIDS a manageable disease in the United States, Europe, Brazil, Japan, Taiwan, and Australia is simply not available or affordable to most of the people in the world. Medicine exists to limit mother-to-child transmission of HIV/AIDS, but the Two-Thirds World cannot afford it. So children continue to be infected and die.

Patent questions and issues of fair trade abound. Pressure on pharmaceutical companies is beginning to make a difference, but politics, patents, fair trade agreements, distribution problems, fair return on investments, and other issues create an ethical and practical quandary. The development of generic copies of some of the highly active anti-retroviral therapies (HAART), and the reduction of costs, should make it possible to sharply increase the number of people who can benefit throughout the world. Breakthroughs are on the rise in South Africa, Brazil, and India, but this is only at the beginning stages.

Kenya, for example, has pills labeled "Lamivudine," "Zidovudine," and "Efavirez" that are the needed anti-retrovirals to fight HIV/AIDS.

A stone's throw away from the laboratory are African men, women, and children suffering and dying because they cannot have the pills. The Western pharmaceutical giants refuse permission for making generic copies, and the African governments won't break patent laws, lest they suffer retribution through investment and trade punishments. Global pressures are mounting for a breakthrough, and hopefully, by the time this book is published, the pills will be available to the people.[14]

Even when anti-retroviral therapy is available at a reduced cost, the ethical dilemmas can be excruciating, as described in chapter 6. Unless therapy is available for all, some will have to go without.

Championing access to medical care for people with HIV/AIDS is not limited to advocating expensive anti-retroviral therapies. Christian love means questioning why only 25 percent of the earth's population has access to 79 percent of the world's available drugs. Persons living with HIV/AIDS in most of the world are hardly receiving any modern medications at all, except for the cheapest antibiotics.

When I visited an AIDS hospice in a Buddhist temple in Thailand, the Christian volunteers from the Netherlands pleaded not only for anti-retroviral therapies, but asked that ordinary painkilling medicines be available. "If Americans and Europeans would even send expired morphine packs that now only have 50 percent efficacy," said one nurse, "it would reduce pain 50 percent more than is now happening for dying women and men in our care." Experiencing unrelenting pain is like being imprisoned and tortured. In the twenty-first century, such suffering is unconscionable, because we have the means to manage such pain. There in the Buddhist temple, I heard anew the words of Hebrews 13:1-3: "Let mutual love continue. Do not neglect to show hospitality to strangers, for by doing that some have entertained angels without knowing it. Remember those who are in prison, as though you were in prison with them; those who are being tortured, as though you yourselves were being tortured."

But whether Christians will hear this cry and respond is yet to be determined. The World Council of Churches has forthrightly declared: (1) "We will advocate for access to health care, and for drugs to treat opportunistic infections, and to prevent mother to child transmission," and (2) "we will support the efforts of those who are campaigning for access to anti-retroviral drugs."[15]

What role will individual churches and religious institutions in the United States play? To my knowledge, theological educators in the United States have been more interested in other issues and, in essence, have been silent on these social justice questions.

Governmental Funding

Finally, demonstrating Christian love in a time of AIDS means joining with other religious and secular organizations in urging greater financial support from governments and international organizations. This calamity is causing not only widespread suffering and death, but also greater poverty, political and economic instability, and decreased educational opportunities for the world's citizens. Money is needed not only for medicines, but for efforts to strengthen the world health care system generally, including the human infrastructure of front-line health workers.[16]

"Mass murder by complacency" is the way Stephen Lewis, the UN secretary-general's special envoy for HIV/AIDS in Africa, describes the lack of funding for HIV/AIDS. Exasperated by the lack of commitment of political leadership around the world, Lewis predicts "there may yet come a day when we have peacetime tribunals to deal with this particular version of crimes against humanity."[17]

During the 1990s the United States allocated about $70 million per year for promoting HIV prevention in the Two-Thirds World. Compare that to the $50 million the Pentagon budgeted to provide the impotence drug Viagra to American troops and military retirees when it first became available![18]

The initial goal of the UN-supported Global Fund for HIV/AIDS, Tuberculosis, and Malaria was $7 to $10 billion annually, but to date contributions have fallen far short. Despite rhetorical commitments, giving has been remarkably stingy from the United States and other countries. Sebastian Mallaby, a journalist writing in the *Washington Post,* pondered why America could spend more than $100 billion for a war in Iraq and yet do so little to combat global AIDS. Mallaby speculated that "a century from now, when historians write about our era, one question will dwarf all others, and it won't be about finance or politics or even terrorism. The question will be, simply, how could a rich and civilized society allow a known and beatable enemy to kill millions of people?"[19] Globally, some 9,000 people a day die from AIDS—about three times as many as died on the infamous and tragic day at the World Trade Center. "Yet, the world does not seem to notice or care," says Thomas Coates, director of the Center for AIDS Prevention Studies.[20]

Slowly, United States elected officials are awakening to the economic, political, and social consequences of global AIDS. Late in President Clinton's administration, the disease finally was identified as a threat to national security and the military became concerned about its impact on world order. At first the Republicans scoffed, but when President George W. Bush took office, he reaffirmed the policy. In 2003 Bush surprised everyone in his State of the Union address when he proposed a $15 billion AIDS package, targeted particularly for Africa and the Caribbean. Reportedly, Bush was influenced by a coalition of forces, including evangelical Christians who lobbied him to respond to the global health emergency. Congress, in a rare bi-partisan effort, endorsed the legislation. The "devil may be in the details," as separate legislation later must actually pass to fund the proposal, and controversy exists about how the funds will be spent in relation to the UN-supported Global Fund, unilateral initiatives of the United States, and programmatic issues such as abstinence education versus condom distribution.

Realistic Idealism

Any time Christians dream of a world without AIDS or address major issues of social justice, critics and cynics are certain to discount these ideas as too idealistic and utopian. Yet Christians are captured by Jesus' vision of the kingdom of God that is both realistic and idealistic. We know that eradicating age-old diseases like malaria and tuberculosis will not be easy, but we also know it is not impossible. We recognize that advocating and attaining debt relief for impoverished nations are not simple, but are not beyond attainment. We are aware that championing better medical care for all God's people is to reach beyond current realities, but it is not beyond the grasp of coming generations. We admit that pushing for more government responsibility and funding to combat HIV/AIDS will require a reordering of political and economic priorities, but we believe that soon leaders will recognize that it is in their national and self-interest to do so. Above all, we believe that God is already at work in the world seeking to achieve these objectives for his suffering children, and that we are called to join in God's liberating and loving mission and ministry.

Richard Feachem, executive director of the UN-related Global Fund, notes that "the global HIV/AIDS pandemic is by far the largest catastrophe to befall humankind in recorded human history." Considerably worse than the Black Death in the middle of the fourteenth century, he projects that "the epidemic isn't going to peak until about 2050, 2060."[21] Christians cannot accept passively such a pessimistic forecast. We must seek to change the world and speed up the timetable for overcoming and overpowering this dreadful disease. Christians are called to reorder missional priorities and extend helping hands in the struggle for a world without AIDS.

8

Ensuring Care, Testing, Counseling, and Treatment

We are witnesses to a genocide by indifference.

—A psychologist and Lutheran laywoman in South Africa

Once when I was in New York City, I made an unscheduled visit to the Spellman Center for HIV-related Diseases at St. Clare's Hospital. I wanted to see the place and people of whom Daniel J. Baxter, MD, had written about in his book, *The Least of These My Brethren: A Doctor's Story of Hope and Miracles on an Inner-City AIDS Ward.* In particular, I had hoped to see the caregiving saint he had described: Director of Pastoral Care, Sister Pascal Conforti.

Of course, I got lost and went to the wrong entrance. I immediately was aware, however, that Sister Pascal must be special. For though I was nearly two blocks away, I was able to get directions from a part-time African American guard who clearly knew of whom I spoke. Once I entered the hospital, I discovered that literally every staff member and patient knew and was known by this caregiver. Graciously, this gray-haired, Italian American, Roman Catholic nun received me, just as she had done with thousands and thousands before me, making me feel immediately like we were cherished friends. Her very being radiated a spirit of Christian care and candor. I understood what Dr. Baxter meant when he said that Sister Pascal eased "the patient's pain that Percocet could not reach," responded "to the loneliness and despair that Prozac could not reach," and understood "the 'difficult' patient that psychiatry could not fathom."[1]

Sister Pascal provides the compassion and companionship to contemporary HIV/AIDS patients of New York that Jesus provided to the lepers of ancient Galilee. A theologian as well as a chaplain, she argues, "God doesn't like AIDS any more than we do." It is a random virus that presently defies "all our efforts to eradicate it completely." She is convinced and convincing that "God is neither cause of our suffering nor is God some kind of divine rescuer who will swoop down and save us." Rather, she proclaims, "God is always with us in the process as co-suffering, compassionate presence." In her words, "God is most obviously present in the physical and spiritual companionship which we provide for our sick brothers and sisters and which in some way they provide for us even as their bodies weaken, . . . God is there when we are there for one another—loving and being loved, laughing together and weeping together, staying with one another, supporting one another in life and in death."

I wish that the global church would adopt the motto of the actors and actresses of America: "We will do whatever it takes, for as long as it takes." In the fight against leprosy and other diseases, the church made precisely that commitment. Now the church is challenged to take that vow with respect to people living with HIV/AIDS around the world. There are four interrelated tasks involved in doing "whatever it takes, for as long as it takes," namely: (1) caring, (2) testing, (3) counseling, and (4) treatment.

Care, Not Cure

Unfortunately, finding a cure or a vaccine to conquer HIV/AIDS remains but a distant scientific dream. We can pray for and support medical research efforts to achieve such scientific breakthroughs, but the world cannot wait until a miracle drug is discovered and distributed. Caring, not curing, becomes our immediate priority.

God is calling Christians to discover new levels of empathy and care. In Galatians 6:9 we are reminded not to "grow weary in doing what is right, for we will reap at harvest time, if we do not give up." In Hebrews 13:3 Christians are instructed: "Remember those who are in prison, as though you were in prison with them; those who are being tortured, as though you yourselves were being tortured." In other words, Christians are called to identify with human suffering. We are not asked to condemn those in prison or speculate why people are imprisoned or being tortured. Instead, we are asked to offer care and hospitality to those in anguish and agony. In an age of great suffering, we are called to join God's angels in loving and caring and healing.

Early in the pandemic, Margaret Gallimore, a nurse for more than twenty-five years, turned her home into an AIDS shelter. Keeping two men at a time, she provided for all their needs, worked as a private duty nurse at night, cooked three meals a day for her "sons," changed their sheets up to five or six times a day, and drove them to doctor appointments. Why did she do it? "That's not the question," she responded. "That's just not the question. The question is why aren't there more people doing it?"[2]

Actually more and more people are now doing it, most by necessity, but many by choice. In the non-governmental area, the Roman Catholic community is leading the way, providing approximately 25 percent of all the care facilities, hospitals, homes, hospices, and other services in the world. From the sordid streets of Calcutta, India, to the shantytowns of South Africa, to the inner city of Denver, to the rural prairie of South Dakota, Catholic nuns in particular have forged a network of care facilities.[3]

Generally, however, the Christian church in the world has failed to live up to the standards of caring and mercy exemplified in the healing ministry of Jesus the Christ. By our own normative expectations, we have failed to offer leadership in stemming or caring for the AIDS pandemic.

This lack of a positive witness has subjected the Christian faith to serious criticism, both from our own believers and from those who do not identify with the Christian faith. Public health authorities sometimes find the church a stumbling block in their efforts at prevention and care. The church has failed to practice what it preaches. We prove more prone to judgment than grace, condemnation than care, and exclusion than inclusion. As Mother Teresa said, "If you are busy judging, you have no time to love."

Instead of relieving anxiety, pain, and suffering, Christians often add guilt and shame. For example, instead of asking the persons, "Where do you hurt and need comfort?" we are inclined to ask, "How did you get infected?"

The church is not alone in such uncaring attitudes and practices. Cultural callousness pervades almost every country and society, and extensive educational efforts are required to break through sexual taboos and judgmental perspectives. The medical community, unfortunately, is also not immune; even doctors and nurses function with fears and often find excuses for not treating patients. Early in the pandemic a woman pastor in rural Missouri wrote me a note: "Yesterday I had to fish out the names of two doctors I keep hidden in my drawer. A family in our church is bringing their son home to die. The doctors here who will treat AIDS patients feel they must do so secretly, for fear of losing other patients. I feel like I'm working the underground railroad."[4]

Increasingly, medical personnel worldwide have been providing yeoman's service in offering medical care. For example, frustrated and angry about the lack of known medical resources, South African doctors have been publicly petitioning their government for anti-retroviral medicines: "We can no longer in good conscience simply continue providing palliative and terminal care for our patients with AIDS, when we know that effective lifesaving treatment is available." They have threatened breaking patent laws, illegally importing generic drugs, engaging in civil disobedience, and getting arrested. They note that those fortunate and rich enough to get the treatment are "like Lazarus, rising from the dead," while "many mothers, fathers, sons, and daughters, are fading and quietly dying."[5]

With advanced treatment in the First World, or industrialized nations, fewer and fewer HIV/AIDS patients have had to be hospitalized on a regular basis. Individuals are able to take care of themselves, utilizing clinics and/or having assistance in their homes. Worldwide, home care is essential. Hospitals and hospices in the Two-Thirds World (non-industrialized countries) are minimal and now often are overflowing with people suffering from HIV/AIDS. For a long time in India, Christian hospitals did not accept AIDS patients and only slowly began taking limited numbers. The lack of medical infrastructure in many impoverished countries makes hospital or hospice care impossible.

Increasingly senior citizens, with and without financial resources, are summoned to care for the lives of young and middle-aged adults and children, especially in Africa and Asia. The World Health Organization (WHO) has noted that older caregivers are often "unsung, unrewarded, and unsupported." In poor health themselves, they are struggling to care for their own sick children and grandchildren while simultaneously dealing with community stigmatization. Often they are forced back to working on farms, preparing meals, cleaning the house, and buying school supplies while taking care of their orphaned grandchildren. In Zimbabwe, elderly women are especially overwhelmed with these caregiving responsibilities. As one older woman from Bulawayo, the guardian of three little children, said, "I am so afraid of what the future has in store for these orphans. If I were to die and leave them, who would look after them?"[6]

Christians since the time of Jesus have understood the care of orphans not as a religious duty, but as a spiritual opportunity to show love and to nurture life. Christians may be divided over condom use or sexual issues, but there is no division on the question of caring for children without parents or family. As I tell congregations, "if you are uncomfortable talking about sex or condoms, you can still make a major difference by helping to provide homes for orphans." At the Beautiful Gate orphanage outside Cape Town, South Africa, over forty children are cared for, thanks to the vision of a Dutch couple, Toby and Aukje Brouwer, who seek to "show the love of Jesus Christ through practical assistance." An incredible young medical doctor, Vaughan Stannard, showed my wife the facilities; I was stunned to enter a room set aside as a hospice for the little children who are dying of AIDS.

Caregiving must also occur in other places, such as prisons. Members of the Central Presbyterian Church in Baltimore and Prison Fellowship work in "The Living Room" of the Maryland Penitentiary to ease the pain of inmates with AIDS. Treated as, one prisoner says, "the lowest of the low," these people receive comfort and care from Christians who share mercy, not judgment—acceptance, not rejection.[7] In Russia, Rev. Elena Stepanova, has launched a United Methodist ministry for people with HIV/AIDS within the prison at Ekaterinburg. With infection rates climbing within prison communities and high levels of short-term incarceration in Russia, the probability for the rapid spread of the disease throughout the country is high. Her mission and ministry are aimed at connecting the importance of caring, education, and future prevention of transmission.

Serving as a caregiver on the frontlines of mercy introduces one to the harsh realities of this virus and illness. There is nothing romantic about AIDS or suffering. Hospital Chaplain David Yeoman bluntly describes some of its painful reality: "Seeing someone's body covered in the purple lesions that come with Kaposi's Sarcoma, seeing people emaciated to the point that they are almost skeletal, seeing them shed skin and vomit hideously, seeing them gasping for breath with respiratory problems, seeing people in their twenties and thirties with dementia."[8]

Not only do patients need treatment and comforting care, but the caregivers themselves also need support and assistance. Burnout is not an uncommon experience among professionals and volunteers. Overwhelmed by daily experiences of suffering and death, they need avenues to express their feelings, to cope with their anxieties and fears, and to articulate their pain and grief.

During a visit to a mental health clinic near three impoverished townships in Johannesburg, South Africa, my wife Bonnie and I listened to a psychologist and two community caregivers tell of their professional and emotional struggles. Regardless of the reason people sought out their clinic, some 80 percent were infected and HIV/AIDS was omnipresent. Lack of financial and physical resources limited their outreach to the endless stream of people at their door. Most of the social work and psychology "professionals" had fled, and the clergy and church "professionals" had never appeared. The intensity of burnout was too great, and they themselves were being threatened by fatigue. All of them had taken orphans into their homes. Thanks to their own incredible personal and spiritual resources, they were staying and serving. A nearby Methodist retreat center, Common Ground, was providing some chance for reflection and renewal. When I asked the three women what sustained them and gave them hope, one replied, "We meet Christ where the suffering is the greatest."

The call is for Christians, professionals and volunteers, to find ways of meeting Christ in constructive engagement. Pastor and professor Janet Everhart reminded an audience in India about how often the wisdom literature of Job, Proverbs, and the Psalms deals with the reality of righteous, good people who suffer. She pointed out that "the most helpful thing Job's friends did for him was not to explain his suffering but to sit with him in silence." Sometimes our calling is "to sit with silence and compassion with people who suffer." Other times, Everhart emphasizes, we are called to be prophetic, speaking clearly about God's love and justice: "Even those who have been shunned are invited into God's community, according to Isaiah and other prophets. The divide between rich and poor, between those who have medical treatment and those who do not, is inconsistent with the prophet's vision of God's community." Jesus, the healer, touched and talked with people who were otherwise shunned. To a menstruating woman who touched him in the crowd, Jesus declared that her faith had healed her. "In New Testament Greek," reports Everhart, "the word for 'heal' and the word for 'save' are the same! To be healed is to be saved, and vice versa."[9]

The saving ministry of Jesus Christ is a healing ministry. Such healing is not the sole domain of medical practitioners, hospitals, or clinics but resides within the power and scope of us all. Caring includes many dimensions and must be individualized to meet individual needs. Being a faithful friend and family member instills hope. Respecting confidentiality, but offering to help, makes a big difference. Touching appropriately, squeezing a hand, or giving a hug offers life and overcomes barriers and fears. Other practical suggestions include:

- Listening and learning
- Spending time together
- Keeping in telephone contact when miles separate
- Holding people in prayer
- Finding ways of helping in personal ways
- Helping negotiate medical or public bureaucracies
- Offering transportation to treatment, to the store, or to a movie
- Cooking favorite foods
- Overcoming isolation and keeping people involved in church and community

Saving and healing are not one-way streets. Establishing meaningful relationships with people living with HIV/AIDS is mutually rewarding. People living with HIV/AIDS have much to share and teach the rest of us. Around the world, they have witnessed and worked for improved health care for all. They have lobbied and educated governments, non-governmental organizations, pharmaceutical companies, the media, and educational institutions. Their positive presence in the world continues to make a difference. The famous "AIDS Quilt," memorializing those who have given their lives in this pandemic, symbolizes both the great loss and the immense contribution these people have made and are continuing to make to ensure better health care and human rights for all the citizens of earth.

Yes, caring, not curing, remains a high priority. It has a saving and healing dimension that is impossible to quantify, but it makes a tremendous difference both in the lives of the receiver and the giver. Upon my return from sub-Saharan Africa, I wrote a Zimbabwean Christian activist, Nontando Margaret Hadebe, that I found it hard to be hopeful amid genocide. Yet I know despair rarely propels action or motivates people to move forward against tremendous odds. She quickly replied that while the challenge of HIV/AIDS is indeed immense, "every drop of assistance makes a difference no matter what it is or what form it takes. I find that one way of keeping myself from not being overwhelmed by the situation in Africa is to do concrete acts of assistance whenever I can—it just breaks the hopelessness and fosters hope."[10]

Once, when I was sightseeing with friends outside of Mumbai (Bombay), India, an elderly Indian woman started visiting with us. She was very friendly, and her family wanted to know what was next on our journey. We indicated we were headed to Calcutta to visit Mother Teresa's house and ministry. A son suddenly commented, "Oh, we don't hear much about her anymore. Mother Teresa doesn't seem to get out much anymore." We refrained from responding or laughing, but a few days later as we stood by her heavy marble crypt, we had to agree! The message is clear: Christian caring is now our responsibility.

Testing, Not Denial

Testing and counseling have always been understood as interrelated, but testing and treatment have often been treated in the past as quite different categories. Of course, they are separate subjects, but their interrelationship is increasingly recognized and emphasized.

Testing is critically important but can never be done in isolation. Early in the pandemic, it was a tremendous medical breakthrough to be able to identify the virus that was baffling the world. Unfortunately, the tests were often done without permission and the results were treated without due confidentiality or care for the individuals involved. Confidentiality was broken and sensitive counseling was not provided. My friend, Ashok Pillai, reported how he was abruptly given the results that he was HIV-positive and bluntly told he was going to die. Word spread to his naval unit, and he was treated worse than a pariah, criminal, or first-century leper. He devoted his life to speaking out against such inhumane behavior and policies. Psychologist Bonnie J. Messer underscores the importance of confidentiality:

> As a counselor or minister or health worker, we have a duty, a moral obligation, to protect the privacy of the persons with whom we work. . . . It is the person with HIV/AIDS who owns the information regarding their medical status. Granted, there are concerns to protect other persons from being exposed to AIDS through social contact, sharing needles, or donating contaminated blood. However, the optimal, ethical stance is that one needs to work with the infected person and encourage them to take responsible actions so that they do not infect others.[11]

Significant changes have been made in the medical establishment around the world, but even today testing can be an excruciating, emotional experience. Due to concerns about stigmatization and discrimination, many fear to get tested. Lack of anonymity and possible negative social consequences cause people to either choose not to be tested or travel long distances, if possible, to get the results. Regardless, it can be a lonely and isolated experience. When a person does receive news of being HIV-positive, he or she is encouraged to get re-tested to avoid false results. People who have reason to think they may have been exposed to the virus must repeat tests every six months or so, since often it takes an unspecified period of time to appear in one's system.

It is crucial for every person to know his or her HIV status. Knowing one's status allows a person to make the most informed and responsible decisions about sexual behavior and life commitments. Mouth tests and blood tests typically require a patient to return to a clinic one to two weeks later for results. Unfortunately, many, for whatever reason, never get their results. In the year 2000, the Centers for Disease Control and Prevention indicated that 30 percent of those who tested positive in the United States never learned of their status because they did not come back and inquire.

Rapid tests are now available, which provide reports within twenty minutes, thus reducing the long and nerve-racking waiting period. Rapid testing, though more expensive, may actually be more cost-effective, since the numbers who receive the results are higher.

Lack of life-giving treatment is recognized as the primary obstacle to widespread testing. People are understandably reluctant to get tested and learn their status if there is no hope for treatment and they run the tremendous risk of losing family, friends, jobs, and social standing. When one of Mozambique's leading journalists, Bento Bango, a forty-four-year-old father of four announced he was HIV-positive, the landlord threw him and his family out of the house.[12] In some cultures and countries, HIV identification can even mean physical violence and abuse. In 2003, police officers in Henan Province, China, beat up residents and smashed their property, arresting thirteen people, in retaliation for their public protest about promised AIDS help that never came.[13] As former U.S. President Bill Clinton has noted:

> Prevention doesn't work unless large numbers of people agree to be tested. They won't agree to be tested if all they will learn is that they are going to die. . . . They should be tested, of course, to save others. But they want to save their own lives, too. . . . More people will stop suffering in silence and be willing to get tested for HIV if we offer treatment that will prolong their lives and spare the lives of others.[14]

Having no hope for treatment or one's future contributes to fatalistic thinking, which in turn can lead to high-risk sexual behavior. For example, studies in the United States find that men who engaged in unprotected anal intercourse outside of sexually exclusive relationships often reflected fatalistic thinking. Lacking a future, they felt less responsibility to protect themselves or others. Men who engage in "safer sex" are more likely to report that they have reasons for living and expectations for tomorrow.[15]

In Kenya, an estimated 700 people are dying daily. The social fabric and governmental order are cracking. For example, up to fifteen prison guards are dying each month and six to ten soldiers every week! Nearly 60 percent of the military's hospital beds in Nairobi are occupied with people suffering from HIV/AIDS. The Kenyan government now has declared this a national disaster and has begun to encourage anonymous "voluntary" testing and counseling.[16] As long as treatment and care, however, lag tragically behind, successful programs of testing and prevention remain problematic.

Competent, Compassionate Counseling

Competent and compassionate counseling is integral to the testing and treatment process of HIV/AIDS. The complexities of the counseling process are far beyond the limits of this book and author, but certain critical elements are important to discuss. Effective and accessible voluntary counseling services are essential in helping individuals to combat this global scourge. Counseling can help people make informed and conscientious decisions about their lives and their future.

The description of tasks and challenges of counseling mentioned in this chapter apply to secular professional psychologists, social workers, therapists, and medical staff, as well as to pastors, professional pastoral counselors, and volunteer church community caregivers. Obviously, persons in certain roles, with different levels of educational training, experience, and licensure, can better handle certain challenges and circumstances. Professional discretion and judgment are required, and forging working partnerships among these and other people can provide a critical team approach to helping people live with HIV/AIDS.

Counseling begins before testing, continues during the testing period, and includes post-testing therapy. It can be focused on providing preventive advice on how HIV is and is not transmitted and include information about "safer sex" such as the ABCs of prevention. Advice might be to help people understand various risks—such as the fact that UNAIDS research indicates "condoms fail to protect against HIV exposure about 10 percent of the time due to incorrect usage and human error."[17] It might involve complex assistance for behavioral change leading to abstinence, partner reduction, or faithfulness. It might only be a simple assertion like "Be wise, condomize" (see chapter 5), or even the adage that "vows of abstinence break more often than condoms." People can be helped to make their own risk assessment to determine how vulnerable they are to the disease and their reasons for concern. If they are contemplating an HIV test, they can discover the meaning, steps, and implications of the process.

If people are found to be infected, they need to understand the possible stages of the disease, how to live with the uncertainties of their health and the probabilities of stigmatization, as well as their own feelings of fear, disbelief, anger, loss, shame, guilt, despair, or depression. Each person's journey is unique, but each person needs assistance in coping not only with his or her feelings, but potential reactions, responses, and even rejection from family and friends.

Telling loved ones—partners, children, parents, and others—can be excruciatingly difficult. Easy assurances to the contrary cannot be given to the counselee. Long-time Colorado AIDS director and pastor, Julian Rush, tells how a son finally wrote his parents to tell them he was HIV-positive. When he opened a letter of response, he found his birth certificate torn in two. People can be amazingly cruel and contrary to the way of love. Fortunately, this extreme rejection increasingly proves the exception rather than the rule; most of us, however, still hesitate because of uncertainty in our particular situation. When Ashok Pillai finally summoned courage to tell his family, his mother embraced him tightly, holding him to her breast. Unfortunately, in many global contexts, people justifiably fear deeply the consequences of revealing their HIV-positive status. As Kalpana Jain notes:

> Acceptance is the most difficult part of disclosure. For the family and people close to the person concerned, it is almost as difficult to accept his/her having HIV, as it is for him/her to come to terms with the confirmation of his/her status. There is a gamut of emotions for the family to handle. In the case of a spouse, betrayal is the most

obvious one. For parents, it could be a mixture of anger, outrage, guilt, as also shock. Acceptance may or may not follow, though after the disclosure, it's acceptance that HIV-positive people crave for.[18]

Counselors need to be alert to signs of suicidal ideation. Non-acceptance and despair can drive people to end their lives, thinking there is no future. No reliable statistics exist, but many HIV-positive people contemplate, if not attempt, suicide or "self-deliverance," as psychotherapist Robert J. Perelli confirms:

> The weight of this disease and the constellation of psy-chosocial stressors (such as guilt, low self-esteem, shame, alienation, fear, stigma, discrimination . . .) that surround it may drive the PWA (person living with AIDS) to con-sider taking his own life. On the physical level, the PWA is subject to debilitating weakness, wasting, constant fever, nagging diarrhea, the potential loss of mobility, the prospect of around-the-clock care, and vulnerability to any number of opportunistic diseases. . . . It is no wonder that the thoughts of suicide are on the mind of everyone afflicted with this disease. The best suicide prevention might be giving the patient the space to vent feelings of despair to lessen the likelihood of unexpressed feeling welling up and overtaking him in a moment of crisis.[19]

Availability of treatment reduces the threat and possibility of sui-cide significantly. A competent and compassionate counselor can also make a difference, helping people to see alternatives and avenues that are hidden to the person under incredible stress.

Quick counseling too often is the norm around the world as medical facilities are swamped with patients, and staff members are inade-quately prepared professionally or personally for the task. Needed is regular empathetic conversation and communication that is medically informed and psychologically insightful. Counseling should extend not just to those infected but to others affected—family, friends, employers, and others. If the African saying "It takes a village to raise a child" has validity, it certainly is true that coping and caring in the AIDS pandemic requires a community, not just isolated individuals.

Helping people move beyond the shock, disbelief, and possible guilt or shame to constructive adjustment back into life, family, and society is not an easy road. Yet people who persevere and develop a positive attitude toward living have repeatedly demonstrated better health and longer life. Creating and cultivating a new or renewed sense of self-worth and purpose makes a difference.

As previously stressed in this chapter, access to life-giving antiretroviral treatments plays a significant role in more positive outcomes. Such treatments not only provide a person and their families new hope but also encourage better prevention and education. When people are denied access because of income or social status, disparity and despair increase.

The counselor's task extends into areas such as preparation for death and death itself, as well as bereavement. No individual counselor or pastor can or probably should do all these things, but they are imperative steps in the journey. "Human beings," Cathie Lyons, a pioneer in health and welfare ministries, has noted, "respond to illness and affliction based on deeply rooted social and religious beliefs."[20] Understanding and ministering in that contextual framework is essential. Drawing deeply from the scriptural resources can provide comfort, especially remembering that Jesus rejected the socio-religious perspective that illness and affliction were divine-earthly retribution. "In a world, which so clearly judged some as sinners and made outcasts of others, came this man Jesus," says Lyons, "who, in forgiving sin and in cleansing the leper, gave a preview of God's more just and merciful kingdom."[21]

Many people are affected by the loss of a person with AIDS, and attention must be given to partners, family members, church, and community. Not only must there be necessary religious preparations and observances but also attention to various psychological and legal issues. For the latter, a unique support group has been developed by Common Ground, a spiritual life center in Johannesburg, South Africa, where fifteen HIV-positive mothers meet regularly to seek emotional and spiritual support, as well as receive guidance on getting one's personal and legal affairs prepared for impending early death.

Most models for professional counseling, of course, are based on ordinary or even extraordinary circumstances of life, not in the face of a sustained global emergency. Individual counseling is limited, as larger and larger support groups become a necessity. In South Africa, for instance, up to 1,000 people are dying daily. Fearing denial and discrimination, many people never reveal their health condition until they are forced by extreme exigency, and their life often ebbs away shortly afterward. Women community caregivers with whom I met indicated they had no chance to offer sustained care and comfort. Confidentiality requirements keep office colleagues from reaching out in open friendship to a fellow worker they are certain is struggling to live with HIV/AIDS.

Pastors and priests reported that they are faced with an overwhelming deluge of funerals week after week. Ten to twenty in one church are not unusual; one pastor reported forty-seven funerals over a two-day period. No seminary ever prepared clergy to conduct assembly-line funerals week after week, month after month. How does one handle "disenfranchised grief" and a cultural community torn apart by endless death and dying?[22] In South Africa people can no longer have "proper" traditional funerals. Coffins of wood sometimes now have to be replaced with cardboard boxes. Sometimes bodies have to be piled in a grave. Grave-digging backhoes operate overtime as the cemeteries expand and expand.

As the pandemic escalates, all the previous methods and models of counseling will be tested and probably new paradigms will emerge to handle the heartbreaking dilemmas of people, families, and communities. Whatever emerges, people always need to know they are not alone—that others care and that God is with them always.

Treatment

"HIV/AIDS is the new apartheid of discrimination and stigmatization," declares the presiding Methodist Bishop of Southern Africa, Rev. Ivan M. Abrahams. "Previously apartheid meant lack of access to opportunities and institutions; now it means lack of access to the life-sustaining anti-retroviral medicines."[23] In these bold words, the bishop frankly describes the new world of globalization, where apartheid is no longer restricted to South Africa but has become the reality of the impoverished ill throughout the Two-Thirds World. Access to medical care and the latest treatments are prerogatives of the powerful and the wealthy, as the world is deeply divided between the "haves" and the "have-nots." Increasingly, voices of justice internationally are demanding that all God's people living with HIV/AIDS have a right to these life-prolonging drugs and that governments have an ethical responsibility to ensure access for all their citizens. Denial of medicines that exist on the market is being challenged, and politicians and pharmaceutical companies are being held account-able for the suffering and death of millions of citizens.

Genocide by indifference has never been acceptable moral behav-ior, but it has been disguised in recent times by international patent disputes, trade treaties, and power politics. Previous holocausts in Nazi Europe, Cambodia, or Rwanda were deliberate massacres of women, men, and children perpetuated by evil people and parties. Today's death toll is just as real, but the perpetrators are disguised as stockholders, health care industry managers, patent lawyers, scien-tists, and government leaders. As Nelson Mandela has repeatedly said: "We have failed to translate our scientific progress into action where it is most needed, in the developing world. This is the global injustice, which can't be tolerated. It is a travesty of human rights on a global scale."[24]

While many treatment discussions primarily focus on anti-retro-viral medications (ARVs), many ill people lack even the most basic medicines and treatment. In Thailand, I heard the cry of Christian Dutch volunteers for expired morphine packs and any type of anti-diarrhea medicine. In rural areas of Africa, people sometimes lack even an aspirin. In sexually-transmitted disease (STD) clinics near the slums of Chennai, India, I heard the health workers complain that they had only the weakest and oldest antibiotics. Sadly, I watched as recently expired medicines were dumped down the drain at the University of Minnesota—a regular practice at other U.S. hospitals and clinics.

There are six main stumbling blocks in the path of universal access. First, a well-developed health service infrastructure simply does not exist in many developing countries. Hospitals, clinics, doc-tors, nurses, technicians, pharmaceutical industries, educational pro-grams, and other types of medical care services are minimal to nonexistent. Further complicating this shortage in many countries has been political corruption, misplacement of priorities, poor health policies, and lack of leadership. All of this complicates immensely, if not prohibits, the effective provision of anti-retroviral drugs.

Many places need well-equipped mobile health units that include modern laboratories and trained medical personnel. They must carry out complicated blood counts, measure viral loads, prescribe appropriate drug combinations, monitor drug resistance, and ensure compliance with prescriptions. They cannot just appear occasionally on the scene, but must have a regular pattern. This is a long-term commitment, not a fly-by-night government scheme or a church's short-term volunteer mission project.

Second, the costs are beyond the means of most people, except for those fortunate to live in nations with significant resources. Because the cost is so overwhelming, only 50,000 infected people use AIDS drugs in sub-Saharan Africa. In 2003, prices began to tumble after strenuous public pressure. GlaxoSmithKline, the world's biggest manufacturer of AIDS drugs, sliced prices in half and promised additional cuts in the future if the UN and others would buy in bulk.[25] Despite signs that price reductions are under way, only a very small percentage of HIV-infected people are likely to benefit. Six African countries in 2003 had made low-cost deals with drug manufacturers, but they still could only afford to provide treatment for 1 to 2 percent of people with HIV/AIDS.[26] Remember that the goal stated at the UN General Assembly Special Session on HIV/AIDS was to provide treatment and care to 3 million people in developing countries by 2005—a significant, but only small, step forward in light of the numbers needing medical assistance. Even as prices have fallen to about one U.S. dollar a day for treatment—the cost of ARVs is still beyond the grasp of most of the world's citizens. The World Health Organization (WHO) through its "3x5 Initiative" hopes to meet the UN goal of 3 million by 2005.[27]

Third, intellectual property rights, trade laws, and patents have kept generics from being distributed. These patent protections exist to protect the companies that invest vast sums of money in producing new drugs. The Tufts Center for the Study of Drug Development claims it costs $802 million to develop a new drug. Former presidential hopeful Ralph Nader's organization, Public Citizen, claimed this was inflated by 75 percent. Nader's group said the cost was more like $240 million. So the controversy goes.[28] An exact figure is not known, but clearly it costs significant money to create new medicines, and those who have invested deserve to be reward generously but fairly.

In case of an "emergency," nations can break the codes. However, many countries are financially subservient to the major powers. They fear irritating the world's power brokers, whom they perceive as being "in bed" with the interests of the pharmaceutical companies. Brazil, however, has broken the patent, and the government is making the medicine available to all who need it. Namibia, Uganda, and South Africa are now producing generic copies.[29] Thailand hopes to have universal access for its citizens by 2005.

Nations like South Africa have to find a solution. Years of "unconscionable obtuseness" by the government prohibited adequate AIDS treatment through the public health system.[30] For example, teachers are dying by the thousands every year—in KwaZulu-Natal, more than fifty-five teachers die per month at the average age of thirty-six. UNICEF estimates 860,000 children in sub-Saharan Africa have lost their teachers to AIDS since the pandemic began. If current trends continue, who will teach the children? Anti-retroviral drugs are urgently needed to prolong the lives and careers of these professionals.[31]

Fourth, health workers fear that patients will not use the medicine properly or faithfully, and as a result, new mutations of the virus may occur, only further complicating the fight against HIV/AIDS. Already in Europe about 10 percent of all newly infected HIV patients are infected with drug-resistant strains. But ethicists emphasize that the possibility of creating drug-resistant strains of a virus is not a justifiable reason for denying drugs to the poor. Roy M. Gulick, MD, of Cornell University, says that because so few are actually getting drugs now in Africa, "the risk of resistance in most African populations right now is very low or zero."[32] Doctors will have to carefully monitor patients to ensure compliance with the drug regimen. Nokuthenjwa Bulana, a woman in a black township of South Africa, is fortunate because she is getting supervised ARVs. Without them, she says, "I think I would be dead now."[33] Unfortunately, she remains the exception, not the norm in South Africa.

Fifth, the lack of a stable food supply and appropriate nutrition makes it nearly impossible for many people to benefit from the medicine. Human hunger and lack of food security are a daunting challenge to making ARVs effective. People cannot take powerful medicines without a proper and dependable diet or on an empty stomach.

Hunger and disease create a vicious circle. Hungry people are more subject to disease. Ill people need money for medicine and have less for food. Sick people find it impossible to work and earn needed money. Recognizing these dilemmas, the UN World Food Program has begun providing special enriched food rations to HIV/AIDS infected people in the Central African Republic and other nations to help people resist opportunistic diseases.[34]

Future famines in Africa are likely to be more devastating than ever before in history. In previous famines the elderly and children were the most likely to die, but many rural Africans have found ways of coping with minimal food supplies. However, AIDS is now killing the young adults whose labor is most needed to work the fields up to sixteen hours a day during times of rain. The elderly are overwhelmed with childcare. If the critical period of food production is missed, families go hungry and national production rates sharply decrease.[35]

Everywhere in Africa, says the UN's Stephen Lewis, "There is absolutely no doubt that hunger and AIDS have come together in a Hecate's brew of horror."[36] In many places there is no one left to till the soil and grow the crops because disease and death stalk the land.

Political turmoil, civil wars, and international conflicts comprise yet a sixth barrier to universal access. In Africa, for example, there is abundant evidence that HIV/AIDS has flourished during political instability and violence. Rape has been used as a weapon of war, and soldiers have wantonly spread the disease. Decades of warfare have wrecked existing medical facilities and other structures in places like Uganda, Sierra Leone, and the Congo. Money has been diverted from health care to warfare.

The United States clearly prioritized the elimination of Saddam Hussein over defeating global HIV/AIDS in 2003. Critics noted that President George W. Bush was willing to spend seemingly any amount in Iraq, but offered only $15 billion over five years for HIV/AIDS in Africa and the Caribbean. Even as Bush was publicizing this offer in a presidential trip to Africa, Congress was attempting to reduce the amount for the first year. For comparison purposes, it should be noted that the Defense Department acknowledged that it was costing the United States $1 billion a week to sustain the occupation of Iraq (others claimed it was more like $2 or $3 billion). Meanwhile, the $10 billion UN Fund to fight HIV/AIDS, tuberculosis, and malaria languished.[37]

These are only six of the obstacles that make universal ARV treatment unavailable, and it is our responsibility to help destroy these stumbling blocks. As the rock star Bono keeps reminding Christian audiences and political gatherings: "We have the drugs but we're not sharing them. I believe history and God will be our judge on this one."[38]

Saving Grace

Grace Matnanga, age thirty, a shoe seller in Lilongwe, Malawi, may soon become yet another AIDS death statistic. First her husband died and then her daughter, Tiyajane, succumbed to AIDS: "When she died, aged three, she was a pitiful, wasted scrap, the ulcers in her throat and mouth making the pain of swallowing more vicious than the pangs of hunger."[39]

If she lived in London or Chicago, Grace could survive, thanks to modern medicine, but she is on the downward dance of death because her fate is to live in Malawi, Africa. She knows anti-retroviral drugs exist and can be purchased for about twenty-eight (U.S.) dollars per month—a greatly reduced figure but an unimaginable sum in a country where the per capita income is only $178. She is a hard-working, attractive, conscientious young woman, quite willing to follow the necessary regime of treatment. She could continue to be a contributing citizen and even adopt orphans into a loving home. But as long as there is no concerted effort to save Grace—and the many Graces of the Two-Thirds World—she is destined to die an early death. Only 1 percent of HIV-positive Africans receive the latest medical treatment; like the other 99 percent, Grace waits and waits as suffering increases and death creeps closer.

Bob Dylan sings confidently that he has been kept from "sleeping in a pine box for all eternity" because of the "saving grace that's over me."[40] The Grace Matnangas of this world do not know Bob Dylan or his music, but his words reflect their fervent prayer.

When Christians speak or sing of God's "saving grace," let us think of Grace Matnanga, and how we might be God's saving grace for her. Caring, testing, counseling, and treatment are integrally related to education and prevention. Her story is the story of every person struggling to live with HIV/AIDS and yearning for life and hope. As compassionate people, Christians can make a difference even for those who find themselves living on the wrong side of the global divide.

9

Global Hope in a Global Emergency

Churches cannot conquer AIDS alone, but it will not happen without us.

—Bishop Felton E. May

A familiar contemporary image of Christian mission and ministry— the "star thrower"—was created by the poet-scientist, Loren Eiseley.[1] It is based on a story that goes something like this: He spotted a man on an unidentified beach in Mexico who was reaching down beside the breaking surf, picking up something, and tossing it back into the ocean. His visitor chided him that tossing a few starfish was ridiculous, since "There are thousands of miles of beach and millions of starfish. You can't possibly believe that what you're doing could possibly make a difference!" In response, the star thrower picked up another starfish, tossed it into the waves, and said, "It makes a difference to this one."

The star thrower stands in opposition to the entire inclination of contemporary culture. In it, hope rather than despair dominates. Life rather than death prevails. The strong reach out to save, not to crush. All cannot be rescued, but since some can, the star throwers of this world continue spinning living starfish beyond the danger points. In this existential essay, Eiseley rejected his evolutionary "survival of the fittest" perspective and joined in the work of the star thrower, not as a scientist but as a fellow sufferer. Parker J. Palmer speculates: "Is there a star thrower at work in the universe, a God who contradicts death, a God whose nature (in the words of Thomas Merton) is 'mercy within mercy within mercy'?"

In confronting the global HIV/AIDS emergency, I believe God is calling each of us to be star throwers—Christians committed to valuing every life, saving and preserving every precious member of God's family despite the difficulties and against all odds. God calls us not only individually to save lives, but also to be a church of star throwers, joining with the whole human race. In the words of Pope John Paul II: "AIDS threatens not just some nations or societies but the whole of humanity. It knows no frontiers of geography, race, age or social condition. The threat is so great, indifference on the part of public authorities, condemnatory or discriminatory practices toward those affected by the virus or self-interested rivalries in the search for a medical answer, should be considered forms of collaboration in this terrible evil which has come upon humanity."[2]

Christian star throwers never accept a vision of defeat and death, but instead are aficionados of love and life, hope and health. What distinguishes the church from many other human organizations is its relentless commitment to compassion and its unconditional love for every human being. The Christian church has never accepted common definitions of "reality." Had we done so, the apostles never would have left Jerusalem, taking the gospel to six continents. If Christians had been realistic, they never would have sent out missionaries with the intent of conquering hunger, defeating illiteracy, translating the Bible into every language, upgrading the status of women and children in every culture, starting new churches, or challenging every disease on earth.

Any sane analysis of statistics would demonstrate that throughout history the problems have always been too great and the resources of the faithful too small. Star throwers are distinguished, however, by their ability to see beyond the ordinary, hope beyond the usual, and act beyond what is expected. In that spirit of faith some Christians around the world are beginning to address the global AIDS pandemic—knowing that God is leading them into the heart of suffering because we worship a God who is an aficionado of love and life, hope and health. We affirm with the Talmud: "If you save one life, you save the whole world."

Awakening a Sleeping Church

Preceding chapters have described the scientific quest for vaccines, new prophylactics, and palliative solutions. Clearly the best minds of the medical world are engaged in the struggle to end HIV/AIDS. Countless non-governmental organizations and foundations are making AIDS a priority health concern. Governments are slowly but surely responding to the leadership of the United Nations (UN) as they address this new global emergency. For example, the new president of Kenya, Mwai Kibaki, has proclaimed a "total war on AIDS" after twenty-four years of denial and inaction by his predecessor.[3] UN Secretary-General Kofi Annan says hopefully, "The people are speaking out now, the conspiracy of silence is broken. . . . "[4]

What is still essentially sleeping on the sideline is the Christian church. Most communities of faith have not yet awakened to the cries of human need or the call of God. When will we Christians, like Jacob, awake from our sleep and say as Jacob did: "Surely the Lord is in this place—and I did not know it" (Genesis 28:16)? God is already at work in loving and liberating ways to rid the world of the HIV virus that is antithetical to God's kingdom on earth. But most of his disciples are sleeping like Jacob in Bethel and Peter and the disciples in the Garden of Gethsemane (Mark 14:37-41).

Despite the urgency of the situation—on the eve of Christ's betrayal and crucifixion—it took three urgent pleas from Jesus to awaken his disciples from their slumber. Twenty years into the pandemic, with some 46 million people infected and at least another 20 million dead—the church has not yet truly responded to the alarm clock of human need or the insistent tugging of the Holy Spirit. But perhaps it is too soon to despair. If it took Jesus three appeals to his faithful apostles, it is likely to take many more to rouse the contemporary church.

The theological task facing the church and seminaries has only just begun. Theologian Edward P. Antonio from Zimbabwe suggests that HIV/AIDS challenges Christian theological thought at many deep levels. Theology must raise important questions about the meaning of life in the face of a disease where there is no "exit visa"; the idea of a loving God amid such global suffering; the sacredness of death when it becomes so commonplace, especially among the young; confidence in modern medicine and science; and the nature of human love and sexuality, when it is in the very act of "making love" that people get infected.

Antonio presses Christians not to be too quick in giving standard answers, but to probe deeply, not letting the church or God "off the hook too quickly." He believes that "Christian hope is founded not only on an affirmation of life, but on the premise of struggling for promoting and preserving life."[5]

A Liturgical Response to the Global Emergency

Slowly the ecumenical church worldwide has begun to respond positively to the crisis. Certain liturgical steps are needed on the journey from indifference to involvement, condemnation to compassion. In *AIDS: The Spiritual Dilemma*, John E. Fortunato noted that theologically there is no ready *answer* to the mystery of this pandemic: "no logical explanation for the pain of those dying, for the fear of those who are ill, for the grief of those left behind." But there must be a *response*.

> We must love each other through this—bearing one another's pain and affirming for each the promise that neither death nor life; nor angels, nor principalities; neither things present, nor things to come; neither Kaposi's nor pneumocystis, nor any syndrome nor anguish nor pain, nor the hatred of those who fear us; nor anything else in all creation, can separate us from the love of God or keep us from the kingdom prepared for us from the beginning of the world.[6]

Confession

Confession needs to be the first liturgical step in the church's constructive engagement with HIV/AIDS. Honesty and humility dictate that the church not pretend it has been in the forefront of the fight against HIV/AIDS in the world. We have been moral laggards in the struggle, not only failing to contribute our substantial resources and energy, but worse yet, often creating pain and prejudice for the infected and posting roadblocks for public health officials.

Let us candidly confess that gay and lesbian persons in the United States, a group that has suffered immensely from the church's discriminatory teachings and treatment, consistently provided early and faithful leadership. They often demonstrated more love and shared more grace than those who specifically claim the name of Christ. Likewise, globally, people living with HIV/AIDS, though stigmatized and sinned against, have repeatedly provided the key leadership necessary to move countries and cultures to address this pandemic. Yet they have been repeatedly overlooked as essential partners and need empowerment in helping the world address this health emergency.[7]

Confession includes both the ecumenical and the evangelical wings of the church. Few have been as open as Terry Wortz, MD, the United Methodist medical director of the Mission Society, who admitted that during a Samaritan's Purse Conference on AIDS, "I repented on my behalf and on behalf of the Mission Society. We have done almost nothing to fight the HIV/AIDS crisis. I prayed that God would give me a vision for how we can help."[8] That would be a fitting prayer for most Christians to utter, regardless of denominational label or theological persuasion. At a Pan-African Lutheran Church Leadership Consultation, people were very explicit:

> We, . . . publicly confess and acknowledge that we have too often contributed to stigmatization and discrimination and that our churches have not always been safe or welcome places for people living with or affected by HIV/AIDS. In some cases Holy Communion has been refused to people living with HIV/AIDS, funerals for people having died from AIDS have been denied, and comfort to the bereaved has not been given. We repent of these sins. We therefore commit ourselves to a faithful and courageous response in

breaking the silence, speaking openly and truthfully about
human sexuality and HIV/AIDS.[9]

At an ecumenical assembly of the South African Christian Leadership Assembly, people acknowledged that as the church of Christ, we
are called to "repent of our past mistakes, and open ourselves to new
directions in which God is leading us."[10] In Mozambique a prayer of
confession declares:

> We confess that the Church has not acted promptly or
> positively to the challenges brought by HIV/AIDS in this
> country.
> We confess that the Church has rejected when it should
> have embraced and judged when it should have shown
> love, compassion, and care.[11]

Changing Our Behavior

Changing our behavior needs to be the second liturgical step in the
church's constructive engagement with HIV/AIDS. The church traditionally asks others to change their behavior. We are quick with moral
solutions and boldly assert sexual prohibitions. We have condemned
others for failing to live up to their own best impulses and highest
norms, but quite frankly the church has fallen far short of its noble
ideals of forgiveness, compassion, and unconditional love. Can the
church itself experience behavior change or just ask others to change?

At their best, every faith community manifests the values of love,
forgiveness, and healing in the way it encourages and ensures supportive care and relationships for people experiencing ill health. Individuals and their families suffering from HIV/AIDS provide a special
opportunity for religious leaders, theological educators, and other
people of the faith to demonstrate how their beliefs graciously
embrace and spiritually transform the human condition in times of
sickness and even death.

Unfortunately, however, Christianity repeatedly has failed to offer
healing care and nurturing relationships. Sometimes adherents have
been mean-spirited and theologically hardhearted, even suggesting,
"AIDS represents the judgment of God." Fortunately, however,
visionary people of faith, who have sought to incarnate their faith in
loving, forgiving, and healing actions, have helped offset these
extreme reactions.

Watching the language we use can be a practical manifestation of changed behavior. Words can heal or hurt, be inclusive or exclusive. The way we speak reflects our own thinking and feelings and can shape the attitudes and actions of others. Avoiding language that is judgmental and stigmatizing is essential. People living with HIV/AIDS prefer to be identified as HIV-positive persons rather than as "victims." Likewise, it is an affront to speak of "innocent victims" since nobody chooses to have HIV and, further, it implies guilt. Beware also of value-laden words like "promiscuous" and "prostitute," as they convey accusatory and derogatory perspectives. Terms like "homosexual" and "gay" are problematic in various areas of the world as they suggest an identity or lifestyle that means something different in the Western world than in Africa or Asia. Thus the phrase "men who have sex with men" or "MSM" increasingly appears in discussions and literature about global AIDS. Language, of course, has limits, and "political correctness" can become absurd, so I am not trying to censor but to sensitize Christians to speak in terms that reflect the spirit of their loving hearts.

Changed behavior may mean staying out of the way if we cannot provide a message of hope, a gift of loving care, or a theology of life. Let us spare the world our self-righteous judgment, remembering Jesus' admonition to look for the beams in our own eyes rather than for the specks in others.

Maake Masango tells how, when his cousin was dying of AIDS, he told the family that he wanted the truth told at his funeral. A service was planned to celebrate his life and to educate the youth who attended. During the service, his grandmother walked to front of the African church and placed her hand on her grandson's coffin. "My grandson," she declared, "no longer has to suffer with AIDS." Turning to the pulpit, she addressed the pastor who was about to preach. "Now talk to them freely about this disease. To us it is not a shame."[12] She broke a conspiracy of silence.

Commitment
Third, Christians are called to commitment. This liturgical step means more than writing additional resolutions, as good and needed as they may be. Translated into common parlance, it means to "walk our talk" or to "put our money where our mouth is." In the ritual language of the Eucharist, it means to respond positively and personally to the invitation: "Ye that do truly and earnestly repent of your sins,

and are in love and charity with your neighbors, and intend to lead a new life, . . . Draw near with faith. . . . "[13]

Leading "a new life" in mission and ministry will prompt Christian laity and clergy to become involved in this global emergency in practical ways. Practical possibilities are endless and vary depending on context, culture, and circumstance. Some possibilities for Christians include:

- Reaching out personally to HIV-infected people and their families with loving care and supportive relationships
- Preparing teams of people in every congregation that can help HIV-infected people and their affected families
- Speaking formally and informally on the subject of HIV/AIDS, especially denouncing the sins of stigmatization and discrimination
- Supporting volunteer AIDS mission experiences that work in partnership with Christians in other countries
- Reshaping denominational and local church budgets to make global HIV/AIDS ministry a high priority
- Encouraging people to live out their faith by becoming involved as scientists, health professionals, medical missionaries, etc., as a vocation or avocation
- Supporting secular and government leaders and organizations in their work for social justice, human rights, and medical advances

This listing, of course, is but a beginning. Later in this chapter, additional illustrations are cited of how Christian commitment currently is being manifested in response to this global emergency.

Courage

Integral to all these steps is a fourth: courage. If churches are to break the conspiracy of silence and to break forth in new ways of mission and ministry, then courageous leaders, lay and clergy, will need to step forth. Fearful silence kills. Preachers need to address HIV/AIDS regularly in their sermons. Young people must be provided educational opportunities to learn about HIV/AIDS. Churches need to reprioritize their budgets and get involved. Stigma and discrimination must be denounced as sins.

This will not happen without persistent and courageous leadership. Biblical scholar William Barclay has noted that the early church was not afraid to take risks of compassion for Christ's sake. In his commentary on Philippians, he writes:

> In the days of the early Christian Church there was an association of men and women called the *parabolani*, the "gamblers." It was their aim and object to visit the prisoners and the sick, especially those who were ill with dangerous and infectious diseases. In A.D. 252, plague broke out in Carthage; the heathen threw out the bodies of their dead, and fled in terror. Cyprian, the Christian bishop, gathered his congregation together and set them to burying the dead and nursing the sick in that plague-stricken city; and by so doing they saved the city, at the risk of their lives, from destruction and desolation. There should be in the Christian an almost reckless courage which is ready to gamble with his life to serve Christ and to serve men. The Church always needs the *parabolani*, the "gamblers" of Christ.[14]

Gambling with one's life is not necessary at this stage of the HIV/AIDS pandemic. By taking reasonable and limited precautions, one can be involved deeply in direct caring and compassionate ministry with infected people without also getting infected. The "gambling" is more in the arena of speaking out, to be identified with people with HIV/AIDS, and to risk one's personal reputation or professional career by being an advocate on this issue and for people who are marginalized and "sinned against." With the great theologian Reinhold Niebuhr, we need to pray for "courage to change the things I can." Too often we are simply satisfied to pray for "the serenity to accept the things I cannot change."[15]

Community

Along with confession, change, commitment, and courage, the fifth liturgical step in the journey of global hope during this global emergency is to embrace a new sense of community. Christian commitment does not mean unilateral initiatives and pious proclamations, but finding new ways of working in partnership with government and non-governmental organizations, people living with HIV/AIDS, people of other religions and other theological persuasions.

Joining hands to fight this disease means moving beyond a provincial perspective to a global spirituality that embraces the whole human family. Christians may need to read anew Albert Camus's book, *The Plague*, especially when Doctor Rieux, an atheist, says to Father Paneloux the priest: "What I hate is death and disease as you well know, and whether you wish it or not we are allies facing death and disease and fighting them together."[16]

AIDS may eventually even transform international politics, predicts futurist John Platt, who envisions the disease uniting countries in a "life-and-death interest that laughs at the nation-state." His optimistic, even utopian, vision, suggests that a "New Deal will be called for . . . paid by canceling other expensive projects—big science, fusion power, space stations, the Strategic Defense Initiative—that will seem increasingly irrelevant in a world dominated by AIDS. . . . The challenge of coping with AIDS at all levels could give the world a new sense of planet-wide interdependence and responsibility for human survival."[17]

The HIV/AIDS global epidemic is a call not only for Christians to respond but also for the great world religions to find ways to work together. There are limited, but encouraging, signs from around the world that faith-based groups can work together. In sub-Saharan Africa, Muslim and Christian organizations have found ways together of communicating to the public about prevention. Speaking to an interfaith religious leadership assembly in Africa, Stephen Lewis, a special envoy of the UN Secretary-General, asked: "Who else is so well-placed to lead? Who else has such a network of voices at the grass-roots level? Who else has access to all communities once a week, every week, across the continent? Who else officiates at the millions of funerals of those who die of AIDS-related illnesses, and better understands the consequences for children and families? Who else works on a daily basis with faith-based, community-based organizations?"[18] The answer, of course, is faith-based groups, including Christian, Muslim, Ba'hai, Hindu, Buddhist, Jewish, Animist, and so forth.

Globalization partly means that we currently inhabit the "world house" Martin Luther King Jr. long ago envisioned. A Christian sense of community can no longer be confined by parochial and prejudicial boundaries that limit our message of health and hope for God's family. In the clear but simple words of Mother Teresa, interfaith works of love reflect the deepest spiritual expressions of our religions:

> Christians, Muslim, Hindus, believers and nonbelievers
>> have the opportunity with us to do works of love
>> have the opportunity with us to share the joy of
>>> loving and come to realize God's presence.
> Hindus become better Hindus.
> Catholics become better Catholics
> Muslims become better Muslims.[19]

Signs of Global Hope

After more than two decades of inaction and indifference, there are signs of hope that the Christian community is beginning to hear the call of God and the cries of God's people. Of course, motivations for involvement are mixed, but God seems to work in human life and politics despite our human limitations and weaknesses.

Belatedly, for example, Christians are recognizing that the body of Christ has AIDS. As Gillian Paterson notes, "Christians are dying, clergy are dying, church leaders are dying. AIDS is not just happening 'out there', and to 'other people': at every level, the Church itself is living with and affected by HIV."[20]

President George W. Bush proposed spending $15 billion on AIDS in Africa and the Caribbean, thanks to the influence of an unlikely coalition of Christian evangelicals and liberal activists. The *Washington Post* reports that evangelicals with deep commitments to "missions in Africa" are important to Bush's political base and his desire to promote himself as a "compassionate conservative."[21] On his 2003 trip to five African countries, Bush repeatedly asserted that Americans were a compassionate people and that "the average citizen cares deeply about the fact that people are dying in record numbers because of HIV/AIDS."[22] Critics correctly noted that his promised $15 billion was insufficient to meet the overwhelming global need, but in fact the president was far ahead of most Americans in terms of compassion and action. Hopefully, he has helped to move the debate to center political stage and church leaders of all persuasions will continue to pressure for greater financial support.

The church's witness in the social justice arena will be greater if it demonstrates that it is ready to take some risks and make some sacrifices to combat this devastating disease. For example, the founder of Methodism, John Wesley, was a great advocate of encouraging governments to act on social causes. However, he did not think government inaction was any excuse for the church to remain uninvolved. He had no hesitancy in chastising governments and society for their failures. "But," as Theodore Runyon has noted, "Wesley did not wait for the government to act. Ministering to the poor and their needs was part of the job description of every Methodist."[23]

If that is the Methodist mandate, why haven't Methodists everywhere formed action agencies to reach out in healing ministries to people living with HIV/AIDS? Why hasn't Wesley's slogan, "the world is my parish," translated into an aggressive and compassionate program against global AIDS? As a United Methodist myself, I find it appalling that my own denomination to date has done so little. United Methodists gave nearly $5 billion in 2000 for all purposes, but only an infinitesimal percentage was dedicated to combating global HIV/AIDS. An analysis of other Protestant denominational budgets, whether mainline or evangelical, would unfortunately reveal a similar pattern.

Lest only the negative be underscored, it is critical to highlight some signs of hope as churches around the world increase their involvement. What follows are but a few examples of what has happened. They also are illustrative of what needs to happen in the immediate years ahead in almost every place.

1. Ecumenical HIV/AIDS consultations (conferences) in Chiang Mai, Thailand; Nairobi, Kenya; and elsewhere. In each case, they have issued theological and practical documents calling the church to action. They have spoken both pastorally and prophetically to the issues facing women, youth, and children, that is, of making antiretroviral treatment available, of eliminating suffocating debt repayments, etc.

2. A comprehensive Global Lutheran World Federation Campaign against HIV/AIDS aimed at empowering local congregations to become healing communities, promoting prevention, reaching out

to orphans, and addressing stigma and discrimination. In Namibia, where Lutherans make up 50 percent of the population, the bishop urged every Lutheran congregation to create a village AIDS committee focusing on home-based care, youth education, and outreach to orphans.[24]

3. The Church of South India has encouraged all twenty national dioceses to initiate programs to address the issues of HIV/AIDS at the local congregation level. Projects have focused on awareness, testing, counseling, and a mobile health unit.

4. The Salvation Army in India has, for more than a decade, worked closely with people living with HIV/AIDS, standing in solidarity with those facing stigmatization and discrimination. The Army has emphasized home care and created special outreach programs to sex workers and their children.

5. The Anglican churches of Africa have spoken and acted boldly to combat HIV/AIDS. In Uganda the church seeks to end discrimination and stigmatization with a strategic program of welcoming people living with HIV/AIDS into the church. In Nigeria clergy and bishops are being educated in the areas of pastoral care and support. In Kenya voluntary counseling and testing kits are provided by church-based clinics. The efficacy of condoms has been openly discussed and endorsed by the church in Tanzania. Peer-education programs for youth along with AIDS prevention training for Sunday school teachers characterize Anglican work in Ghana. Thousands and thousands of women volunteers are providing compassionate support for people who are sick and dying.

6. The National Council of Churches of India held a training workshop for all its member churches and set forth an ambitious program for education, prevention, care, and treatment. The theological schools of India are creating a theological curriculum to educate future pastors for AIDS mission and ministry.

7. Throughout the world, Catholic bishops have been adopting HIV/AIDS policies. As the Nigerian Catholic bishops declared, "In today's world there are only two categories: those infected and those affected by HIV/AIDS." Catholic Health Services in Nigeria is "committed to administering the 'medicine of love' to all infected and affected by HIV/AIDS."

8. The Inter-Religious Council of Uganda (Anglican, Muslim, Roman Catholic, Protestant, and Orthodox) has developed a five-

year strategic plan and program, focusing especially on orphans and prevention.

9. The United Methodist Board of Global Ministries has established in Zimbabwe an orphanage and sponsored educational awareness and prevention programs targeted at youth. United Methodists in Africa, Asia, Latin America, and the Caribbean are training community-based primary health care teams. They have also joined other Christians in lobbying the United States Congress for greater funding to fight AIDS.

10. Campus Crusade, World Vision, and Samaritan's Purse have increased their commitment to AIDS education and prevention, with special emphasis on programs of abstinence and fidelity in marriage. Franklin Graham challenged evangelical Christians to attack AIDS "with the same level of commitment, zeal, money, and resources that we have rightly applied toward combating international terrorism."[25]

11. Presbyterians are distributing home-care kits for AIDS patients in Africa who don't have access to medical care. Presbyterian congregations are paired with African counterparts, and the Presbyterian Church, U.S.A., has increased funding for global AIDS at a time when the denomination has generally been reducing its expenditures.

12. The Methodist Church of Southern Africa has promoted frank discussion of sex and HIV/AIDS, created poverty relief programs for affected households, and promoted anti-retroviral medicine to prevent mother-child transmission. Fundamental to their strategy and implementation plan is the belief that "HIV/AIDS is not the judgment of God on the infected, but an opportunity for Methodists to love and care for the affected."[26]

13. Roman Catholics in South Africa have sought to provide theological reflection for the AIDS pandemic. A book, *Responsibility in a Time of AIDS,* resulted from a conference in which theologians and laity wrestled with the complexities of moral teachings and the tragedy unfolding in their society. In particular, they have sought to defuse the negative "condom controversy" articulated by their bishops and instead focused on ways the church can be involved in prevention and care.[27]

Hopeful Models: Partnerships to Save Lives

A particularly hopeful model for Christian involvement has been developed by the Global AIDS Interfaith Alliance. It is aimed at mobilizing congregations in a partnership to save lives. By connecting African and American local communities of faith, it builds a bridge of hope in the struggle against HIV/AIDS.

This particular project focused on Malawi, Africa. A team traveled there to gather accurate and timely information. During the immersion experience, they met with the Anglican bishop, Catholic Development Commission, missionaries of various faiths, and youth leaders. They visited various HIV/AIDS prevention and care projects, including clinics, orphan care programs, home-based care, women's empowerment, and youth education programs. Special attention was given to the peril of women and children. In total, they identified more than twenty different projects churches could support. With the assistance of photographs and video footage, they were able to vividly share how the pandemic is impacting this beautiful African nation.

At their first conference introducing the possibilities of this partnership, twenty-one congregations were represented. The goals of the conference were to educate participants about the HIV/AIDS crisis in sub-Saharan Africa; learn about the experiences of other congregations that were in partnerships with African projects; and provide details about how to partner to save lives. Drawing upon medical personnel, university professors, foundation officials, church leaders, and others, they shared what was happening in Africa and how communities of faith can make a difference. Congregations were asked to consider supporting projects at the level of at least $5,000 a year over a three-year period. Support for initiating this project was received from The John M. Lloyd Foundation and the William and Gretchen Kimball Fund.

Hopefully, similar denominational and ecumenical models and projects will emerge in the immediate years ahead. My experience working with the Park Hill United Methodist Church in Denver, Colorado, has demonstrated that local congregations are eager to find ways to get involved. In this case, the church working in partnership with projects in India, helped to sponsor workshops at two seminar-

ies, provided Christmas gifts to over 800 forgotten AIDS patients in a
public hospital, and sponsored two women living with HIV as community caregivers. People outside the church also got interested, and
almost an equal number of gifts came from non-members as church
members. In a two-year period, they raised nearly $15,000.

Building upon the Park Hill experience, I was able to get the Rocky
Mountain United Methodist Conference for the first time to commit
funds targeted at global AIDS. In the first year, these funds were used
to sponsor a prison ministry for men with HIV in Russia, an African
orphanage, funds for an outreach program in Namakkal, India, to
stop mother-to-child HIV transmission, and a multi-church Denver
program focused on HIV/AIDS education and prevention in the
African American community. The United Methodist General Board
of Global Ministries and the Iliff School of Theology have supported
my own involvement at the Center for Global Pastoral Ministry.

Of special concern is the need to create an appropriate HIV/AIDS
theological curriculum in every context and country. As the disease
escalates, pastors and seminarians throughout the world are ill prepared to deal with the complex issues of biblical interpretation, theology, pastoral care, community work, and social advocacy.

Theological colleges and seminaries everywhere are overworked
and understaffed. Bound by tradition, they address curriculum change
reluctantly. In the United States we have a saying that it is easier to
move a cemetery than a seminary! However, a model curriculum has
been developed for Africa, and in India the accrediting/degree-grant-
ing Serampore College has begun to outline requirements for the
future. At a day-long seminar in Mizoram, India, with the leadership
of the fifty Protestant and Orthodox leaders of theological institutions, I was greatly encouraged by their willingness to challenge religious and societal "taboos" so they can talk about sexuality in order to
save lives in Christ's name.

The curriculum designed in Africa has five units focusing on
HIV/AIDS: (1) human sexuality, (2) biblical studies, (3) theology, (4)
counseling, and (5) program development. The goals of the curriculum are to:

- Reduce and finally eradicate the spread and impact of
  HIV/AIDS in Africa

- Strengthen the churches' role and capacity to respond to the HIV/AIDS pandemic
- Equip Christian workers with the necessary knowledge, skills, and attitude to serve their churches and society more effectively in the struggle against the HIV/AIDS epidemic
- Increase the capacity of students of theological institutions in designing, implementing, and monitoring of HIV/AIDS prevention, care, and support intervention programs in their communities of work
- Exploit the Christian church's own internal resources and heritage[28]

These various models of constructive engagement—for individuals, local congregations, denominations, and divinity schools—offer hope for a future world without AIDS. South African Archbishop Desmond Tutu once said, during the darkest days of apartheid, that he believed justice and equality would triumph. Asked how he could be so hopeful, he responded that Christians by nature are prisoners of hope. We do not pretend to know how or when AIDS will be conquered, but we are confident that ultimately God's way of life and love, hope and health, will prevail.

Since I fervently believe that global HIV/AIDS is not a "liberal" or an "evangelical" issue, but a call by God to respond to an urgent human crisis with the healing spirit of Jesus Christ, I am hopeful that congregations, denominations, ecumenical organizations, and other faith-based community initiatives will discover creative involvement. Mission takes on new meaning in our time as

- We begin to acknowledge that we are all HIV-positive and that the body of Christ has AIDS.
- Local congregations, conferences, dioceses, etc., identify and create global partnerships for mutual HIV/AIDS ministry.
- Christians work together ecumenically to address urgent health needs such as HIV/AIDS, malaria, and tuberculosis.
- People and congregations invest their money, intellect, energy, and time in addressing this global pandemic.
- The church becomes an advocate for social justice, particularly related to increasing governmental and non-governmental

funding and issues regarding the role of pharmaceutical companies.

- Individuals and congregations broaden their spiritual life to pray for those infected and affected by HIV/AIDS.
- People begin to become personally involved in God's liberating and loving ministry of healing in the world.

Faith, Hope, and Love

This call for personal involvement in God's liberating and loving ministry of healing is ultimately why this book has been written. Readers are invited to go beyond just understanding the global pandemic and to ponder how they can personally make a difference. Compassionate people inevitably find practical ways to care. It is an invitation to become a star thrower that refuses to accept a vision of defeat and death, but instead becomes an aficionado of love and life, hope and health.

The biographers of Francis of Assisi report he was a fastidious young man. He was especially afraid of leprosy and lepers. When he saw a leper, he literally would hold his nose and send a messenger to give his alms. One day, just at the beginning point of his conversion, he unexpectedly met a leper. He started to recoil, but then remembering his newfound Christian faith, it is said that "he slipped off his horse and ran to kiss the man. When the leper put out his hand as if to receive some alms, Francis gave him money and a kiss."[29] In doing so, he rediscovered Christ.

In becoming compassionate Christian companions of people with AIDS, we too have a chance of rediscovering Christ. In Paul's immortal words in 1 Corinthians 13, it is faith, hope, and love that characterize being a Christian. Christian faith calls us to work on the medical frontiers, stand in solidarity with the suffering, promote prevention and treatment, and struggle to raise the status of women everywhere. Christian hope demands our political involvement in matters of social justice and to envision a world without HIV/AIDS. Christian love prompts us to speak out against stigmatization and discrimination, living lives of compassion and caring. Mother Teresa, when asked how she maintained hope amid death and poverty, replied that "we must always realize that we can do no great things, only small things with great love."

Love, however, is never abstract, but always personal. It becomes incarnated when we pull ourselves close to the bedside of a loved one and seek to provide care and compassion. Love is when we hold their hand and share their pain. Love is when they say they are thirsty and we lift the straw to their lips. Love is when they feel sick and we fetch a basin, wrap an arm around their spasm-wracked shoulders, and wipe the sweat from their forehead.

Love is not some sexy movie star or romantic film scene, but love is when we say, "Let me help you sit up." Ultimately "love is not a smoldering glance across the dance floor, the clink of crystal, a leisurely picnic spread upon a sandy beach. It is the squeeze of a hand." It is saying: "I'm here. I'll be here no matter how long the struggle. Water? You need water? Here. Drink. Let me straighten your pillow."[30]

In an age of incredible suffering, let us personally join God's merciful angels in loving and caring and healing. Doing so will be a way of visiting the sick as Jesus commanded (Matthew 25:36). It will be discovering a "means of grace" as deeply spiritual and meaningful as partaking in Holy Communion or being baptized.[31] It will be experiencing anew the splendor of God's grace. Yes, as we do it to "one of the least" of God's children, we will be doing it to Christ.

Appendix

Avoiding HIV/AIDS

What follows is a short summary of how one can and cannot get the HIV virus. Many other more detailed lists are available by contacting various AIDS agencies or checking Web sites such as those listed in chapter 1.

These lists are designed to provide helpful information to persons so they can avoid the disease and yet provide helpful care, companionship, and compassion to those already infected. It should be noted that there is no such activity as "safe" sex—all of life has an element of risk, but it is possible to have "safer sex" by substantially reducing the likelihood of HIV infection. The transmission of HIV and these guidelines apply equally to all persons, regardless of sexual orientation.

You Cannot Get HIV by:
- Casual contact through sneezes, coughs, toilet seats, eating utensils, telephones, hand shaking, dry kissing, touching, hugging, and massage
- Insect bites
- Masturbation
- Abstinence from sex

You Could Get HIV by:

- Having unprotected vaginal, anal, or oral sex (that is, without a latex condom) with a person who has the virus (Condoms, however, can break or tear, thereby eliminating protection.)
- Infected semen, urine, or blood in open skin wounds
- Sharing injection needles with a person who has the virus
- Getting blood or blood products that have the virus
- Engaging in mouth-to-mouth wet kissing with an infected person
- An infected mother passing the virus to her baby during pregnancy, during birth, or after birth through breast feeding
- Reusing condoms or sharing dildos or other sex toys

Notes

Introduction

1. Sean O'Casey, *Drums of Father Ned,* act III, 1958.

2. Robert McAfee Brown, ed., *Karios: Three Prophetic Challenges to the Church* (Grand Rapids: Eerdmans, 1990), 3.

3. See Emil Brenner, *The Word and the Church* (London: SCM, 1931), 108.

4. D. T. Niles, quoted in Donald E. Messer, *A Conspiracy of Goodness: Contemporary Images of Christian Mission* (Nashville: Abingdon, 1992), 27.

5. Kofi Annan (opening statement, International Partnership Against HIV/AIDS in Africa, New York City, December 6–7, 1999). Annan has repeated this perspective and phrase in many speeches.

6. Ibid.

7. "Pan-African Lutheran Church Leaders Committed to 'Breaking the Silence,'" Lutheran World Federation Global Campaign against HIV/AIDS. Launched July 5, 2002. Available at http://www.lutheranworld.org/News/LWI/EN/972.EN.html.

8. Ronald Nicolson, *God in AIDS?* (London: SCM, 1996), 10.

9. Bonginjalo Goba, *The AIDS Pandemic in Uganda and Tanzania* (Cape Town: Centre for South-South Relations, 1995), quoted in Nicolson, *God in AIDS?* 10.

10. Mother Teresa, quoted in Michael J. Christensen, *The Samaritan's Imperative: Compassionate Ministry to People Living with AIDS* (Nashville: Abingdon, 1991), 197.

11. This section benefits from Gerald J. Stine, *AIDS Update 2002* (Upper Saddle River, N.J.: Prentice Hall, 2002), 24–31.

1. The Church and Global AIDS

1. N. M. Samuel, personal communication.

2. The declaration was endorsed in a UN General Assembly special session (June 2001), "Global Crisis—Global Action." See http://www.un.org/ga/aids/coverage/.

3. United Nations, *Declaration of Commitment on HIV/AIDS, A/s-26/L.2* (New York, 2001), sec. 2, http://www.un.org/ga/aids/coverage/FinalDeclarationHIVAIDS.html.

4. Quoted in Christopher S. Wren, "Powell, at U.N., Asks War on AIDS," *New York Times,* June 26, 2001, www.newyorktimes.com. See also http://www.un.org/ga/aids/statements/docs/usaE.html.

5. Gerald J. Stine, *AIDS Update 2002* (Upper Saddle River, N.J.: Prentice Hall, 2002), xxiii.

6. Excerpt from a statement presented by Bishop Felton Edwin May to the House International Task Force on HIV-AIDS Congressional Briefing, Feb. 26, Rayburn House Office Building, Washington, D.C. See also http://www.bwconf.org/BWC_News/UMConnection/2002/March20-02issue/DeanCol032902.html.

7. Nontando Hadebe (director of Institute for Contextual Theology, South Africa), e-mail message to author, July 20, 2001.

8. Kevin Sack, "Epidemic Takes Toll on Black Women," *New York Times*, July 3, 2001, www.newyorktimes.com.

9. Bob Herbert, "A Black AIDS Epidemic," *New York Times*, June 4, 2001, www.newyorktimes.com.

10. Quoted in Wren, "Powell, at U.N."

11. Quoted in Sabin Russell, "AIDS Meeting Opens with Conflict/Dispute over Gay Speaker—Delays U.N. Conference," *San Francisco Chronicle*, June 26, 2001.

12. Quoted at http: http://www.guardian.co.uk/comment/story/0,3604,531453,00.html by Pieter-Dirk Uys "AIDS is a Laughing Matter," *The Guardian,* August 3, 2001.

13. Ibid.

14. The Balm in Gilead, "AIDS Facts—Kenya," http://www.balmingilead.org/aidsfacts/aidsfacts_kenya.asp.

15. Pascoal Mocumbi, "A Time for Frankness on AIDS and Africa," *New York Times*, June 20, 2001, www.newyorktimes.com.

16. Ibid.

17. U.S. National Intelligence Council (NIC), *The Next Wave of HIV/AIDS: Nigeria, Ethiopia, Russia, India, and China*, Washington, D.C., September 2002, 8.

18. Ibid., 24.

19. Seth Mydans, "Fighting AIDS: A New War Is Killing Cambodians," *New York Times,* July 7, 2001, www.newyorktimes.com.

20. http://www.globalfamilydoctor.com/publications/news/december/10.htm.

21. NIC, *The Next Wave of HIV/AIDS*, 4. See also Elisabeth Rosenthal, "China Now Facing an AIDS Epidemic, a Top Aide Admits," *New York Times*, August 24, 2001, www.newyorktimes.com.

22. NIC, *The Next Wave of HIV/AIDS*, 16, indicates that "Chinese media report that people selling blood in Qinghai, Henan, and Shaanxi claim that they earn between $12 and $25 for each bag of donated blood—a large sum of money in these poor provinces. Some farmers report donating blood 50 times in two months."

23. Richard Feachem, *Global Fund Observer Newsletter,* no. 2, Aidspan, January 10, 2003, www.aidspan.org/gfo/archives/newsletter/issue2.htm.

24. Bill Gates, "Slowing the Spread of AIDS in India," *New York Times*, November 9, 2002.

25. NIC, *The Next Wave of HIV/AIDS,* 12.

26. Michael Wines, "Rise of H.I.V. in Russia Is Quickening, Official Says," *New York Times*, May 22, 2003, A11.

27. Estimates vary widely, depending on source and methods of calculation. A widely used source for estimated number of people living with HIV/AIDS is the UNAIDS/WHO Epidemiological Fact Sheet, which can be obtained by an Internet search and will provide their latest estimates and reports. See also http://www.avert.org/uksummary.htm.

28. Feachem, *Global Fund Observer,* no. 2.

29. Ray Martin, e-mail message to author, March 6, 2003. Support for the parentless children can be provided by sending a donation to Syamalevwe Children, Global Health Council, 20 Palmer Court, White River Junction, Vermont 05001.

30. George F. MacLeod, *Only One Way Left: Church Prospect* (Glasgow: Iona Community, 1956).

31. This edited paragraph and the remainder of this section draws upon my essay, "Homosexuality and Ecclesiology," first presented to the United Methodist Council of Bishops in Minneapolis, May 2, 2002. It was first published in *Focus*, Boston University School of Theology (fall 2002): 10ff.

32. Peter C. Hodgson, *Revisioning the Church: Ecclesial Freedom in the New Paradigm* (Philadelphia: Fortress Press, 1988), 39.

33. Ibid. Hodgson claims that "on the basis of the inclusion of women, the inclusion of marginalized groups who were not present or visible in the time of Jesus, such as racial minorities or homosexuals, must also be affirmed."

34. See Dietrich Bonhoeffer, *The Communion of Saints: A Dogmatic Inquiry into the Sociology of the Church* (New York: Harper & Row, 1963), 86, 146–47.

35. Richard B. Hays, "Awaiting the Redemption of our Bodies," in *Virtues & Practices in the Christian Tradition: Christian Ethics after MacIntyre,* ed. Nancey Murphy, Brad J. Kallenberg, and Mark Thiessen Nation (Harrisburg, Pa.: Trinity Press International, 1997), 211.

36. Luke Timothy Johnson, "Debate and Discernment, Scripture and the Spirit," in Hays, *Virtues and Practices,* 217.

37. Ibid., 215.

38. World Council of Churches, "Plan of Action: The Ecumenical Response to HIV/AIDS in Africa" (Global Consultation on the Ecumenical Response to the Challenge of HIV/AIDS in Africa, Nairobi, Kenya, November 25–28, 2001), 2.

39. Martin Luther King Jr., *Where Do We Go from Here: Chaos or Community?* (Boston: Beacon, 1967), 167.

40. Mother Teresa, *Words to Love By* (Notre Dame: Ave Maria, 1983), 79.

2. We Are All HIV-positive

1. John Howard Griffin, *Black Like Me* (Boston: Houghton Mifflin, 1961).

2. Gerald J. Stine, *Aids Update 2002* (Upper Saddle River, N.J.: Prentice Hall, 2002), 10. See Arthur Ashe, *A Hard Road to Glory: A History of the African-American Athlete* (New York: Warner Books, 1988).

3. The trilogy of *The Masque of the Red Death* includes *The Divine Punishment, Saint of the Pit,* and *You Must Be Certain of the Devil,* all released between 1986 and 1998. Her brother, Philip-Dimitri Galás, died in 1986 from AIDS.

4. Daniel J. Baxter, *The Least of These My Brethren: A Doctor's Story of Hope and Miracles on an Inner-City AIDS Ward* (New York: Harmony Books, 1997), 57. Italics in original.

5. Ibid., 57–58. Italics in original.

6. José Ignacio Cabezón, "Meditations on HIV/AIDS," (working paper), Iliff School of Theology, Denver, Colo.

7. Janice A. Burns, *Sarah's Song: A True Story of Love and Courage* (New York: Warner Books, 1995).

8. David Satcher, quoted in "The Faith and Public Health Partnership," *Faith and Health* (winter 1995): 6.

9. See Cindy Patton, *Globalizing AIDS* (Minneapolis: University of Minnesota Press, 2002), 34ff.

10. Ibid., 31.

11. Christian Conference of Asia, Hong Kong, "Summary Report," appendix 2 (report, Consultation on AIDS: A Challenge for Religious Response, November 25–30, 2001, Chiang Mai, Thailand), 19–20.

3. Facing and Responding to Sexual Realities

1. For example, see Jeremy Seabrook, *Love in a Different Culture: Men Who Have Sex with Men in India* (London: Verso, 1999); Shivananda Khan, *Safe Sex & Risky Identities* and *Conference Report: Emerging Gay Identities in India—Implications for Sexual Health* (London: Naz, 1995); Arno Schmitt and Jehoeda Sofer, eds., *Sexuality*

and Eroticism among Males in Moslem Societies (Binghamton, N.Y.: Haworth, 1992); William Hoffman, "Here Comes Ashok Row Kavi, the Larry Kramer of India," *POZ* (July 1998); and José Ignacio Cabezón, "Homosexuality and Buddhism," in *Homosexuality and World Religions,* ed. Arlene Swidler (Valley Forge, Pa.: Trinity Press International, 1993).

2. Gillian Paterson, "Church Leadership and HIV/AIDS: The New Commitment," 3. Pdf available at www.e-alliance.ch/media/media-3860.pdf.

3. Heather Snidle, "HIV and AIDS: An Introduction," in *Christ in AIDS: An Educational, Pastoral and Spiritual Approach to HIV/AIDS* (Cardiff: Cardiff Academic), 26.

4. Cathie Lyons, afterword to Terry Boyd's "Living With AIDS: A Personal Journey," by Terry Boyd, Focus Paper #4, AIDS Ministry Network Alert, March 17, 1989, 8.

5. Andres Tapia, "How Churches Can Get Involved," *Christianity Today,* August 7, 1987, 16.

6. Michael J. Christensen, *The Samaritan's Imperative: Compassionate Ministry to People Living with AIDS* (Nashville: Abingdon, 1991), 42.

7. Quoted in Elizabeth Kastor, "The Conflict of a Gay Conservative," *Washington Post,* June 8, 1987, national weekly edition. Regarding the percentage of gay people in the general problem, estimates range from .8 percent to 10 percent, with increased probability of 2–3 percent. Projections vary considerably, as scientific research is difficult due to political reasons, and because people are not necessarily honest or forthcoming in reporting their own sexual behavior.

8. John J. McNeill, *Taking a Chance on God: Liberating Theology for Gays, Lesbians, and Their Lovers, Families, and Friends* (Boston: Beacon, 1988), 38.

9. Melvin E. Wheatley, Open Letter to the United Methodist Rocky Mountain Conference, Denver, Colorado, October 12, 1981.

10. See Joseph Nicolosi and Ruth L. Fuller, "What Does Science Teach about Human Sexuality?" in *Caught in the Crossfire: Helping Christians Debate Homosexuality,* eds. Sally B. Geis and Donald E. Messer (Nashville: Abingdon, 1994), 67–88.

11. See Charles N. Crutchfield, "My Witness," *United Methodist Reporter,* May 29, 1987; James V. Heidinger II, "Bishop Crutchfield, AIDS and Methodism," *Good News* (July/August, 1987); Jean Caffey Lyles, "Bishop Practiced Gay Lifestyle, Pair Say," *Arizona Republic* (Phoenix), June 6, 1987; and Emily Yoffe, "The Gay Bishop: The Double Life of Finis Crutchfield," *Texas Monthly* 15, no. 10, October 1987.

12. Martin E. Marty, "M.E.M.O.: Tears," *Christian Century,* November 30, 1988, 1111.

13. Henri Nouwen, *The Road to Daybreak: A Spiritual Journey* (New York: Doubleday, 1988), 200.

14. Estimate at the end of 1995 by the Joint United Nations Program on HIV/AIDS (UNAIDS). See http://www.hivpositive.com/f-HIVyou/f-Statistics/UN-AIDS.html.

15. Cited in J. A. Grunbaum et al., *Youth Risk Behavior Surveillance, United States, 2001,* MMWR CDC Surveillance Summaries 2002; 51 (SS-4): 1–64.

16. See Donald E. Messer, *A Conspiracy of Goodness: Contemporary Images of Christian Mission* (Nashville: Abingdon, 1992).

17. Wheatley, Open Letter.

18. "AIDS Virus Spreads in Latin America: WHO Prediction 'Conservative,'" *Toronto Globe and Mail*, March 9, 1991, A1.

19. "A Latin AIDS Meeting Opens Its Ears to What Was Once Unmentionable," New York Times, January 16, 1989, A6.

20. "Service of Word and Table IV," *United Methodist Book of Worship* (Nashville: United Methodist Publishing House, 1992), 45.

21. Gerald J. Stine, *AIDS Update 2002* (Upper Saddle River, N.J.: Prentice Hall, 2002), 14.

22. James B. Nelson, "Responding to, Learning from AIDS," *Christianity and Crisis*, May 19, 1986, 179–80.

23. World Council of Churches, "Plan of Action: The Ecumenical Response to HIV/AIDS in Africa," Global Consultation on the Ecumenical Response to the Challenge of HIV/AIDS, Nairobi, Kenya, November 25–28, 2001.

24. Ibid.

25. Franklin Graham, cited in Michael Kress, "Religion in the Age of AIDS," *Religion & Ethics Newsweekly,* 2003, 6. Available at http://www.pbs.org/wnet/religionandethics/pdfs/religionguide2003.pdf.

26. See Swidler, *Homosexuality and World Religions*. Also Geis and Messer, *Caught in the Crossfire.*

27. See Tolbert McCarroll, *Morning Glory Babies: Children with AIDS and the Celebration of Life* (New York: St. Martin's, 1988).

28. Michael Specter, "The Vaccine," *New Yorker*, February 3, 2003, 54–65.

29. Ibid., 54.

30. Ibid., 56.

4. Stigmatization and Discrimination

1. Kalpana Jain, *Positive Lives: The Story of Ashok and Others with HIV* (New Delhi: Penguin Books, 2002), 100–104.

2. Philip J. Hilts, "Ties to Church Are Sundered by AIDS," *New York Times*, September 8, 1992, A9.

3. World Council of Churches, "Plan of Action: The Ecumenical Response to HIV/AIDS in Africa," Global Consultation on the Ecumenical Response to the Challenge of HIV/AIDS, Nairobi, Kenya, November 25–28, 2001, 3.

4. Ibid.

5. Frederick Herzog, "A New Spirituality: Shaping Doctrine at the Grass Roots," *Christian Century*, July 30–August 6, 1986, 681.

6. Ibid.

7. For further discussion, see Donald E. Messer, *A Conspiracy of Goodness: Contemporary Images of Christian Mission* (Nashville: Abingdon, 1992), 97ff.

8. Opening statement, Workshop on HIV/AIDS Awareness, United Theological College, Bangalore, India, February 16, 2001. Citation source was listed as "The Pit," an adapted form of the quotation from Deliver Ministries, "Freedom from Homosexuality," http://members.aol.com/Delivermin/index.html.

9. Gillian Paterson, "Church, AIDS and Stigma," 2002. Pdf available at http://www.e-alliance.ch/media/media-3859.pdf

10. Calle Almedal, e-mail message to Ray Martin, December 5, 2001.

11. Kofi Annan, "Message on World AIDS Day 2002," e-mail from Calle Almedal to author, November 29, 2002.

12. "Stigma, discrimination are barriers to reversing AIDS spread," *Daily News Online* (Republic of Botswana), March 4, 2003.

13. Jain, *Positive Lives,* 30.

14. Ibid., 33–34.

15. Albert and Etta Mae Mutti, *Dancing in a Wheelchair: One Family Faces HIV/AIDS* (Nashville: Abingdon, 2001), 123–24.

16. Jain, *Positive Lives,* 7.

17. Paterson, "Church, AIDS and Stigma."

18. United Nations, *Declaration of Commitment on HIV/AIDS,* A/s-26/L.2 (United Nations Special Session, New York, 2001), http://www.un.org/ga/aids/coverage/FinalDeclarationHIVAIDS.html.

19. See "Society Should Change Attitude toward Sexual Minorities," *The Hindu* (Bangalore, India), February 17, 2001.

20. Jain, *Positive Lives,* 69.

21. Gideon Byamugisha, *Breaking the Silence on HIV/AIDS in Africa: How Can Religious Institutions Talk about Sexual Matters in Their Communities?* (Kampala, Uganda: Tricolour Designers & Printers, 2000), 29–30.

22. John S. Spong, "A Priest Dies of AIDS," *Christian Century,* October 24, 1990, 960.

23. Njongonkulu Ndungane, cited in "Quote, Unquote" section, *Christian Century,* December 18–31, 2002, 15.

24. "1,500 Attend Funeral of Courageous AIDS Fighter," *New York Times,* April 12, 1990, C19.

5. Women, Children, and HIV/AIDS

1. Musa W. Dube, *International Review of Mission* (October 2002), cited in "Century Marks, *Christian Century,* May 3, 2003, 6.

2. Robert Bilheimer, *Letters From the World of AIDS,* Letter 7, April 6, 2001, Fisherman's Cove, Chennai, India. http://www.thebody.com/closerwalkfilm/journal7/journal7.html.

3. Lawrence K. Altman, "Women Catch Up to Men in Global H.I.V. Cases," *New York Times,* November 27, 2002.

4. Statistic from the American Association for World Health, 2000.

5. Ibid. These UN statistics are from on the 2002 annual report of the United Nations.

6. Mabel Bianco, "Sexism Fuels Women's AIDS Risks," *Newsday,* December 2, 2002. Quoted from *Alliance for Microbicide Development Biweekly News Digest* 3, no. 3, December 6, 2002. Available at http://www.microbicide.org/publications/digest/thenews.digest_vol3no13.pdf.

7. Nicole Itano, "Researchers in Africa Ask If Diaphragms Block HIV," *Women's Enews,* December 1, 2002. Available at http://www.womensenews.org/article.cfm/dyn/aid/1128/context/cover/.

8. "Traditional Culture Spreading HIV/AIDS," Arusha, Tanzania, AF-AIDS Internet forum 2002, March 28, 2003. Available at http://www.cirp.org/news/irinnews03-28-03/.

9. Seth Mydans, "Fighting AIDS: A New War Is Killing Cambodians," *New York Times,* July 7, 2001, www.newyorktimes.com.

10. Cited in Marie Cocco, "Foreign AIDS Policy Is Sexist," *Denver Post,* July 12, 2002.

11. Martha Frase-Blunt, "The Sugar Daddies' Kiss of Death," *Washington Post,* October 6, 2002, B4.

12. His father, King Sobhuza, married at least 120 wives. See "Swaziland King's Polygamy Remarks Condemned," AF-AIDS Internet forum 2002, March 19, 2003. Available at http://www.irinnews.org/AIDSreport.asp?ReportID=1883.

13. UNICEF studies and statistics cited in Michael Kelly SJ, "Addressing the Susceptibility of Youth to HIV Infection," African Jesus AIDS Network (AJAN), May 11/12, 2002. Available at http://www.jesuitaids.net/susceptibility.htm.

14. Peter Piot, quoted in "Men Can Change Course of AIDS Epidemic" (Joint United Nations Programme on HIV/AIDS 2000, New Delhi, India, March 6, 2000). Available at http://gbgm-umc.org/programs/wad00/men.stm.

15. Gillian Paterson, "Global HIV/AIDS Epidemic: Understanding the Issues," Norwegian Church Aid, http://www.nca.no/article/articleview/2381/1/277/.

16. Lyndsay Griffiths, "Charity Chronicles Spread of Sex Tourism," Reuters, May 16, 1995.

17. Kalpana Jain, *Positive Lives: The Story of Ashok and Others with HIV* (New Delhi: Penguin Books, 2002), 59–60.

18. Jimmy Carter is quoted in "Three Wise Men," *POZ*, June 2002, 12. Citation is from an on-the-road e-journal in *www.slate.com*. See http://slate.msn.com/id/2062757/entry/2062993/. See also Samwel Kere and Clare Barasa, "A Dawn for Twilight Girls," *Profile Magazine: East African Standard*, January 11–17, 2003, online edition, http://www.eastandard.net/profile/features/ feat1.htm.

19. Reuters, "U.S. Experts Warn of Honduras AIDS Risk to Women," February 3, 1996. Summary available at http://www.aidsinfobbs.org/library/cdcsums/1996/0761.

20. Antonio de Moya, quoted in David Gonzalez, "As AIDS Ravages Caribbean, Governments Confront Denial," *New York Times*, May 18, 2003.

21. See "Traditional Culture Spreading HIV/AIDS" (see n. 8); and Beatrix Nyakisumo, "Kenya—A Vile Custom That Must Go . . . ," *Africanews*, AF-AIDS Internet forum, May 1997. The latter is available at http://www.peacelink.it/afrinews/14_issue/p6.html.

22. See Rodrick Mukumbira, "Women," *Africanews*, AF-AIDS Internet forum 2002, April 29, 2003; and Joshua Chigodora, "Widows and HIV/AIDS," AF-AIDS Internet forum 2002, April 30, 2003. See http://archives.healthdev.net/gender -aids/msg00524.html.

23. Bianco, "Sexism."

24. Jennifer Butler, "Alarmed by Global Progress on Reproductive Rights, the Religious Right Storms the United Nations," Religious Consultation, report 6, no. 1, 2002, 11.

25. Reuters, "HIV-Positive TV Muppet Worries U.S. Lawmakers," July 15, 2002.

26. African Women's Sexual & Reproductive Health & Rights Partnership (resolution, African Women's Sexual & Reproductive Health and Rights Conference, Johannesburg, February 4–7, 2003). Female genital mutilation (FGM) is a traditional practice affecting an estimated 85–115 million women and children, according to the World Health Organization in 1994. It occurs in over thirty African countries.

27. Itano, "Researchers."

28. Stacie Stukin, "Kiss and Gel," *POZ*, June 2003, 34.

29. Ibid. Thailand study cited was in the *Journal of Acquired Immune Deficiency Syndromes*, cited by Reuters in "Husbands Implicated in HIV transmission among

Thai Women, " available at http://www.hivandhepatitis.com/recent/transmission/122900.html.

30. Gonzalez, "As AIDS Ravages."

31. See http://www.childline.org.zw/docs/resdoc1999.doc.

32. Stephen Lewis, quoted by John J. Goldman in "Iraq War Would Quash Efforts to Fight AIDS UN Africa Envoy Says," *Los Angelese Times,* January 9, 2003. Available at http://www.globalpolicy.org/security/issues/iraq/attack/2003/0109aids.htm. Lewis is the UN Secretary-General's Special Envoy for HIV/AIDS in Africa.

33. Ibid.

34. "How AIDS Discriminates Against The Poor," reprinted in *Religious Consultation Report* 6, no. 1 (2002) from *Our Planet* 12, no. 2, 12.

35. Jacqueline Long, "HIV/AIDS Will Impact Women's History, Destiny," *Out Front Colorado,* February 26, 2003, 15.

36. See Christopher Jimu, "Picture Grim on HIV/AIDS in Malawi Defence Force," *The Chronicle,* March 31, 2003, *thechronicle@africa-online.net* (e-mail forum). The report cites the army commander General Joseph Chimbayo as saying that factors predisposing soldiers to AIDS are "that they feel invincible, have ready cash stacked in their wallets but do not carry condoms. They are additionally under extreme peer pressure to have sex and act aggressively and they place the 'conquest' syndrome as important to them."

37. Bono, "Mr. President, Africa Needs Us," *Washington Post,* January 27, 2003, A19.

38. Lewis, in Goldman, "Iraq War."

39. Musa W. Dube, "Preaching to the Converted: Unsettling the Christian Church" in *Southern African Region Consultation* 51, no. 4 (March 26–29, 2001), 10. Available at http://www.warc.ch/24gc/rw014/03.html.

40. Ibid., 5.

41. Madipoane Masenya, "Trapped between Two Canons: African–South African Christian Women in the HIV/AIDS Era" (unpublished paper), University of South Africa, Pietersburg, South Africa, 1, 5.

42. Anna Mary Mukamwezi Kayonga, "African Women and Morality in Mugambi," in *Moral Issues in African Christianity,* ed. J. N. K. and A. Nasimiyu-Wasike (Nairobi, Kenya: Acton, 1999), 145.

43. Dube, "Preaching to the Converted," 5.

44. Masenya, "Trapped," 8.

6. The ABCs of Prevention

1. Richard Stearns, president of World Vision, quoted in "AIDS as WMD," *Christian Century*, May 3, 2003, 6.

2. See Seth C. Kalichman, *Preventing AIDS: A Sourcebook for Behavioral Interventions* (Mahwah, N.J.: Erlbaum, 1998), 2.

3. See Michael Carter, "Oral Sex Has Near-Zero HIV Risk According To New San Francisco Study," *Aidsmap*, November 8, 2002, http://www.aidsmap.com/news/newsdisplay2.asp?newsId=1738. This study contradicts a previous widely reported study in San Francisco that indicated 8 percent of all HIV infections among gay men were due to oral sex. A recent Spanish study of heterosexual couples also concludes that oral sex is not a route of transmission. Note, however, that most guidelines for "safer" sex recommend avoiding oral sex without condoms or a "safe" partner.

4. See Brenda Almond, "Personal Issues and Personal Dilemmas," in *AIDS—A Moral Issue: the Ethical, Legal and Social Aspects*, ed. Brenda Almond (New York: St. Martin's, 1990), 166.

5. David Serwadda, "Beyond Abstinence," *Washington Post,* May 16, 2003.

6. Cited from the Web site of the Bill and Melinda Gates Foundation, December 3, 2002, www.gatesfoundation.org. The list of "proven tools" they include are: Educational and social-marketing campaigns detailing the ways in which AIDS can be prevented; behavioral-change programs that encourage abstinence and safer sexual practices; access to, and increased distribution of, condoms; voluntary counseling and HIV testing (VCT) so people can learn if they are infected and how they can avoid passing the virus to others; prevention and treatment of STDs that increase the risk of HIV infection; protection of blood supplies and reduction of transmission in health care settings and among injecting drug users; enhancement of reproductive health services, anti-retroviral drugs, and VCT to prevent mother-to-child transmission.

7. Data from Paul Webster, "US Triples AIDS Spending in Africa," AF-AIDS 2002 Internet forum, May 8, 2003. See http://archives.hst.org.za/af-aids/msg00904.html. The confusing legislation suggests teaching that a mutually faithful monogamous relationship also qualifies as a form of "abstinence."

8. Associated Press, "U.S. House Approves Global AIDS Bill," *The Globe and Mail*, May 1, 2003.

9. Elizabeth Aquilera, "Who's counting? Disclosing Number of Sexual Partners a Sensitive Subject," *Denver Post*, May 11, 2003, 4L.

10. Anne Bayley, *One New Humanity: The Challenge of AIDS* (London: SPCK, 1996), 32, 34.

11. Edward C. Green, *Rethinking AIDS Prevention: How the Experts Went Wrong* (Westport, Conn.: Praeger, 2003).

12. Ibid.

13. Ibid.

14. Charlene Smith, "Journalists Form Association to Fight AIDS," AF-AIDS 2000 Internet forum, May 2003. See http://archives.hst.org.za/af-aids/msg00910.html.

15. Donald G. McNeil Jr., "Global War on AIDS Runs Short of Key Weapon," *New York Times,* October 9, 2002.

16. Quoted in Sabin Russell, "Drugs, Contraceptives Failing to Conquer Virus: Many Tools Are Low-Tech, Underused," *San Francisco Chronicle*, July 12, 2002.

17. Emily Wax, "In Another Break with Past, Kenyans See Hope on AIDS," *Washington Post,* May 21, 2003, A.

18. Donald G. McNeil Jr., "AIDS and Death Hold No Sting for Fatalistic Men at African Bar," *New York Times*, November 29, 2001, A14.

19. Christoph Benn, plenary presentation (United Nations General Assembly Special Session on HIV/AIDS, New York, June 27, 2001). It is reprinted in *International Review of Mission* XC, no. 359, 471–72. See also http://www.un.org/ga/aids/coverage/.

20. Eamonn McCann, "Pope Must Face Facts of Life and Death," *Belfast Telegraph*, November 29, 2001, online edition.

21. Karen DeYoung, "AIDS Challenges Religious Leaders," *Washington Post*, August 15, 2001, online edition, www.washingtonpost.com.

22. Ibid.

23. Gunther Simmermacher (editor of *Southern Cross*), "Condoms and the Church," AF-AIDS 2002 Internet forum, December 4–10, 2002, *http://archives. healthdev.net/af-aids*.

24. Quoted in Ibid. Bishop Rixen was rebuked by the Vatican and by São Paulo Archbishop Claudio Hummes, who called such arguments "unacceptable." The Catholic position is based on Pope Paul VI's *Humane Vitae* (1968), which contended that every act of sexual intercourse must remain open to procreation. "Every action" that intervened with possible conception was banned. Specifically, it stated that the "lesser evil" concept justifies no exceptions, "even for the gravest reasons . . . even when the intention is to safeguard or promote individual, family, or social well-being."

25. Colin Powell, quoted in "Quote, Unquote" section in *Christian Century*, February 27–March 6, 2002, 15.

26. Michael Specter, "The Vaccine" *New Yorker*, February 3, 2003, 55.

27. Religious Consultation on Population, Reproductive Health, and Ethics, "Update: Microbicides as AIDS Prevention," *TRC Newsletter,* http://www.religious-consultation.org/News_Tracker/UN_report_on_condom_debate.htm.

28. Stacie Stukin, "Kiss and Gel," *POZ,* June 2002, 34–35.

29. Lynne Altenroxel, "Baby Nevirapine," *Toronto Star,* July 14, 2003, 5.

30. Almond, "Personal Issues and Personal Dilemmas," 167.

31. William Henry Barcus III, "The Gospel Imperative," in *The Gospel Imperative in the Midst of AIDS: Towards a Prophetic Pastoral Theology,* ed. Robert H. Iles (Wilton, Conn.: Morehouse, 1989), 9.

32. Quoted in Dennis McClean, "Countering HIV/AIDS Stigma and Discrimination," AF-AIDS 2000 Internet forum, May 9, 2003. Available at http://archives.healthdev.net/af-aids.

33. See George Schmid (Department of HIV/AIDS, World Health Organization), "Transmission of AIDS in Africa," AF-AIDS Internet forum, April 14, 2003. Available at http://archives.healthdev.net/af-aids.

34. Kalichman, *Preventing AIDS.*

35. Russell, "Drugs, Contraceptives Failing to Conquer Virus."

36. See "Circumcision Does Not Prevent AIDS Virus," *Independent,* July 21, 2003, online edition.

37. See Robert McAfee Brown, *Theology in a New Key: Responding to Liberation Themes* (Philadelphia: Westminister, 1978).

38. David Patient, "Blessing the Condoms in South Africa," AF-AIDS 2002 Internet forum, http://archives.heathdev.net/af-aids. Reprinted in *Religious Consultation Report* 6, no. 2 (2003), 7.

39. Words quoted from advertisement published on World AIDS Day (December 1, 2001) by Catholics for a Free Choice, Washington, D.C. See http://www.kaisernetwork.org/adwatch/print_ads/Newspaper%20Bishops%20in%20line%20CFFC.pdf. See also www.condoms4life.org.

40. Bishop Joseph Humper, quoted in "Religious Leaders Must Provide AIDS Education in Africa," General Board of Global Ministries, United Methodist Church, April 39, 2001, http://gbgm-umc.org/global_news/full_article.cfm?articleid=548.

41. Lucy Y. Steinitz, "Compassionate Conspiracy: AIDS Action in Namibia," *Christian Century,* May 17, 2000, 571–72.

42. Unidentified bishop quoted in Patient, "Blessing the Condoms."

43. Serwadda, "Beyond Abstinence."

44. Edward C. Green, "Culture Clash and AIDS Prevention" *The Responsive Community* 14, no. 4 (2003): 4–9. Available at http://www.aidsuganda.org/pdf/Comments_on_ABC1.pdf.

45. See Edward C. Green, "New Challenges to the AIDS Prevention Paradigm," *Anthropology News*, September 2003, for further discussion of these paradigms.

7. A World without AIDS

1. Cited by Stephen Lewis (UN Secretary-General's Special Envoy for HIV/AIDS in Africa), "The Lack of Funding for HIV/AIDS Is Mass Murder by Complacency," *AllAfrica*, January 8, 2003, www.AllAfrica.com.

2. Cited from Stan D'Souza, "UN World Population Projection: The 2002 Revision and the Impact on AIDS," *AJA News*, African Jesuit AIDS Network, May 2003, *www.jesuitaids.net*. Discussions about world population trends would note that of the 8.9 billion people projected in 2050, 1.2 billion will live in the "more developed regions," while 7.7 billion will live in the "less developed regions" (up from 4.9 billion in those areas in 2000).

3. Albert Schweitzer, *Out of My Life and Thought* (New York: Holt, 1933).

4. Sallie McFague, *Models of God: Theology for an Ecological Nuclear Age* (Philadelphia: Fortress Press, 1987), 52.

5. Gabriel Garcia Marquez, *Love in a Time of Cholera* (New York: Penguin, 1989).

6. SARS, *severe acute respiratory syndrome*, first emerged as a global disease in 2003.

7. Aaron Sachs, "HIV/AIDS Cases Rise at Record Rates," in Lester R. Brown, Nicholas Lenssen, and Hal Kane, *Vital Signs 1995: The Trends That Our Shaping Our Future*, Worldwatch Institute (New York: Norton, 1995), 98.

8. "Four Horsemen of the Apocalypse?" *The Economist,* May 3, 2003, 74.

9. Maxwell Madzikanga (Zimbabwe), "Empowering PLWHAs," AF-AIDS 2002 Internet forum, May 20, 2003. See http://archives.hst.org.za/af-aids/msg00921.html

10. "Four Horsemen," 73.

11. Pius K. Kamau, "African AIDS and American Medicine," *Journal of the National Medical Association* 95, no. 5 (May 2003), 403. Available at http://www.nmanet.org/A7_A8RJN0503.pdf.

12. Terry Mattingly, "What's the Problem?" *Good News*, September/October 2001, 24.

13. Sheryl Henderson Blunt, "Bono Tells Christians: Don't Neglect Africa," *Christianity Today*, April 22, 2002.

14. For example, former President Bill Clinton's foundation has negotiated agreements with generic drug manufacturers to cut prices of AIDS drugs and with five major medical companies to discount price of two diagnostic tests for thirteen developing countries. See Celia W. Dugger, "Clinton Gets Give Companies to Reduce the Cost of AIDS Tests," *The New York Times,* January 15, 2004, p. A11.

15. "Plan of Action: The Ecumenical Response to HIV/AIDS in Africa" (World

Council of Churches, Nairobi, Kenya, November 25–28, 2001), 5. Available at http://www.wcc-coe.org/wcc/news/press/01/hiv-aids-plan.html.

16. See Helen Epstein and Lincoln Chen, "Can AIDS Be Stopped?" *New York Review*, March 14, 2002, 29.

17. Lewis, "Lack of Funding for HIV/AIDS."

18. See "Viagra is a $50 Million Pentagon Budget Item," *New York Times*, October 4, 1998. Although the actual amount spent proved to be considerably less, it does illustrate our priorities!

19. Sebastian Mallaby, "Why Focus on Iraq and Not AIDS?" *Washington Post*, October 15, 2002.

20. Nicole Crawford, "HIV Needs Psychology," *Monitor on Psychology*, November 2002, 36. Coates says 3,500 died on 9/11 and that 8,300 people die daily of AIDS. The respected journal, *The Economist,* claimed in "AIDS, the Long War," July 13, 2002, that nearly 9,000 die daily—"three times as many people as died in the terrorist attack on the World Trade Center."

21. Richard Feachem, cited in *Global Fund Observer (GFO) Newsletter*, January 10, 2003, www.aidspan.org/gfo/archives/newsletter/issue2.htm.

8. Ensuring Care, Testing, Counseling, and Treatment

1. This quotation and following come from notes from personal conversations and documents shared by Sister Pascal Conforti, OSU. See her unpublished lecture, "Spirituality and HIV Mental Health Practice"and alsoDaniel Baxter, *The Least of These My Brethren: A Doctor's Story of Hope and Miracles on an Inner-city AIDS Ward* (New York: Harmony Books, 1997), 130-77.

2. Cited by Skip Hollandsworth, "AIDS: Seven Days in the Crisis," *D Magazine,* March 1988, 53.

3. Berakhah House, in Sioux Falls, South Dakota, is the only care residence in my home state. *Berakhah* means blessing in Hebrew.

4. Anonymous woman in Carthage, Missouri, personal communication to author, March 4, 1989.

5. Zackie Achmat, "An Open Letter from Six South African Doctors" AF-AIDS 2002 Internet forum, April 28, 2003. Available at http://www.childrenfirst.org.za/shownews?mode=content&id=15899&refto=2290&PHPSESSID=89c0aac31b07c4f1c05eb12577016c8f.

6. World Health Organization, "African Elders Bear Hardships of Care for Orphans, AIDS Sufferers," *AllAfrica*, December 11, 2002, www.AllAfrica.com.

7. See Cal Thomas, "'Living Room' for the Dying Eases Last Days for Inmates with AIDS," *Los Angeles Times Syndicate*.

8. David Yeoman, "Dying into Life," in *Christ in AIDS*, ed. Heather Snidle and David Yeoman (Cardiff: Cardiff Academic, 1997), 144.

9. Janet Everhart, "AIDS: Theological, Biblical, and Pastoral Responses" (unpublished paper, Serampore College, Mizoram, India, 2002). Used with permission.

10. Nontando Margaret Hadebe, e-mail message to author, July 25, 2003.

11. Bonnie J. Messer, "Issues Related to Counseling Persons with HIV/AIDS" (lecture, Bangalore, India, February 2000). Used with permission.

12. Jose Tembe, *BBC News*, "Mozambique Moved by HIV Story," AF-AIDS 2002 Internet forum, June 26, 2003.

13. "China's Abuses in AIDS," *International Herald Tribune*, June 2003, 13.

14. William Jefferson Clinton, "AIDS Is Not a Death Sentence," *New York Times*, December 1, 2002.

15. Seth C. Kalichman, *Preventing AIDS: A Sourcebook for Behavioral Interventions* (Mahwah, N.J.: Erlbaum, 1998), 13.

16. *BBC News*, "AIDS Burdens Kenya Prison Warders," AF-AIDS 2002 Internet forum, June 23, 2003.

17. "UNAIDS Report: Condoms Fail to Protect Against HIV 10 Percent of the Time," Healthwatch, *The Advocate*, June 24, 2003, www.advocate.com.

18. Kalpana Jain, *Positive Lives: The Story of Ashok and Others with HIV* (New Delhi: Penguin, 2002), 109.

19. Robert J. Perelli, *Ministry to Persons with AIDS: A Family Systems Approach* (Minneapolis: Augsburg Fortress, 1991), 26.

20. Cathie Lyons, "The Healing Ministry of the Church in the Second Decade of AIDS," *HIV/AIDS Focus Paper* 19, January 1993. Available at http://gbgm-umc.org/health/hivfocus/focus019.cfm

21. Ibid.

22. See Ruth L. Fuller, Sally B. Geis, and Julian Rush, "Lovers and Significant Others," in *Disenfranchised Grief: New Directions, Challenges, and Strategies for Practice*, ed. Kenneth Doka (Champaign, Ill.: Research Press, 2002).

23. Rev. Ivan M. Abrahams, in discussion with author, Johannesburg, South Africa, July 2003.

24. Nelson Mandela, quoted in Sarah Boseley, "Mandela Calls for Extra Funds," *The Guardian*, July 15, 2003.

25. Kayode Soyinka, ed. "It's All about Profit, Stupid," *Africa Today* 9, no. 5 (May 2003): 29–31.

26. John Kiwanulka Ssemakula, "13th ICASA: Challenges to Scaling Up ARV Treatment in Africa" AF-AIDS 2002 Internet forum, June 7, 2003. Available at http://archives.hst.org.za/af-aids/msg00944.html.

27. John Donnelly, "AIDS Treatment Plan Targets 3 Million Poor," *The Boston Globe,* October 3, 2003, p. 1.

28. "Saving Grace: How Much Does It Really Cost to Manufacture a Drug?" *Africa Today* 9, no. 5 (May 2003).

29. Christof Maletsky, "Namibian Firm Will Produce AIDS Drugs, Says Minister," AF-AIDS 2002 Internet forum, June 11, 2003. Available at http://archives .healthdev.net/af-aids/msg00976.html.

30. "South Africa Addresses AIDS," editorial. *New York Times,* August 18, 2003.

31. Natal Witness, "KwaZulu-Natal Teachers Dying in Their Thousands," AF-AIDS 2002 Internet forum, April 11, 2003. Available at http://archives.healthdev .net/af-aids/msg00963.html.

32. Donald G. McNeil Jr., "Broad Study Finds Significant Resistance to AIDS Drugs," *New York Times,* July 15, 2003.

33. Alastair Leithead, "Townships Hold Breath for HIV Decision," AF-AIDS 2002 Internet forum, June 6, 2003.

34. *IRIN PlusNews,* "WFP Food AID for HIV/AIDS-Infected People" AF-AIDS 2002 Internet forum, June 17, 2003. Available at http://www.irinnews.org/ AIDSreport.asp?ReportID=2145.

35. See Alex DeWall, "What AIDS Means in A Famine," *New York Times,* November 19, 2002.

36. Lewis, "Lack of Funding."

37. See Paul S. Zeitz, "Waging a Global Battle More Efficiently," *New York Times,* March 1, 2003; Donald E. Messer, "Reflections on HIV/AIDS in South Africa: 'Genocide by Indifference,'" *United Methodist News Service,* August 2003; and Ben Hirschler, "AIDS Fund Faces Shortfall as Donors Meet in Paris," *Reuters,* July 15, 2003.

38. BBC World News Service, "Bono: World AIDS Day 2002, Part 2," BBCi, December 2002, http://www.bbc.co.uk/.

39. "Grace Matnanga, Shoe Seller," *Africa Today* 9, no. 5 (May 2003): 20.

40. Bob Dylan, "Saving Grace," *Saved,* Special Rider Music © 1980. See p. iv.

9. Global Hope in a Global Emergency

1. This material is extracted from Donald E. Messer, *A Conspiracy of Goodness: Contemporary Images of Christian Mission* (Nashville: Abingdon, 1994), 108–10.

2. Pope John Paul II, Caritas Internationalis Statement for the World AIDS Campaign 2002, Tanzania, September 1990, cited at http://www.cafod.org.uk/ archive/hivaids/aids_caritas2002.shtml

3. Emily Wax, "In Another Break with Past, Kenyans See Hope on AIDS," *Washington Post,* May 21, 2003, A01.

4. "Annan Says Silence Surrounding HIV/AIDS Is Broken," *Washington File*, April 24, 2001, http://uinofo.state.gov/topical/pol/usandun/01042510.htm.

5. Notes of author from lectures given by Edward P. Antonio, The Iliff School of Theology, at the consultation on AIDS of the National Council of Churches, Mumbai, India, February 2003, and the lecture "What Does Christian Theology Have to Say about AIDS?" at Iliff School of Theology, Denver, Colorado, April 24, 2003.

6. John E. Fortunato, *AIDS: The Spiritual Dilemma* (San Francisco: Harper & Row, 1987), 88–89.

7. A principle known as GIPA, the Greater Involvement of People with AIDS, was recognized by the United Nations and included in the Paris Declaration of 1994.

8. "Christians from 87 Countries Gathered, Committing 'to Reach out to a Dying World,'" *Heartbeat* 24 (fall 2002): 3.

9. Taken from the Pan-African Lutheran Church Leadership Consultation in response to the HIV/AIDS pandemic, Nairobi, Kenya, May 2002. Distributed through the AF-AIDS Internet forum, August 21, 2003. Available at http://www.nigeria-aids.org/MsgRead.cfm?ID=1729.

10. "Being Real Christians in the Real South Africa" (statement, South African Christian Leadership Assembly, Pretoria, South Africa, July 7–11, 2003), 10.

11. HIV/AIDS Christian Network (prayer of dedication, Mozambique, July 16, 2003).

12. World Council of Churches, cited in "Faith Based Organisations in the Fight against HIV/AIDS and Stigma," AF-AIDS Internet forum, August 21, 2003. Available at http://www.wcc-coe.org/wcc/news/press/01/hiv-aids-plan.html.

13. "A Service of Word and Table IV," Daily Study Bible, *United Methodist Book of Worship* (Nashville: United Methodist Publishing House, 1992).

14. William Barclay, *The Letters to the Philippians, Colossians, and Thessalonians*, Daily Study Bible (Philadelphia: Westminister, 1959), 62–63.

15. Reinhold Niebuhr's famous "serenity prayer" says: "God, grant me the serenity to accept the things I cannot change; courage to change the things I can; and wisdom to know the difference."

16. Albert Camus, *The Plague*, translated by Stuart Gilbert (New York: Vintage, 1972), 202.

17. John Platt, "The Future of AIDS," *Futurist*, November/December 1987, 10–17. Cited by Susan Palmer in *AIDS as an Apocalyptic Metaphor in North America* (Toronto: University of Toronto Press, 1997), 171.

18. Stephen Lewis, quoted at the African Religious Leaders Assembly on Children and HIV/AIDS in Nairobi, Kenya, June 10, 2003. Cited in "Faith Based Organisations (FBOs) in the Fight against HIV/AIDS and Stigma," AF-AIDS Internet Forum. Available at http://www.hivandhepatitis.com/recent/developing/061902e.html.

19. Mother Teresa, *Words to Love By* (Notre Dame: Ave Maria, 1983), 35.

20. Gillian Paterson, "Church Leadership and HIV/AIDS: The New Commitment." Pdf available at http://www.e-alliance.ch/media/media-3860.pdf.

21. Mike Allen and Paul Blustein, "Unlikely Allies Influenced Bush to Shift Course on AIDS Relief," *Washington Post,* January 30, 2003, A01.

22. See http://www.achap.org/news/boston_globe.htm.

23. Theodore Runyon, *The New Creation* (Nashville: Abingdon, 1998), 189.

24. Lutheran World Federation, "Pan-African Lutheran Church Leaders Committed to 'Breaking the Silence,'" and "Healing Influence of Church Community Can Bring About Transformation," May 7, 2002, http://www.lutheranworld.org.

25. Cited by Michael Kress in "Religion in the Age of AIDS," *Religion & Ethics NewsWeekly,* 2003, 9.

26. Cited from a booklet: Methodist Church of Southern Africa Connexional Task Force on HIV/AIDS, *The Methodist Response to HIV/AIDS in Southern Africa: Strategy and Implementation Plan* (Johannesburg, South Africa: Methodist Church of Southern Africa, n.d.).

27. See Stuart C. Bate OMI, ed., *Responsibility in a Time of AIDS: A Pastoral Response by Catholic Theologians and AIDS Activists in Southern Africa* (Pretoria, South Africa.: Cluster Publications, 2003).

28. Musa W. Dube, "HIV and AIDS Curriculum for Theological Institutions in Africa," University of Botswana, December 11, 2001, 7. Dr. Dube is the World Council of Churches Southern African Regional Consultant.

29. St. Bonaventure, "The Life of St. Francis, I.5," in Ewart Cousins, ed., *Bonaventure and the Coincidence of Opposites,* Classics of Western Spirituality series (London: SPCK, 1978); quoted in Thomas of Celano, "The Second Life of St. Francis," in *St. Francis of Assisi: Writings and Early Biographies: English Omnibus of the Sources for the Life of St. Francis,* edited by Marion A. Habig, 3rd ed. (Chicago: Franciscan Herald Press, 1973), 9.

30. Adapted from Mike Harden in *Columbus Dispatch,* December 27, 1987, quoted by Donald J. Shelby in "What Brings Us Together," May 1, 1988. Shelby cites Harden in a sermon preached in Santa Monica First United Methodist Church.

31. See John Wesley, "On Visiting the Sick," Sermon 98. Available at http://gbgm-umc.org/umw/wesley/serm-098.stm.

Selected Bibliography

Akukwe, Chinua. "Responding to the HIV/AIDS Tragedy in Africa: The Need for Global Action and the Role of Christian Health Missionaries." *The Christian Connections for International Health (CCIH) Forum*, no. 6 (November 1999).

Almond, Brenda, ed. *AIDS—A Moral Issue: The Ethical, Legal and Social Aspects*. New York: St. Martin's, 1990.

Amos, William E., Jr. *When AIDS Comes to Church*. Philadelphia: Westminster, 1988.

Barnett, Tony, and Alan Whiteside. *AIDS in the Twenty-First Century: Disease and Globalization*. New York: Palgrave Macmillan, 2002.

Bate, Stuart C., OMI, ed. *Responsibility in a Time of AIDS: A Pastoral Response by Catholic Theologians and AIDS Activists in Southern Africa*. Linden, South Africa: St. Augustine College, 2003.

Baxter, Daniel, MD. *The Least of These My Brethren: A Doctor's Story of Hope and Miracles on an Inner-City AIDS Ward*. New York: Harmony, 1997.

Bayley, Anne. *One New Humanity: The Challenge of AIDS*. London: SPCK, 1996.

Boyd, Terry. *Living with AIDS: One Christian's Struggle*. Lima, Ohio: C.S.S., 1990.

Byamugisha, Gideon. *Breaking the Silence on HIV/AIDS in Africa: How Can Religious Institutions Talk about Sexual Matters in Their Communities?* Kampala, Uganda: Tricolour, 2000.

Byamugisha, Gideon, Lucy Y. Steinitz, Glen Williams, and Phumzile Zondi. *Journeys of Faith: Church-based Responses to HIV and AIDS in Three Southern African Countries*. Pietermaritzburg, South Africa: Cluster, 2002.

Carter, Nancy A. *Created and Loved by God: An HIV/AIDS Ministry Covenant to Care Handbook*. New York: Health and Welfare Ministries, United Methodist General Board of Global Ministries, 1995.

Chandorikar, S. M. *AIDS: Biblical Resources and Christian Responsibility*. Pune, India: Navjeevan, 2003.

Christensen, Michael J. *The Samaritan's Imperative: Compassionate Ministry to People Living with AIDS*. Nashville: Abingdon, 1991.

Corea, Gena. *The Invisible Epidemic: The Story of Women and AIDS*. New York: HarperCollins, 1992.

Doka, Kenneth J. *AIDS, Fear and Society: Challenging the Dreaded Disease*. Washington, D.C.: Taylor & Francis, 1997.

Eberstadt, Nicholas. "The Future of AIDS." *Foreign Affairs* 81, no. 6 (November/December 2002).

Fortunato, John E. *AIDS: The Spiritual Dilemma*. San Francisco: Harper & Row, 1987.

Fountain, Daniel E. "AIDS Care as an Avenue for Ministry in Congo," *The Christian Connections for International Health (CCIH) Forum*, no. 6 (November 1999).

Geis, Sally B., and Donald E. Messer, eds. *Caught in the Crossfire: Helping Christians Debate Homosexuality*. Nashville: Abingdon, 1994.

Global Health Challenge: Essays on AIDS. London: Commonwealth Secretariat, 2001.

Graham, Larry Kent. *Discovering Images of God: Narratives of Care among Lesbians and Gays*. Louisville: Westminster John Knox, 1997.

Green, Edward C. "The Impact of Religious Organizations in Promoting HIV/AIDS Prevention," *Christian Connections for International Health (CCIH) Forum*, no. 11 (October 2001).

———. *Rethinking AIDS Prevention: Learning from Successes in Developing Countries*. Westport, Conn.: Praeger, 2003.

Hallman, David G., ed. *AIDS Issues: Confronting the Challenge*. New York: Pilgrim, 1989.

Iles, Robert H., ed. *The Gospel Imperative in the Midst of AIDS: Towards a Prophetic Pastoral Theology*. Wilton, Conn.: Morehouse, 1989.

Jain, Kalpana. *Positive Lives: The Story of Ashok and Others with HIV*. New Delhi: Penguin, 2002.

Kain, Craig D., ed. *No Longer Immune: A Counselor's Guide to AIDS*. Alexandria, Va.: American Association for Counseling and Development, 1989.

Kalichman, Seth C. *Preventing AIDS: A Sourcebook for Behavioral Interventions*. Mahwah, N.J.: Lawrence Erlbaum, 1998.

Kalra, R. M. *Preventing AIDS among Industrial Workers in India (Special Reference to the Third World Countries)*. New Delhi: Vikas, 1999.

Keenan, James F., S.J., with Jon D. Fuller, Lisa Sowle Cahill, and Kevin Kelly, eds. *Catholic Ethicists on HIV/AIDS Prevention*. New York: Continuum, 2000.

Mann, Jonathan, Daniel J. M. Tarantola, and Thomas W. Netter, eds. *AIDS in the World: A Global Report*. Cambridge, Mass.: Harvard University Press, 1991.

Map International. *Choosing Hope: The Christian Response to the HIV/AIDS Epidemic—Curriculum Modules for Theological and Pastoral Training Institutions.* Nairobi, Kenya, 1996.

———. *Helpers for a Healing Community: A Pastoral Counseling Manual for AIDS.* Nairobi, Kenya: Map International, 1996.

Marshall, Joretta L. *Counseling Lesbian Partners.* Louisville: Westminster John Knox, 1997.

McElrath, Karen, ed. *HIV and AIDS: A Global View.* Westport, Conn.: Greenwood, 2002.

Melton, J. Gordon. *The Churches Speak on AIDS: Official Statements from Religious Bodies and Ecumenical Organizations.* Detroit: Gale Research, 1989.

Messer, Donald E. *A Conspiracy of Goodness: Contemporary Images of Christian Ministry.* Nashville: Abingdon, 1992.

———. "HIV/AIDS: The Challenge to Theological Education," *National Council of Churches Review.* National Council of Churches in India (March 2002): 175–93.

Miller, Riva, and Robert Bor. *AIDS: A Guide to Clinical Counseling.* London: Science, 1989.

Monette, Paul. *Borrowed Time: An AIDS Memoir.* New York: Harcourt Brace Jovanovich, 1988.

Muchiri, John. *HIV/AIDS—Breaking the Silence: A Guide Book for Pastoral Caregivers.* Nairobi, Kenya: Paulines Africa, 2002.

Mutti, Fritz, and Etta Mae Mutti. *Dancing in a Wheelchair.* Nashville: Abingdon, 2001.

Nicolson, Ronald. *God in AIDS?* London: SCM, 1996.

Palmer, Susan. *AIDS as an Apocalyptic Metaphor in North America.* Toronto: University of Toronto Press, 1997.

Patton, Cindy. *Fatal Advice: How Safe-Sex Education Went Wrong.* Durham, N.C.: Duke University Press, 1996.

———. *Globalizing AIDS.* Minneapolis: University of Minnesota Press, 2002.

———. *Inventing AIDS.* New York: Routledge, 1990.

Richardson, Ann, and Dietmar Bolle, eds. *Wise before Their Time: People from around the World Living with AIDS and HIV Tell Their Stories.* London: HarperCollins, 1992.

Russell, Letty M., ed. *The Church with AIDS: Renewal in the Midst of Crisis.* Louisville, Ky.: Westminster John Knox, 1990.

Samuel, N. M., MD. "The Future." *AIDS.* Edited by B. P. Rajan. Madras, India: The Tamilnadu Dr. M.G. R. Medical University, 1993.

Shelp, Earl E., and Ronald H. Sunderland. *AIDS and the Church: The Second Decade.* Louisville, Ky.: Westminster John Knox, 1992.

Shilts, Randy. *And the Band Played On: Politics, People and the AIDS Epidemic*. New York: St. Martin's, 1987.

Skjelmerud, Anne, and Christopher Tusubira. *Confronting AIDS Together*. Oslo, Norway: Centre for Partnership in Development, 1997.

Snidle, Heather and David Yeoman. *Christ in AIDS: An Educational, Pastoral and Spiritual Approach to HIV/AIDS*. Cardiff: Cardiff Academic, 1997.

Stine, Gerald J. *AIDS Update 2002: An Annual Overview of Acquired Immune Deficiency Syndrome*. Upper Saddle River, N.J.: Prentice Hall, 2002.

Swindler, Arlene, ed. *Homosexuality and World Religions*. Valley Forge, Pa.: Trinity Press International, 1993.

Vanita, Ruth, and Saleem Kidwai, eds. *Same-Sex Love in India: Readings from Literature and History*. New York: St. Martin's, 2000.

Voluntary Health Services, Chennai, India. *Training of Peer Educators in STDs and HIV/AIDS Prevention*. Training manual, n.d.

Weatherford, Ronald Jeffrey, and Carole Boston. *Somebody's Knocking at Your Door: AIDS and the African-American Church*. Binghamton, New York: Haworth Pastoral, 1999.

Wezeman, Phyllis Vos. *Creative Compassion: Activities for Understanding HIV/AIDS*. Cleveland: Pilgrim, 1991.

Whiltshire, Susan Ford. *Seasons of Grief and Grace: A Sister's Story of AIDS*. Nashville: Vanderbilt University Press, 1994.

White, Ryan, and Marie Cunningham. *My Own Story*. New York: Penguin, 1992.

Woodward, James, ed. *Embracing the Chaos: Theological Responses to AIDS*. London: SPCK, 1990.

World Council of Churches. *Facing AIDS; The Challenge, the Churches' Response: A WCC Study Document*. Geneva: WCC, 1997.

———. *Facing AIDS: Education in the Context of Vulnerability HIV/AIDS*. Geneva: WCC, 1999.

———. *Healing and Wholeness: The Churches' Role in Health*. Study by the Christian Medical Commission, 1990.

———. "Health, Faith, and Healing," *International Review of Mission* XC, nos. 356/357 (January/April 2001).